OTHER BOOKS

How Highly Effective People Speak

Eloquence

How Legendary Leaders Speak

Influential Leadership

Public Speaking Mastery

The 7 Keys to Confidence

Trust is Power

Influence

Decoding Human Nature

The Psychology of Persuasion

How Visionaries Speak

The Eloquent Leader

The Language of Leadership

The Psychology of Communication

The Charisma Code

Available on Amazon

Claim These Free Resources that Will Help You Unleash the Power of Your Words and Speak with Confidence. Visit www.speakforsuccesshub.com/toolkit for Access.

18 Free PDF Resources

30 Free Video Lessons

2 Free Workbooks

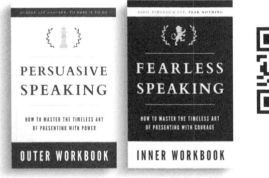

Claim These Free Resources that Will Help You Unleash the Power of Your Words and Speak with Confidence. Visit www.speakforsuccesshub.com/toolkit for Access.

18 Free PDF Resources

12 Iron Rules for Captivating Story, 21 Speeches that Changed the World, 341-Point Influence Checklist, 143 Persuasive Cognitive Biases, 17 Ways to Think On Your Feet, 18 Lies About Speaking Well, 137 Deadly Logical Fallacies, 12 Iron Rules For Captivating Slides, 371 Words that Persuade, 63 Truths of Speaking Well, 27 Laws of Empathy, 21 Secrets of Legendary Speeches, 19 Scripts that Persuade, 12 Iron Rules For Captivating Speech, 33 Laws of Charisma, 11 Influence Formulas, 219-Point Speech-Writing Checklist, 21 Eloquence Formulas

30 Free Video Lessons

We'll send you one free video lesson every day for 30 days, written and recorded by Peter D. Andrei. Days 1-10 cover authenticity, the prerequisite to confidence and persuasive power. Days 11-20 cover building self-belief and defeating communication anxiety. Days 21-30 cover how to speak with impact and influence, ensuring your words change minds instead of falling flat. Authenticity, self-belief, and impact – this course helps you master three components of confidence, turning even the most high-stakes presentations from obstacles into opportunities.

2 Free Workbooks

We'll send you two free workbooks, including long-lost excerpts by Dale Carnegie, the mega-bestselling author of *How to Win Friends and Influence People* (5,000,000 copies sold). *Fearless Speaking* guides you in the proven principles of mastering your inner game as a speaker. *Persuasive Speaking* guides you in the time-tested tactics of mastering your outer game by maximizing the power of your words. All of these resources complement the Speak for Success collection.

DECODING HUMAN NATURE

THE UNDERGROUND GUIDE TO EMOTIONAL INTELLIGENCE

Peter Andrei

DECODING HUMAN NATURE

SPEAK FOR SUCCESS COLLECTION BOOK

VIII

SPEAK
TRUTH
WELL
PRESS

A SUBSIDIARY OF SPEAK TRUTH WELL LLC
800 Boylston Street
Boston, MA 02199

SPEAK
TRUTH
WELL LLC

SPEAK FOR SUCCESS COLLECTION

Printed in the United States of America
40 39 38 37 36 35 34 33 32 31

While the author has made every effort to provide accurate internet addresses at the
time of publication, neither the publisher nor the author assumes any responsibility for
errors, or for changes that occur after publication. Further, the publisher does not
have any control over and does not assume any responsibility for author or third-party
websites or their content.

www.speakforsuccesshub.com/toolkit

FREE RESOURCES FOR OUR READERS

We believe in using the power of the internet to go above and beyond for our readers. That's why we created the free communication toolkit: 18 free PDF resources, 30 free video lessons, and even 2 free workbooks, including long-lost excerpts by Dale Carnegie, the mega-bestselling author of *How to Win Friends and Influence People*. (The workbooks help you put the most powerful strategies into action).

We know you're busy. That's why we designed these resources to be accessible, easy, and quick. Each PDF resource takes just 5 minutes to read or use. Each video lesson is only 5 minutes long. And in the workbooks, we bolded the key ideas throughout, so skimming them takes only 10 minutes each.

Why give so much away? For three reasons: we're grateful for you, it's useful content, and we want to go above and beyond. Questions? Feel free to email Peter directly at pandreibusiness@gmail.com.

www.speakforsuccesshub.com/toolkit

WHY DOES THIS HELP YOU?

I

The PDF resources cover topics like storytelling, logic, cognitive biases, empathy, charisma, and more. You can dig deeper into the specific topics that interest you most.

II

Many of the PDF resources are checklists, scripts, example-compilations, and formula-books. With these practical, step-by-step tools, you can quickly create messages that work.

III

With these free resources, you can supplement your reading of this book. You can find more specific guidance on the areas of communication you need to improve the most.

IV

The two workbooks offer practical and actionable guidance for speaking with complete confidence (*Fearless Speaking*) and irresistible persuasive power (*Persuasive Speaking*).

V

You can even learn from your phone with the free PDFs and the free video lessons, to develop your skills faster. The 30-lesson course reveals the secrets of building confidence.

VI

You are reading this because you want to improve your communication. These resources take you to the next level, helping you learn how to speak with power, impact, and confidence. We hope these resources make a difference. They are available here:

www.speakforsuccesshub.com/toolkit

From the desk of Peter Andrei
Speak Truth Well LLC
800 Boylston Street
Boston, MA 02199
pandreibusiness@gmail.com

May 15, 2021

What is Our Mission?

To whom it may concern:

The Wall Street Journal reports that public speaking is the world's biggest fear – bigger than being hit by a car. According to Columbia University, this pervasive, powerful, common phobia can reduce someone's salary by 10% or more. It can reduce someone's chances of graduating college by 10% and cut their chances of attaining a managerial or leadership position at work by 15%.

If weak presentation kills your good ideas, it kills your career. If weak communication turns every negotiation, meeting, pitch, speech, presentation, discussion, and interview into an obstacle (instead of an opportunity), it slows your progress. And if weak communication slows your progress, it tears a gaping hole in your confidence – which halts your progress.

Words can change the world. They can improve your station in life, lifting you forward and upward to higher and higher successes. But they have to be strong words spoken well: rarities in a world where most people fail to connect, engage, and persuade; fail to answer the question "why should we care about this?"; fail to impact, inspire, and influence; and, in doing so, fail to be all they could be.

Now zoom out. Multiply this dynamic by one thousand; one million; one billion. The individual struggle morphs into a problem for our communities, our countries, our world. Imagine the many millions of paradigm-shattering, life-changing, life-saving ideas that never saw the light of day. Imagine how many brilliant convictions were sunk in the shipyard. Imagine all that could have been that failed to be.

Speak Truth Well LLC solves this problem by teaching ambitious professionals how to turn communication from an obstacle into an engine: a tool for converting "what could be" into "what is." There is no upper limit: inexperienced speakers can become self-assured and impactful; veteran speakers can master the skill by learning advanced strategies; masters can learn how to outperform their former selves.

We achieve our mission by producing the best publications, articles, books, video courses, and coaching programs available on public speaking and communication, and at non-prohibitive prices. This combination of quality and accessibility has allowed Speak Truth Well to serve over 70,000 customers in its year of launch alone (2021). Grateful as we are, we hope to one day serve millions.

Dedicated to your success,

Peter Andrei
President of Speak Truth Well LLC
pandreibusiness@gmail.com

PROLOGUE:

This three-part prologue reveals my story, my work, and the practical and ethical principles of communication. It is not a mere introduction. It will help you get more out of the book. It is a preface to the entire 15-book Speak for Success collection. It will show you how to use the information with ease, confidence, and fluency, and how to get better results faster. If you want to skip this, flip to page 42, or read only the parts of interest.

I

page XIII

MY STORY AND THE STORY OF THIS COLLECTION

how I discovered the hidden key to successful communication, public speaking, influence, and persuasion

II

page XXI

THE 15-BOOK SPEAK FOR SUCCESS COLLECTION

confidence, leadership, charisma, influence, public speaking, eloquence, human nature, credibility - it's all here

III

page XXIV

THE PRACTICAL TACTICS AND ETHICAL PRINCIPLES

how to easily put complex strategies into action and how to use the power of words to improve the world

I

MY STORY AND THE STORY OF THIS COLLECTION

how I discovered the hidden key to successful communication, public speaking, influence, and persuasion (by reflecting on a painful failure)

HOW TO GAIN AN UNFAIR ADVANTAGE IN YOUR CAREER, BUSINESS, AND LIFE BY MASTERING THE POWER OF YOUR WORDS

I WAS SITTING IN MY OFFICE, TAPPING A PEN against my small wooden desk. My breaths were jagged, shallow, and rapid. My hands were shaking. I glanced at the clock: 11:31 PM. "I'm not ready." Have you ever had that thought?

I had to speak in front of 200 people the next morning. I had to convince them to put faith in my idea. But I was terrified, attacked by nameless, unreasoning, and unjustified terror which killed my ability to think straight, believe in myself, and get the job done.

Do you know the feeling?

After a sleepless night, the day came. I rose, wobbling on my tired legs. My head felt like it was filled with cotton candy. I couldn't direct my train of thoughts. A rushing waterfall of unhinged, self-destructive, and meaningless musings filled my head with an uncompromising cacophony of anxious, ricocheting nonsense.

"Call in sick."

"You're going to embarrass yourself."

"You're not ready."

I put on my favorite blue suit – my "lucky suit" – and my oversized blue-gold wristwatch; my "lucky" wristwatch.

"You're definitely not ready."

"That tie is ugly."

"You can't do this."

The rest went how you would expect. I drank coffee. Got in my car. Drove. Arrived. Waited. Waited. Waited. Spoke. Did poorly. Rushed back to my seat. Waited. Waited.

Waited. Got in my car. Drove. Arrived home. Sat back in my wooden seat where I accurately predicted "I'm not ready" the night before.

Relieved it was over but disappointed with my performance, I placed a sheet of paper on the desk. I wrote "MY PROBLEMS" at the top, and under that, my prompt for the evening: "What did I do so badly? Why did everything feel so off? Why did the speech fail?"

"You stood in front of 200 people and looked at... a piece of paper, not unlike this one. What the hell were you thinking? You're not fooling anyone by reading a sentence and then looking up at them as you say it out loud. They know you're reading a manuscript, and they know what that means. You are unsure of yourself. You are unsure of your message. You are unprepared. Next: Why did you speak in that odd, low, monotone voice? That sounded like nails on a chalkboard. And it was inauthentic. Next: Why did you open by talking about yourself? Also, you're not particularly funny. No more jokes. And what was the structure of the speech? It had no structure. That, I feel, is probably a pretty big problem."

I believed in my idea, and I wanted to get it across. Of course, I wanted the tangible markers of a successful speech. I wanted action. I wanted the speech to change something in the real world. But my motivations were deeper than that. I wanted to see people "click" and come on board my way of thinking. I wanted to captivate the audience. I wanted to speak with an engaging, impactful voice, drawing the audience in, not repelling them. I wanted them to remember my message and to remember me. I wanted to feel, for just a moment, the thrill of power. But not the petty, forceful power of tyrants and dictators; the justified power – the earned power – of having a good idea and conveying it well; the power of Martin Luther King and John F. Kennedy; a power harnessed in service of a valuable idea, not the personal privilege of the speaker. And I wanted confidence: the quiet strength that comes from knowing your words don't stand in your way, but propel you and the ideas you care about to glorious new mountaintops.

Instead, I stood before the audience, essentially powerless. I spoke for 20 painful minutes – painful for them and for me – and then sat down. I barely made a dent in anyone's consciousness. I generated no excitement. Self-doubt draped its cold embrace over me. Anxiety built a wall between "what I am" and "what I could be."

I had tried so many different solutions. I read countless books on effective communication, asked countless effective communicators for their advice, and consumed countless courses on powerful public speaking. Nothing worked. All the "solutions" that didn't really solve my problem had one thing in common: they treated communication as an abstract art form. They were filled with vague, abstract pieces of advice like "think positive thoughts" and "be yourself." They confused me more than anything else. Instead of illuminating the secrets I had been looking for, they shrouded the elusive but indispensable skill of powerful speaking in uncertainty.

I knew I had to master communication. I knew that the world's most successful people are all great communicators. I knew that effective communication is the bridge between "what I have" and "what I want," or at least an essential part of that bridge. I knew that without effective communication – without the ability to influence, inspire, captivate, and move – I would be all but powerless.

I knew that the person who can speak up but doesn't is no better off than the person who can't speak at all. I heard a wise man say "If you can think and speak and write, you are absolutely deadly. Nothing can get in your way." I heard another wise man say "Speech is power: speech is to persuade, to convert, to compel. It is to bring another out of his bad sense into your good sense." I heard a renowned psychologist say "If you look at people who are remarkably successful across life, there's various reasons. But one of them is that they're unbelievably good at articulating what they're aiming at and strategizing and negotiating and enticing people with a vision forward. Get your words together... that makes you unstoppable. If you are an effective writer and speaker and communicator, you have all the authority and competence that there is."

When I worked in the Massachusetts State House for the Department of Public Safety and Homeland Security, I had the opportunity to speak with countless senators, state representatives, CEOs, and other successful people. In our conversations, however brief, I always asked the same question: "What are the ingredients of your success? What got you where you are?" 100% of them said effective communication. There was not one who said anything else. No matter their field – whether they were entrepreneurs, FBI agents, political leaders, business leaders, or multimillionaire donors – they all pointed to one skill: the ability to convey powerful words in powerful ways. Zero exceptions.

Can you believe it? It still astonishes me.

My problem, and I bet this may be your obstacle as well, was that most of the advice I consumed on this critical skill barely scratched the surface. Sure, it didn't make matters worse, and it certainly offered some improvement, but only in inches when I needed progress in miles. If I stuck with the mainstream public speaking advice, I knew I wouldn't unleash the power of my words. And if I didn't do that, I knew I would always accomplish much less than I could. I knew I would suffocate my own potential. I knew I would feel a rush of crippling anxiety every time I was asked to give a presentation. I knew I would live a life of less fulfillment, less success, less achievement, more frustration, more difficulty, and more anxiety. I knew my words would never become all they could be, which means that I would never become all I could be.

To make matters worse, the mainstream advice – which is not wrong, but simply not deep enough – is everywhere. Almost every article, book, or course published on this subject falls into the mainstream category. And to make matters worse, it's almost impossible to know that until you've spent your hard-earned money and scarce time with the resource. And even then, you might just shrug, and assume that shallow, abstract advice is all there is to the "art" of public speaking. As far as I'm concerned, this is a travesty.

I kept writing. "It felt like there was no real motive; no real impulse to action. Why did they need to act? You didn't tell them. What would happen if they didn't? You didn't tell them that either. Also, you tried too hard to put on a formal façade; you spoke in strange, twisted ways. It didn't sound sophisticated. And your mental game was totally off. You let your mind fill with destructive, doubtful, self-defeating thoughts. And your preparation was totally backward. It did more to set bad habits in stone than it did to set you up for success. And you tried to build suspense at one point but revealed the final point way too early, ruining the effect."

I went on and on until I had a stack of papers filled with problems. "That's no good," I thought. I needed solutions. Everything else I tried failed. But I had one more idea: "I remember reading a great speech. What was it? Oh yeah, that's right: JFK's inaugural address. Let me go pull it up and see why it was so powerful." And that's when everything changed.

I grabbed another sheet of paper. I opened JFK's inaugural address on my laptop. I started reading. Observing. Analyzing. Reverse-engineering. I started writing down what I saw. Why did it work? Why was it powerful? I was like an archaeologist, digging through his speech for the secrets of powerful communication. I got more and more excited as I kept going. It was late at night, but the shocking and invaluable discoveries I was making gave me a burst of energy. It felt like JFK – one of the most powerful and effective speakers of all time – was coaching me in his rhetorical secrets, showing me how to influence an audience, draw them into my narrative, and find words that get results.

"Oh, so that's how you grab attention."

"Aha! So, if I tell them this, they will see why it matters."

"Fascinating – I can apply this same structure to my speech."

Around 3:00 in the morning, an epiphany hit me like a ton of bricks. That night, a new paradigm was born. A new opportunity emerged for all those who want to unleash the unstoppable power of their words. This new opportunity changed everything for me and eventually, tens of thousands of others. It is now my mission to bring it to millions, so that good people know what they need to know to use their words to achieve their dreams and improve the world.

Want to hear the epiphany?

The mainstream approach: Communication is an art form. It is unlike those dry, boring, "academic" subjects. There are no formulas. There are no patterns. It's all about thinking positive thoughts, faking confidence, and making eye contact. Some people are naturally gifted speakers. For others, the highest skill level they can attain is "not horrible."

The consequences of the mainstream approach: Advice that barely scratches the surface of the power of words. Advice that touches only the tip of the tip of the iceberg. A limited body of knowledge that blinds itself to thousands of hidden, little-known communication strategies that carry immense power; that blinds itself to 95% of what great communication really is. Self-limiting dogmas about who can do what, and how great communicators become great. Half the progress in twice the time, and everything that entails: missed opportunities, unnecessary and preventable frustration and anxiety, and confusion about what to say and how to say it. How do I know? Because I've been there. It's not pretty.

My epiphany, the new Speak for Success paradigm: Communication is as much a science as it is an art. You can study words that changed the world, uncover the hidden secrets of their power, and apply these proven principles to your own message. You can discover precisely what made great communicators great and adopt the same strategies. You can do this without being untrue to yourself or flatly imitating others. In fact, you can do this while being truer to yourself and more original than you ever have been before. Communication is not unpredictable, wishy-washy, or abstract. You can apply predictable processes and principles to reach your goals and get results. You can pick and choose from thousands of little-known speaking strategies, combining your favorite to create a unique communication approach that suits you perfectly. You can effortlessly use the same tactics of the world's most transformational leaders and speakers, and do so automatically, by default, without even thinking about it, as a matter of effortless habit. That's power.

The benefits of the Speak for Success paradigm: Less confusion. More confidence. Less frustration. More clarity. Less anxiety. More courage. You understand the whole iceberg of effective communication. As a result, your words captivate others. You draw them into a persuasive narrative, effortlessly linking your desires and their motives. You know exactly what to say. You know exactly how to say it. You know exactly how to keep your head clear; you are a master of the mental game. Your words can move mountains. Your words are the most powerful tools in your arsenal, and you use them to seize opportunities, move your mission forward, and make the world a better place. Simply put, you speak for success.

Fast forward a few years.

I was sitting in my office at my small wooden desk. My breaths were deep, slow, and steady. My entire being – mind, body, soul – was poised and focused. I set my speech manuscript to the side. I glanced at the clock: 12:01 AM. "Let's go. I'm ready."

I had to speak in front of 200 people the next morning. I had to convince them to put faith in my idea. And I was thrilled, filled with genuine gratitude at the opportunity to do what I love: get up in front of a crowd, think clearly, speak well, and get the job done.

I slept deeply. I dreamt vividly. I saw myself giving the speech. I saw myself victorious, in every sense of the word. I heard applause. I saw their facial expressions. I rose. My head was clear. My mental game was pristine. My mind was an ally, not an obstacle.

"This is going to be fun."

"I'll do my best, and whatever happens, happens."

"I'm so lucky that I get to do this again."

I put on my lucky outfit: the blue suit and the blue-gold watch.

"Remember the principles. They work."

"You developed a great plan last night. It's a winner."

"I can't wait."

The rest went how you would expect. I ate breakfast. Got in my car. Drove. Arrived. Waited. Waited. Waited. Spoke. Succeeded. Walked back to my seat. Waited. Waited. Waited. Got in my car. Drove. Arrived home. Sat back in my wooden seat where I accurately predicted "I'm ready" the night before.

I got my idea across perfectly. My message succeeded: it motivated action and created real-world change. I saw people "click" when I hit the rhetorical peak of my speech. I saw them leaning forward, totally hushed, completely absorbed. I applied the proven principles of engaging and impactful vocal modulation. I knew they would remember me and my message; I engineered my words to be memorable. I felt the thrilling power of giving a great speech. I felt the quiet confidence of knowing that my words carried weight; that they could win hearts, change minds, and help me reach the heights of my potential. I tore off the cold embrace of self-doubt. I defeated communication anxiety and broke down the wall between "what I am" and "what I could be."

Disappointed it was over but pleased with my performance, I placed a sheet of paper on the desk. I wrote "Speak Truth Well" and started planning what would become my business.

To date, we have helped tens of thousands of people gain an unfair advantage in their career, business, and life by unleashing the power of their words. And they experienced the exact same transformation I experienced when they applied the system.

If you tried to master communication before but haven't gotten the results you wanted, it's because of the mainstream approach; an approach that tells you "smiling at the audience" and "making eye contact" is all you need to know to speak well. That's not exactly a malicious lie – they don't know any better – but it is completely incorrect and severely harmful.

If you've been concerned that you won't be able to become a vastly more effective and confident communicator, I want to put those fears to rest. I felt the same way. The people I work with felt the same way. We just needed the right system. One public speaking book written by the director of a popular public speaking forum – I won't name names – wants you to believe that there are "nine public speaking secrets of the world's top minds." Wrong: There are many more than nine. If you feel that anyone who would boil down communication to just nine secrets is either missing something or holding it back, you're right. And the alternative is a much more comprehensive and powerful system. It's a system that gave me and everyone I worked with the transformation we were looking for.

Want to Talk? Email Me:

PANDREIBUSINESS@GMAIL.COM

This is My Personal Email.
I Read Every Message and
Respond in Under 12 Hours.

Visit Our Digital Headquarters:

WWW.SPEAKFORSUCCESSHUB.COM

See All Our Free Resources,
Books, Courses, and Services.

II

THE 15-BOOK SPEAK FOR SUCCESS COLLECTION

confidence, leadership, charisma, influence, public speaking, eloquence, human nature, credibility – it's all here, in a unified collection

....A Brief Overview..

- I wrote *How Highly Effective People Speak* to reveal the hidden patterns in the words of the world's most successful and powerful communicators, so that you can adopt the same tactics and speak with the same impact and influence.

- I wrote *Eloquence* to uncover the formulas of beautiful, moving, captivating, and powerful words, so that you can use these exact same step-by-step structures to quickly make your language electrifying, charismatic, and eloquent.

- I wrote *How Legendary Leaders Speak* to illuminate the little-known five-step communication process the top leaders of the past 500 years all used to spread their message, so that you can use it to empower your ideas and get results.

- I wrote *Influential Leadership* to expose the differences between force and power and to show how great leaders use the secrets of irresistible influence to develop gentle power, so that you can move forward and lead with ease.

- I wrote *Public Speaking Mastery* to shatter the myths and expose the harmful advice about public speaking, and to offer a proven, step-by-step framework for speaking well, so that you can always speak with certainty and confidence.

- I wrote *The 7 Keys to Confidence* to bring to light the ancient 4,000-year-old secrets I used to master the mental game and speak in front of hundreds without a second of self-doubt or anxiety, so that you can feel the same freedom.

- I wrote *Trust is Power* to divulge how popular leaders and career communicators earn our trust, speak with credibility, and use this to rise to new heights of power, so that you can do the same thing to advance your purpose and mission.

- I wrote *Decoding Human Nature* to answer the critical question "what do people want?" and reveal how to use this knowledge to develop unparalleled influence, so that people adopt your idea, agree with your position, and support you.

- I wrote *Influence* to unearth another little-known five-step process for winning hearts and changing minds, so that you can know with certainty that your message will persuade people, draw support, and motivate enthusiastic action.

- I wrote *The Psychology of Persuasion* to completely and fully unveil everything about the psychology behind "Yes, I love it! What's the next step?" so that you can use easy step-by-step speaking formulas that get people to say exactly that.

- I wrote *How Visionaries Speak* to debunk common lies about effective communication that hold you back and weaken your words, so that you can boldly share your ideas without accidentally sabotaging your own message.

- I wrote *The Eloquent Leader* to disclose the ten steps to communicating with power and persuasion, so that you don't miss any of the steps and fail to connect, captivate, influence, and inspire in a crucial high-stakes moment.

- I wrote *The Language of Leadership* to unpack the unique, hidden-in-plain-sight secrets of how presidents and world-leaders build movements with the laws of powerful language, so that you use them to propel yourself forward.

- I wrote *The Psychology of Communication* to break the news that most presentations succeed or fail in the first thirty seconds and to reveal proven, step-by-step formulas that grab, hold, and direct attention, so that yours succeeds.

- I wrote *The Charisma Code* to shatter the myths and lies about charisma and reveal its nature as a concrete skill you can master with proven strategies, so that people remember you, your message, and how you electrified the room.

You Can Learn More Here:
www.speakforsuccesshub.com/series

HOW HIGHLY EFFECTIVE PEOPLE SPEAK

HOW HIGH PERFORMERS USE PSYCHOLOGY TO INFLUENCE WITH EASE

PETER D. ANDREI

ELOQUENCE

THE HIDDEN SECRET OF WORDS THAT CHANGE THE WORLD

PETER D. ANDREI

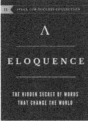

HOW LEGENDARY LEADERS SPEAK

451 PROVEN COMMUNICATION STRATEGIES OF THE WORLD'S TOP LEADERS

PETER D. ANDREI

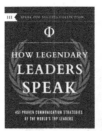

INFLUENTIAL LEADERSHIP

HOW POWERFUL WORDS CREATE REMARKABLE RESULTS

PETER D. ANDREI

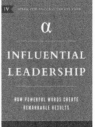

PUBLIC SPEAKING MASTERY

HOW TO SPEAK WITH CONFIDENCE, IMPACT, AND INFLUENCE

PETER D. ANDREI

THE 7 KEYS TO CONFIDENCE

HOW TO LEAD, SPEAK, AND LIVE WITH COURAGE

PETER D. ANDREI

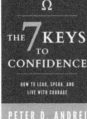

TRUST IS POWER

HOW TO COMMUNICATE IN A WORLD THAT DOUBTS EVERYTHING

PETER D. ANDREI

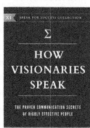

DECODING HUMAN NATURE

THE UNDERGROUND GUIDE TO EMOTIONAL INTELLIGENCE

PETER D. ANDREI

INFLUENCE

THE PSYCHOLOGY OF WORDS THAT WIN HEARTS AND CHANGE MINDS

PETER D. ANDREI

THE PSYCHOLOGY OF PERSUASION

HOW TO USE PROVEN SPEAKING PATTERNS TO MAKE YOUR IDEAS IRRESISTIBLE

PETER D. ANDREI

HOW VISIONARIES SPEAK

THE PROVEN COMMUNICATION SECRETS OF HIGHLY EFFECTIVE PEOPLE

PETER D. ANDREI

THE ELOQUENT LEADER

10 STEPS TO COMMUNICATION THAT PROPELS YOU FORWARD

PETER D. ANDREI

THE LANGUAGE OF LEADERSHIP

HOW GREAT LEADERS USE THE LAWS OF POWERFUL LANGUAGE TO GET RESULTS

PETER D. ANDREI

THE PSYCHOLOGY OF COMMUNICATION

THE UNDERGROUND GUIDE TO PERSUASIVE PRESENTATIONS AND EASY ELOQUENCE

PETER D. ANDREI

THE CHARISMA CODE

MASTERING INFLUENCE, PUBLIC SPEAKING, AND THE ART OF COMMUNICATION

PETER D. ANDREI

III

PRACTICAL TACTICS AND ETHICAL PRINCIPLES

how to easily put complex strategies into action and how to use the power of words to improve the world in an ethical and effective way

MOST COMMUNICATION BOOKS

HAVE YOU READ ANOTHER BOOK ON COMMUNICATION? If you have, let me remind you what you probably learned. And if you haven't, let me briefly spoil 95% of them. "Prepare. Smile. Dress to impress. Keep it simple. Overcome your fears. Speak from the heart. Be authentic. Show them why you care. Speak in terms of their interests. To defeat anxiety, know your stuff. Emotion persuades, not logic. Speak with confidence. Truth sells. And respect is returned."

There you have it. That is most of what you learn in most communication books. None of it is wrong. None of it is misleading. Those ideas are true and valuable. But they are not enough. They are only the absolute basics. And my job is to offer you much more.

Einstein said that "if you can't explain it in a sentence, you don't know it well enough." He also told us to "make it as simple as possible, but no simpler." You, as a communicator, must satisfy both of these maxims, one warning against the dangers of excess complexity, and one warning against the dangers of excess simplicity. And I, as someone who communicates about communication in my books, courses, and coaching, must do the same.

THE SPEAK FOR SUCCESS SYSTEM

The Speak for Success system makes communication as simple as possible. Other communication paradigms make it even simpler. Naturally, this means our system is more complex. This is an unavoidable consequence of treating communication as a deep and concrete science instead of a shallow and abstract art. If you don't dive into learning communication at all, you miss out. I'm sure you agree with that. But if you don't dive *deep*, you still miss out.

THE FOUR QUADRANTS OF COMMUNICATION

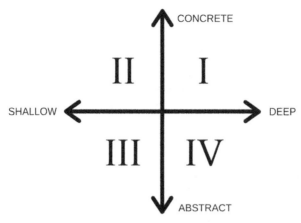

FIGURE VIII: There are four predominant views of communication (whether it takes the form of public speaking, negotiation, writing, or debating is irrelevant). The first view is that communication is concrete and deep. The second view is that communication is concrete and shallow. The third view is that communication is shallow and abstract. The fourth view is that communication is deep and abstract.

WHAT IS COMMUNICATION?

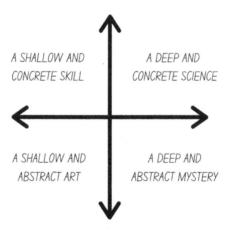

FIGURE VII: The first view treats communication as a science: "There are concrete formulas, rules, principles, and strategies, and they go very deep." The second view treats it as a skill: "Yes, there are concrete formulas, rules, and strategies, but they don't go very deep." The third view treats it as an art: "Rules? Formulas? It's not that complicated. Just smile and think positive thoughts." The fourth view treats it as a mystery: "How are some people such effective communicators? I will never know…"

WHERE WE STAND ON THE QUESTION

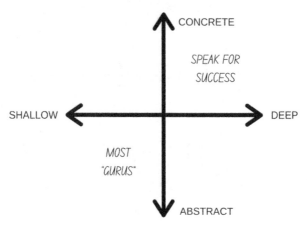

FIGURE VI: Speak for Success takes the view that communication is a deep and concrete science. (And by "takes the view," I mean "has discovered.") Most other writers, thought-leaders, public speaking coaches, and individuals and organizations in this niche treat communication as a shallow and abstract art.

This doesn't mean the Speak for Success system neglects the basics. It only means it goes far beyond the basics, and that it doesn't turn simple ideas into 200 pages of filler. It also doesn't mean that the Speak for Success system is unnecessarily complex. It is as simple as it can possibly be. In this book, and in the other books of the Speak for Success collection, you'll find simple pieces of advice, easy formulas, and straightforward rules. You'll find theories, strategies, tactics, mental models, and principles. None of this should pose a challenge. But you'll also find advanced, complicated tactics. These might.

What is the purpose of the guide on the top of the next page? To reveal the methods that make advanced strategies easy. When you use the tactics revealed in this guide, the difficulty of using the advanced strategies drops dramatically. If the 15-book Speak for Success collection is a complete encyclopedia of communication, to be used like a handbook, then this guide is a handbook for the handbook.

A SAMPLING OF EASY AND HARD STRATEGIES

Easy and Simple	Hard and Complicated
Use Four-Corner Eye Contact	The Fluency-Magnitude Matrix
Appeal to Their Values	The VPB Triad
Describe the Problem You Solve	The Illusory Truth Effect
Use Open Body Language	Percussive Rhythm
Tell a Quick Story	Alliterative Flow
Appeal to Emotion	Stacking and Layering Structures
Project Your Voice	The Declaratory Cascade
Keep it as Simple as Possible	Alternating Semantic Sentiments

THE PRACTICAL TACTICS

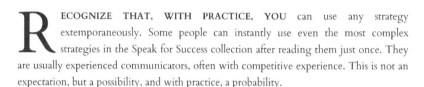

RECOGNIZE THAT, WITH PRACTICE, YOU can use any strategy extemporaneously. Some people can instantly use even the most complex strategies in the Speak for Success collection after reading them just once. They are usually experienced communicators, often with competitive experience. This is not an expectation, but a possibility, and with practice, a probability.

CREATE A COMMUNICATION PLAN. Professional communication often follows a strategic plan. Put these techniques into your plan. Following an effective plan is not harder than following an ineffective one. Marshall your arguments. Marshall your rhetoric. Stack the deck. Know what you know, and how to say it.

DESIGN AN MVP. If you are speaking on short notice, you can create a "minimum viable plan." This can be a few sentences on a notecard jotted down five minutes before speaking. The same principle of formal communication plans applies: While advanced strategies may overburden you if you attempt them in an impromptu setting, putting them into a plan makes them easy.

MASTER YOUR RHETORICAL STACK. Master one difficult strategy. Master another one. Combine them. Master a third. Build out a "rhetorical stack" of ten strategies you can use fluently, in impromptu or extemporaneous communication. Pick strategies that come fluently to you and that complement each other.

PRACTICE THEM TO FLUENCY. I coach a client who approached me and said he wants to master every strategy I ever compiled. That's a lot. As of this writing, we're 90 one-hour sessions in. To warm up for one of our sessions, I gave him a challenge: "Give an impromptu speech on the state of the American economy, and after you stumble, hesitate, or falter four times, I'll cut you off. The challenge is to see how long you can go." He spoke for 20 minutes without a single mistake. After 20 minutes, he brought the impromptu speech to a perfect, persuasive, forceful, and eloquent conclusion. And he naturally and fluently used advanced strategies throughout his impromptu speech. After he closed the speech (which he did because he wanted to get on with the session), I asked him if he thought deeply about the strategies he used. He said no. He used them thoughtlessly. Why? Because he practiced them. You can too. You can practice them on your own. You don't need an audience. You don't need a coach. You don't even need to speak. Practice in your head. Practice ones that resonate with you. Practice with topics you care about.

KNOW TEN TIMES MORE THAN YOU INTEND TO SAY. And know what you do intend to say about ten times more fluently than you need to. This gives your mind room to relax, and frees up cognitive bandwidth to devote to strategy and rhetoric in real-time. Need to speak for five minutes? Be able to speak for 50. Need to read it three times to be able to deliver it smoothly? Read it 30 times.

INCORPORATE THEM IN SLIDES. You can use your slides or visual aids to help you ace complicated strategies. If you can't remember the five steps of a strategy, your slides can still follow them. Good slides aren't harder to use than bad slides.

USE THEM IN WRITTEN COMMUNICATION. You can read your speech. In some situations, this is more appropriate than impromptu or extemporaneous speaking. And if a strategy is difficult to remember in impromptu speaking, you can write it into your speech. And let's not forget about websites, emails, letters, etc.

PICK AND CHOOSE EASY ONES. Use strategies that come naturally and don't overload your mind. Those that do are counterproductive in fast-paced situations.

TAKE SMALL STEPS TO MASTERY. Practice one strategy. Practice it again. Keep going until you master it. Little by little, add to your base of strategies. But never take steps that overwhelm you. Pick a tactic. Practice it. Master it. Repeat.

MEMORIZE AN ENTIRE MESSAGE. Sometimes this is the right move. Is it a high-stakes message? Do you have the time? Do you have the energy? Given the situation, would a memorized delivery beat an impromptu, in-the-moment, spontaneous delivery? If you opt for memorizing, using advanced strategies is easy.

USE ONE AT A TIME. Pick an advanced strategy. Deliver it. Now what? Pick another advanced strategy. Deliver it. Now another. Have you been speaking for a while? Want to bring it to a close? Pick a closing strategy. For some people, using advanced strategies extemporaneously is easy, but only if they focus on one at a time.

MEMORIZE A KEY PHRASE. Deliver your impromptu message as planned, but add a few short, memorized key phrases throughout that include advanced strategies.

CREATE TALKING POINTS. Speak from a list of pre-written bullet-points; big-picture ideas you seek to convey. This is halfway between fully impromptu speaking and using a script. It's not harder to speak from a strategic and persuasively-advanced list of talking points than it is to speak from a persuasively weak list. You can either memorize your talking points, or have them in front of you as a guide.

TREAT IT LIKE A SCIENCE. At some point, you struggled with a skill that you now perform effortlessly. You mastered it. It's a habit. You do it easily, fluently, and thoughtlessly. You can do it while you daydream. Communication is the same. These tactics, methods, and strategies are not supposed to be stuck in the back of your mind as you speak. They are supposed to be ingrained in your habits.

RELY ON FLOW. In fast-paced and high-stakes situations, you usually don't plan every word, sentence, and idea consciously and deliberately. Rather, you let your subconscious mind take over. You speak from a flow state. In flow, you may flawlessly execute strategies that would have overwhelmed your conscious mind.

LISTEN TO THE PROMPTS. You read a strategy and found it difficult to use extemporaneously. But as you speak, your subconscious mind gives you a prompt: "this strategy would work great here." Your subconscious mind saw the opportunity and surfaced the prompt. You execute it, and you do so fluently and effortlessly.

FOLLOW THE FIVE-STEP CYCLE. First, find truth. Research. Prepare. Learn. Second, define your message. Figure out what you believe about what you learned. Third, polish your message with rhetorical strategies, without distorting the precision with which it conveys the truth. Fourth, practice the polished ideas. Fifth, deliver them. The endeavor of finding truth comes before the rhetorical endeavor. First, find the right message. Then, find the best way to convey it.

CREATE YOUR OWN STRATEGY. As you learn new theories, mental models, and principles of psychology and communication, you may think of a new strategy built around the theories, models, and principles. Practice it, test it, and codify it.

STACK GOOD HABITS. An effective communicator is the product of his habits. If you want to be an effective communicator, stack good communication habits (and break bad ones). This is a gradual process. It doesn't happen overnight.

DON'T TRY TO USE THEM. Don't force it. If a strategy seems too difficult, don't try to use it. You might find yourself using it anyway when the time is right.

KNOW ONLY ONE. If you master one compelling communication strategy, like one of the many powerful three-part structures that map out a persuasive speech, that can often be enough to drastically and dramatically improve your impact.

REMEMBER THE SHORTCOMING OF MODELS. All models are wrong, but some are useful. Many of these complex strategies and theories are models. They represent reality, but they are not reality. They help you navigate the territory, but they are not the territory. They are a map, to be used if it helps you navigate, and to be discarded the moment it prevents you from navigating.

DON'T LET THEM INHIBIT YOU. Language flows from thought. You've got to have something to say. And *then* you make it as compelling as possible. And *then* you shape it into something poised and precise; persuasive and powerful; compelling and convincing. Meaning and message come first. Rhetoric comes second. Don't take all this discussion of "advanced communication strategies," "complex communication tactics," and "the deep and concrete science of communication" to suggest that the basics don't matter. They do. Tell the truth as precisely and boldly as you can. Know your subject-matter like the back of your hand. Clear your mind and focus on precisely articulating exactly what you believe to be true. Be authentic. The advanced strategies are not supposed to stand between you and your audience. They are not supposed to stand between you and your authentic and spontaneous self – they are supposed to be integrated with it. They are not an end in themselves, but a means to the end of persuading the maximum number of people to adopt truth. Trust your instinct. Trust your intuition. It won't fail you.

MASTERING ONE COMMUNICATION SKILL

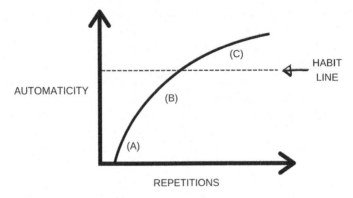

FIGURE V: Automaticity is the extent to which you do something automatically, without thinking about it. At the start of building a communication habit, it has low automaticity. You need to think about it consciously (A). After more repetitions, it gets easier and more automatic (B). Eventually, the behavior becomes more automatic than deliberate. At this point, it becomes a habit (C).

MASTERING COMMUNICATION

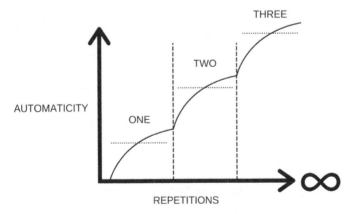

FIGURE IV: Layer good communication habits on top of each other. Go through the learning curve over and over again. When you master the first good habit, jump to the second. This pattern will take you to mastery.

THE FOUR LEVELS OF KNOWING

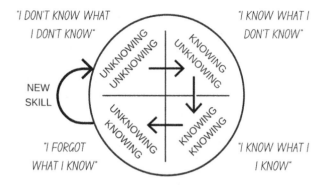

FIGURE III: First, you don't know you don't know it. Then, you discover it and know you don't know it. Then, you practice it and know you know it. Then, it becomes a habit. You forget you know it. It's ingrained in your habits.

REVISITING THE LEARNING CURVE

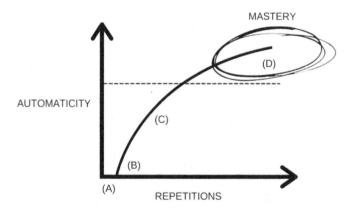

FIGURE II: Note the stages of knowing on the learning curve: unknowing unknowing (A), knowing unknowing (B), knowing knowing (C), unknowing knowing (D).

WHAT'S REALLY HAPPENING?

Have you ever thought deeply about what happens when you communicate? Let's run through the mile-high view.

At some point in your life, you bumped into an experience. You observed. You learned. The experience changed you. Your neural networks connected in new ways. New rivers of neurons began to flow through them.

The experience etched a pattern into your neurobiology representing information about the moral landscape of the universe; a map of *where we are, where we should go, and how we should make the journey.* This is meaning. This is your message.

Now, you take the floor before a crowd. Whether you realize it or not, you want to copy the neural pattern from your mind to their minds. You want to show them where we are, where we should go, and how we should make the journey.

So, you speak. You gesture. You intone. Your words convey meaning. Your body language conveys meaning. Your voice conveys meaning. You flood them with a thousand different inputs, some as subtle as the contraction of a single facial muscle, some as obvious as your opening line. Your character, your intentions, and your goals seep into your speech. Everyone can see them. Everyone can see you.

Let's step into the mind of one of your audience members. Based on all of this, based on a thousand different inputs, based on complex interactions between their conscious and nonconscious minds, the ghost in the machine steps in, and by a dint of free will, acts as the final arbiter and makes a choice. A mind is changed. You changed it. And changing it changed you. You became more confident, more articulate, and deeper; more capable, more impactful, and stronger.

Communication is connection. One mind, with a consciousness at its base, seeks to use ink or pixels or airwaves to connect to another. Through this connection, it seeks to copy neural patterns about the present, the future, and the moral landscape. Whatever your message is, the underlying connection is identical. How could it not be?

IS IT ETHICAL?

By "it," I mean deliberately using language to get someone to do or think something. Let's call this rhetoric. We could just as well call it persuasion, influence, communication, or even leadership itself.

The answer is yes. The answer is no. Rhetoric is a helping hand. It is an iron fist. It is Martin Luther King's dream. It is Stalin's nightmare. It is the "shining city on the hill." It is the iron curtain. It is "the pursuit of happiness." It is the trail of tears. It is "liberty, equality, and brotherhood." It is the reign of terror. Rhetoric is a tool. It is neither good nor evil. It is a reflection of our nature.

Rhetoric can motivate love, peace, charity, strength, patience, progress, prosperity, common sense, common purpose, courage, hope, generosity, and unity. It can also sow the seeds of division, fan the flames of tribalism, and beat back the better angels of our nature.

Rhetoric is the best of us and the worst of us. It is as good as you are. It is as evil as you are. It is as peace-loving as you are. It is as hate-mongering as you are. And I know what you are. I know my readers are generous, hardworking people who want to build a better future for themselves, for their families, and for all humankind. I know that if you have these tools in your hands, you will use them to achieve a moral mission. That's why putting them in your hands is my mission.

Joseph Chatfield said "[rhetoric] is the power to talk people out of their sober and natural opinions." I agree. But it is also the power to talk people out of their wrong and harmful opinions. And if you're using rhetoric to talk people out of their sober opinions, the problem isn't rhetoric, it's you.

In the *Institutes of Rhetoric*, Roman rhetorician Quintilian wrote the following: "The orator then, whom I am concerned to form, shall be the orator as defined by Marcus Cato, a good man, skilled in speaking. But above all he must possess the quality which Cato places first and which is in the very nature of things the greatest and most important, that is, he must be a good man. This is essential not merely on account of the fact that, if the powers of eloquence serve only to lend arms to crime, there can be nothing more pernicious than eloquence to public and private welfare alike, while I myself, who have labored to the best of my ability to contribute something of the value to oratory, shall have rendered the worst of services to mankind, if I forge these weapons not for a soldier, but for a robber."

Saint Augustine, who was trained in the classical schools of rhetoric in the 3rd century, summed it up well: "Rhetoric, after all, being the art of persuading people to accept something, whether it is true or false, would anyone dare to maintain that truth should stand there without any weapons in the hands of its defenders against falsehood; that those speakers, that is to say, who are trying to convince their hearers of what is untrue, should know how to get them on their side, to gain their attention and have them eating out of their hands by their opening remarks, while these who are defending the truth should not? That those should utter their lies briefly, clearly, plausibly, and these should state their truths in a manner too boring to listen to, too obscure to understand, and finally too repellent to believe? That those should attack the truth with specious arguments, and assert falsehoods, while these should be incapable of either defending the truth or refuting falsehood? That those, to move and force the minds of their hearers into error, should be able by their style to terrify them, move them to tears, make them laugh, give them rousing encouragement, while these on behalf of truth stumble along slow, cold and half asleep?"

THE ETHICS OF PERSUASION

R EFER BACK TO THIS ETHICAL GUIDE as needed. I created this in a spirit of humility, for my benefit as much as for the benefit of my readers. And you don't have to choose between efficacy and ethics. When I followed these principles, my words became more ethical *and* more powerful.

FOLLOW THESE TWELVE RULES. Do not use false, fabricated, misrepresented, distorted, or irrelevant evidence to support claims. Do not intentionally use specious, unsupported, or illogical reasoning. Do not represent yourself as informed or as an "expert" on a subject when you are not. Do not use irrelevant appeals to divert attention from the issue at hand. Do not cause intense but unreflective emotional reactions. Do not link your idea to emotion-laden values, motives, or goals to which it is not related. Do not hide your real purpose or self-interest, the group you represent, or your position as an advocate of a viewpoint. Do not distort, hide, or misrepresent the number, scope, or intensity of bad effects. Do not use emotional appeals that lack a basis of evidence or reasoning or that would fail if the audience examined the subject themselves. Do not oversimplify complex, gradation-laden situations into simplistic two-valued, either/or, polar views or choices. Do not pretend certainty where tentativeness and degrees of probability would be more accurate. Do not advocate something you do not believe (Johannesen et al., 2021).

APPLY THIS GOLDEN HEURISTIC. In a 500,000-word book, you might be able to tell your audience everything you know about a subject. In a five-minute persuasive speech, you can only select a small sampling of your knowledge. Would learning your entire body of knowledge result in a significantly different reaction than hearing the small sampling you selected? If the answer is yes, that's a problem.

SWING WITH THE GOOD EDGE. Rhetoric is a double-edged sword. It can express good ideas well. It can also express bad ideas well. Rhetoric makes ideas attractive; tempting; credible; persuasive. Don't use it to turn weakly-worded lies into well-worded lies. Use it to turn weakly-worded truths into well-worded truths.

TREAT TRUTH AS THE HIGHEST GOOD. Use any persuasive strategy, unless using it in your circumstances would distort the truth. The strategies should not come between you and truth, or compromise your honesty and authenticity.

AVOID THE SPIRIT OF DECEIT. Wrong statements are incorrect statements you genuinely believe. Lies are statements you know are wrong but convey anyway. Deceitful statements are not literally wrong, but you convey them with the intent to mislead, obscure, hide, or manipulate. Hiding relevant information is not literally lying (saying you conveyed all the information would be). Cherry-picking facts is not literally lying (saying there are no other facts would be). Using clever innuendo to twist reality without making any concrete claims is not literally lying (knowingly making a false accusation would be). And yet, these are all examples of deceit.

ONLY USE STRATEGIES IF THEY ARE ACCURATE. Motivate unified thinking. Inspire loving thinking. These strategies sound good. Use the victim-perpetrator-benevolence structure. Paint a common enemy. Appeal to tribal psychology. These strategies sound bad. But when reality lines up with the strategies that sound bad, they become good. They are only bad when they are inaccurate or move people down a bad path. *But the same is true for the ones that sound good.* Should Winston Churchill have motivated unified thinking? Not toward his enemy. Should he have avoided appealing to tribal psychology to strengthen the Allied war effort? Should he have avoided painting a common enemy? Should he have avoided portraying the victimization of true victims and the perpetration of a true perpetrator? Should he have avoided calling people to act as the benevolent force for good, protecting the victim and beating back the perpetrator? Don't use the victim-perpetrator-benevolence structure if there aren't clear victims and perpetrators. This is demagoguery. Painting false victims disempowers them. But if there are true victims and perpetrators, stand up for the victims and stand against the perpetrators, calling others to join you as a benevolent force for justice. Don't motivate unified thinking when standing against evil. Don't hold back from portraying a common enemy when there is one. Some strategies might sound morally suspect. Some might sound inherently good. But it depends on the situation. Every time I say "do X to achieve Y," remember the condition: "if it is accurate and moves people up a good path."

APPLY THE TARES TEST: truthfulness of message, authenticity of persuader, respect for audience, equity of persuasive appeal, and social impact (TARES).

REMEMBER THE THREE-PART VENN DIAGRAM: words that are authentic, effective, and true. Donald Miller once said "I'm the kind of person who wants to present my most honest, authentic self to the world, so I hide backstage and rehearse honest and authentic lines until the curtain opens." There's nothing dishonest or inauthentic about choosing your words carefully and making them more effective, as long as they remain just as true. Rhetoric takes a messy marble brick of truth and sculpts it into a poised, precise, and perfect statue. It takes weak truths and makes them strong. Unfortunately, it can do the same for weak lies. But preparing, strategizing, and sculpting is not inauthentic. Unskillfulness is no more authentic than skillfulness. Unpreparedness is no more authentic than preparedness.

APPLY FITZPATRICK AND GAUTHIER'S THREE-QUESTION ANALYSIS. For what purpose is persuasion being employed? Toward what choices and with what consequences for individual lives is it being used? Does the persuasion contribute to or interfere with the audience's decision-making process (Lumen, 2016)?

STRENGTHEN THE TRUTH. Rhetoric makes words strong. Use it to turn truths strong, not falsities strong. There are four categories of language: weak and wrong, strong and wrong, weak and true, strong and true. Turn weak and true language into strong and true language. Don't turn weak and wrong language into strong and wrong language, weak and true language into strong and wrong language, or strong and true language into weak and true language. Research. Question your assumptions. Strive for truth. Ensure your logic is impeccable. Defuse your biases.

START WITH FINDING TRUTH. The rhetorical endeavor starts with becoming as knowledgeable on your subject as possible and developing an impeccable logical argument. The more research you do, the more rhetoric you earn the right to use.

PUT TRUTH BEFORE STYLE. Rhetorical skill does not make you correct. Truth doesn't care about your rhetoric. If your rhetoric is brilliant, but you realize your arguments are simplistic, flawed, or biased, change course. Let logic lead style. Don't sacrifice logic to style. Don't express bad ideas well. Distinguish effective speaking from effective rational argument. Achieve both, but put reason and logic first.

AVOID THE POPULARITY VORTEX. As Plato suggested, avoid "giving the citizens what they want [in speech] with no thought to whether they will be better or worse as a result of what you are saying." Ignore the temptation to gain positive reinforcement and instant gratification from the audience with no merit to your message. Rhetoric is unethical if used solely to appeal rather than to help the world.

CONSIDER THE CONSEQUENCES. If you succeed to persuade people, will the world become better or worse? Will your audience benefit? Will you benefit? Moreover, is it the best action they could take? Or would an alternative help more? Is it an objectively worthwhile investment? Is it the best solution? Are you giving them all the facts they need to determine this on their own?

CONSIDER SECOND- AND THIRD-ORDER IMPACTS. Consider not only immediate consequences, but consequences across time. Consider the impact of the action you seek to persuade, as well as the tools you use to persuade it. Maybe the action is objectively positive, but in motivating the action, you resorted to instilling beliefs that will cause damage over time. Consider their long-term impact as well.

APPLY THE FIVE ETHICAL APPROACHES: seek the greatest good for the greatest number (utilitarian); protect the rights of those affected and treat people not as means but as ends (rights); treat equals equally and nonequals fairly (justice); set the good of humanity as the basis of your moral reasoning (common good); act consistently with the ideals that lead to your self-actualization and the highest potential of your character (virtue). Say and do what is right, not what is expedient, and be willing to suffer the consequences of doing so. Don't place self-gratification, acquisitiveness, social status, and power over the common good of all humanity.

APPLY THE FOUR ETHICAL DECISION-MAKING CRITERIA: respect for individual rights to make choices, hold views, and act based on personal beliefs and values (autonomy); the maximization of benefits and the minimization of harms, acting for the benefit of others, helping others further their legitimate interests; taking action to prevent or remove possible harms (beneficence); acting in ways that cause no harm, avoid the risk of harm, and assuring benefits outweigh costs (non-maleficence); treating others according to a defensible standard (justice).

USE ILLOGICAL PROCESSES TO GET ETHICAL RESULTS. Using flawed thinking processes to get good outcomes is not unethical. Someone who disagrees should stop speaking with conviction, clarity, authority, and effective paralanguage. All are irrelevant to the truth of their words, but impact the final judgment of the audience. You must use logic and evidence to figure out the truth. But this doesn't mean logic and evidence will persuade others. Humans have two broad categories of cognitive functions: system one is intuitive, emotional, fast, heuristic-driven, and generally illogical; system two is rational, deliberate, evidence-driven, and generally logical. The best-case scenario is to get people to believe right things for right reasons (through system two). The next best case is to get people to believe right things for wrong reasons (through system one). Both are far better than letting people believe wrong things for wrong reasons. If you don't use those processes, they still function, but lead people astray. You can reverse-engineer them. If you know the truth, have an abundance of reasons to be confident you know the truth, and can predict the disasters that will occur if people don't believe the truth, don't you have a responsibility to be as effective as possible in bringing people to the truth? Logic and evidence are essential, of course. They will persuade many. They should have persuaded you. But people can't always follow a long chain of reasoning or a complicated argument. Persuade by eloquence what you learned by reason.

HELP YOUR SELF-INTEREST. (But not at the expense of your audience or without their knowledge). Ethics calls for improving the world, and you are a part of the world – the one you control most. Improving yourself is a service to others.

APPLY THE WINDOWPANE STANDARD. In Aristotle's view, rhetoric reveals how to persuade and how to defeat manipulative persuaders. Thus, top students of rhetoric would be master speakers, trained to anticipate and disarm the rhetorical tactics of their adversaries. According to this tradition, language is only useful to the extent that it does not distort reality, and good writing functions as a "windowpane," helping people peer through the wall of ignorance and view reality. You might think this precludes persuasion. You might think this calls for dry academic language. But what good is a windowpane if nobody cares to look through it? What good is a windowpane to reality if, on the other wall, a stained-glass window distorts reality but draws people to it? The best windowpane reveals as much of reality as possible while drawing as many people to it as possible.

RUN THROUGH THESE INTROSPECTIVE QUESTIONS. Are the means truly unethical or merely distasteful, unpopular, or unwise? Is the end truly good, or does it simply appear good because we desire it? Is it probable that bad means will achieve the good end? Is the same good achievable using more ethical means if we are creative, patient, and skillful? Is the good end clearly and overwhelmingly better than any bad effects of the means used to attain it? Will the use of unethical means to achieve a good end withstand public scrutiny? Could the use of unethical means be justified to those most affected and those most impartial? Can I specify my ethical criteria or standards? What is the grounding of the ethical judgment? Can I justify the reasonableness and relevancy of these standards for this case? Why are these the best criteria? Why do they take priority? How does the communication succeed or fail by these standards? What judgment is justified in this case about the degree of ethicality? Is it a narrowly focused one rather than a broad and generalized one? To whom is ethical responsibility owed – to which individuals, groups, organizations, or professions? In what ways and to what extent? Which take precedence? What is my responsibility to myself and society? How do I feel about myself after this choice? Can I continue to "live with myself?" Would I want my family to know of this choice? Does the choice reflect my ethical character? To what degree is it "out of character?" If called upon in public to justify the ethics of my communication, how adequately could I do so? What generally accepted reasons could I offer? Are there precedents which can guide me? Are there aspects of this case that set it apart from others? How thoroughly have alternatives been explored before settling on this choice? Is it less ethical than some of the workable alternatives? If the goal requires unethical communication, can I abandon the goal (Johannesen et al., 2007)?

VIEW YOURSELF AS A GUIDE. Stories have a hero, a villain who stands in his way, and a guide who helps the hero fulfill his mission. If you speak ineffectively, you are a nonfactor. If you speak deceitfully, you become the villain. But if you convey truth effectively, you become the guide in your audience's story, who leads them, teaches them, inspires them, and helps them overcome adversity and win. Use your words to put people on the best possible path. And if you hide an ugly truth, ask yourself this: "If I found out that *my* guide omitted this, how would I react?"

KNOW THAT THE TRUTH WILL OUT. The truth can either come out in your words, or you can deceive people. You can convince them to live in a fantasy. And that might work. Until. Until truth breaks down the door and storms the building. Until the facade comes crashing down and chaos makes its entry. Slay the dragon in its lair before it comes to your village. Invite truth in through the front door before truth burns the building down. Truth wins in the end, either because a good person spreads, defends, and fights for it, or because untruth reveals itself as such by its consequences, and does so in brutal and painful fashion, hurting innocents and perpetrators alike. Trust and reputation take years to create and seconds to destroy.

MAXIMIZE THE TWO HIERARCHIES OF SUCCESS: honesty *and* effectiveness. You could say "Um, well, uh, I think that um, what we should… should uh… do, is that, well… let me think… er, I think if we are more, you know… fluid, we'll be better at… producing, I mean, progressing, and producing, and just more generally, you know, getting better results, but… I guess my point is, like, that, that if we are more fluid and do things more better, we will get better results than with a bureaucracy and, you know how it is, a silo-based structure, right? I mean… you know what I mean." Or, you could say "Bravery beats bureaucracy, courage beats the status quo, and innovation beats stagnation." Is one of those statements truer? No. Is one of them more effective? Is one of them more likely to get positive action that instantiates the truth into the world? Yes. Language is not reality. It provides signposts to reality. Two different signposts can point at the same truth – they can be equally and maximally true – and yet one can be much more effective. One gets people to follow the road. One doesn't. Maximize honesty. Then, insofar as it doesn't sacrifice honesty, maximize effectiveness. Speak truth. And speak it well.

APPLY THE WISDOM OF THIS QUOTE. Mary Beard, an American historian, author, and activist, captured the essence of ethical rhetoric well: "What politicians do is they never get the rhetoric wrong, and the price they pay is they don't speak the truth as they see it. Now, I will speak truth as I see it, and sometimes I don't get the rhetoric right. I think that's a fair trade-off." It's more than fair. It's necessary.

REMEMBER YOUR RESPONSIBILITY TO SOCIETY. Be a guardian of the truth. Speak out against wrongdoing, and do it well. The solution to evil speech is not less speech, but more (good) speech. Create order with your words, not chaos. Our civilization depends on it. Match the truth, honesty, and vulnerable transparency of your words against the irreducible complexity of the universe. And in this complex universe, remember the omnipresence of nuance, and the dangers of simplistic ideologies. (Inconveniently, simplistic ideologies are persuasive, while nuanced truths are difficult to convey. This is why good people need to be verbally skilled; to pull the extra weight of conveying a realistic worldview). Don't commit your whole mind to an isolated fragment of truth, lacking context, lacking nuance. Be precise in your speech, to ensure you are saying what you mean to say. Memorize the logical fallacies, the cognitive biases, and the rules of logic and correct thinking. (Conveniently, many rhetorical devices are also reasoning devices that focus your inquiry and help you explicate truth). But don't demonize those with good intentions and bad ideas. If they are forthcoming and honest, they are not your enemy. Rather, the two of you are on a shared mission to find the truth, partaking in a shared commitment to reason and dialogue. The malevolent enemy doesn't care about the truth. And in this complex world, remember Voltaire's warning to "cherish those who seek the truth but beware of those who find it," and Aristotle's startling observation that "the least deviation from truth [at the start] is multiplied a thousandfold." Be cautious in determining what to say with conviction. Good speaking is not a substitute for good thinking. The danger zone is being confidently incorrect. What hurts us most is what we know that just isn't so. Remember these tenets and your responsibility, and rhetoric becomes the irreplaceable aid of the good person doing good things in difficult times; the sword of the warrior of the light.

KNOW THAT DECEPTION IS ITS OWN PUNISHMENT. Knowingly uttering a falsehood is a spoken lie of commission. Having something to say but not saying it is a spoken lie of omission. Knowingly behaving inauthentically is an acted-out lie of commission. Knowingly omitting authentic behavior is an acted-out lie of omission. All these deceptions weaken your being. All these deceptions corrupt your own mind, turning your greatest asset into an ever-present companion you can no longer trust. Your conscience operates somewhat autonomously, and it will call you out (unless your repeated neglect desensitizes it). You have a conscious conscience which speaks clearly, and an unconscious conscience, which communicates more subtly. A friend of mine asked: "Why do we feel relieved when we speak truth? Why are we drawn toward it, even if it is not pleasant? Do our brains have something that makes this happen?" Yes, they do: our consciences, our inner lights, our inner north stars. And we feel relieved because living with the knowledge of our own deceit is often an unbearable burden. You live your life before an audience of one: yourself. You cannot escape the observation of your own awareness; you can't hide from yourself. Everywhere you go, there you are. Everything you do, there you are. Some of the greatest heights of wellbeing come from performing well in this one-man theater, and signaling virtue to yourself; being someone you are proud to be (and grateful to observe). Every time you lie, you tell your subconscious mind that your character is too weak to contend with the truth. And this shapes your character accordingly. It becomes true. And then what? Lying carries its own punishment, even if the only person who catches the liar is the liar himself.

BE A MONSTER (THEN LEARN TO CONTROL IT). There is nothing moral about weakness and harmlessness. The world is difficult. There are threats to confront, oppressors to resist, and tyrants to rebuff. (Peterson, 2018). There are psychopaths, sociopaths, and Machiavellian actors with no love for the common good. There is genuine malevolence. If you are incapable of being an effective deceiver, then you are incapable of being an effective advocate for truth: it is the same weapon, pointed in different directions. If you cannot use it in both directions, can you use it at all? Become a monster, become dangerous, and become capable of convincing people to believe in a lie... and then use this ability to convince them to believe in the truth. The capacity for harm is also the capacity for harming harmful entities; that is to say, defending innocent ones. If you can't hurt anyone, you can't help anyone when they need someone to stand up for them. Words are truly weapons, and the most powerful weapons in the world at that. The ability to use them, for good *or* for bad, is the prerequisite to using them for good. There is an archetype in our cultural narratives: the well-intentioned but harmless protagonist who gets roundly defeated by the villain, until he develops his monstrous edge and integrates it, at which point he becomes the triumphant hero. Along similar lines, I watched a film about an existential threat to humanity, in which the protagonist sought to convey the threat to a skeptical public, but failed miserably because he lacked the rhetorical skill to do so. The result? The world ended. Everyone died. The protagonist was of no use to anyone. And this almost became a true story. A historical study showed that in the Cuban Missile Crisis, the arguments that won out in the United States mastermind group were not the best, but those argued with the most conviction. Those with the best arguments lacked the skill to match. The world (could have) ended. The moral? Speak truth... well.

MASTERING COMMUNICATION, ONE SKILL AT A TIME

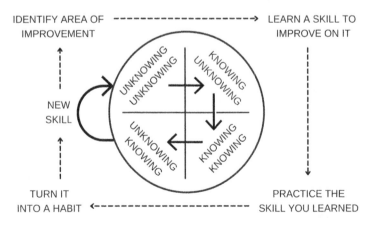

FIGURE I: The proven path to mastery.

decoding

....

verb

    to convert a coded message into intelligible language

human nature

....

noun

    the general psychological characteristics, feelings, and behavioral traits of humankind, regarded as shared by all humans

CONTENTS

MY 7P MODEL

Rhetoric, Motivated by Love, Guided by Reason, and Aimed at Truth, Is a Powerful Force for the Greatest Good.

POLITICAL DISCLAIMER

Throughout this book, and throughout all my books, I draw examples of communication strategies from the political world. I quote from the speeches of many of America's great leaders, like JFK and MLK, as well as from more recent political figures of both major parties. Political communication is ideal for illustrating the concepts revealed in the books. It is the best source of examples of words that work that I have ever found. I don't use anything out of the political mainstream. And it is by extensively studying the inaugural addresses of United States Presidents and the great speeches of history that I have discovered many of the speaking strategies I share with you.

My using the words of any particular figure to illustrate a principle of communication is not necessarily an endorsement of the figure or their message. Separate the speaker from the strategy. After all, the strategy is the only reason the speaker made an appearance in the book at all. Would you rather have a weak example of a strategy you want to learn from a speaker you love, or a perfect example of the strategy from a speaker you detest?

For a time, I didn't think a disclaimer like this was necessary. I thought people would do this on their own. I thought that if people read an example of a strategy drawn from the words of a political figure they disagreed with, they would appreciate the value of the example as an instructive tool and set aside their negative feelings about the speaker. "Yes, I don't agree with this speaker or the message, but I can clearly see the strategy in this example and I now have a better understanding of how it works and how to execute it." Indeed, I suspect 95% of my readers do just that. You probably will, too. But if you are part of the 5% who aren't up for it, don't say I didn't warn you, and please don't leave a negative review because you think I endorse this person or that person. I don't, as this is strictly a book about communication.

DECODING HUMAN NATURE

THE UNDERGROUND GUIDE TO EMOTIONAL INTELLIGENCE

SPEAK FOR SUCCESS COLLECTION BOOK

VIII

DECODING HUMAN NATURE CHAPTER

I

WHAT DO PEOPLE WANT?

How to Discover the Hidden
Programming of Human Desire

WHY DO WE DO THE THINGS WE DO?

W HY DO SOME LEADERS INSPIRE MASS MOVEMENTS of people to take drastic action toward achieving a worthy goal? Why do some businesses succeed in even the worst of economic circumstances, while others fall apart and fail after only a little turbulence? Why do some people know how to effortlessly captivate the attention of others, driving them to invest their energy in a mission? Why are some political leaders renowned for the force of their words and the impact of their ideas? Why are some proposals in the public sphere so persuasive and powerful that they quickly dominate the national discourse? There is a simple answer.

Why do people do what they do? Say what they say? Hire who they hire? Fire who they fire? Associate with who they associate with? Buy what they buy? Think what they think? Love who they love? Work with who they work with? Vote for who they vote for? Follow who they follow? Listen to who they listen to? Ignore who they ignore? Fight who they fight? Cooperate with who they cooperate with? Strive for what they strive for? And, occasionally, die for what they die for?

The answer to all these questions is both irreducibly simple and incredibly complex: we do what we do because of the desires driving us. This is superficially simple: *we do what we do because of what we want.* Seems easy: too easy to be the subject of a book. But it gets complex, not least of all because if "People do what they do because of what they want," we must surely ask the next question: "What do they want?"

This book is an attempt to answer that question.

WHO AM I? WHY SHOULD YOU TRUST ME?

I am not a psychologist. I prefer to be upfront about that fact. You will find no obfuscation in these pages. This book is an *exploration* into a subject, not a *lecture:* if you read it, you are joining me on a journey, not sitting in my classroom. The journey? Answering the question we are both curious about.

There are probably more qualified people out there who could have written this book. The only problem is that they haven't. That's not to say I'm bereft of any knowledge on the subject: I have read 300 books on psychology, watched hundreds of hours of educational material on the subject, and read thousands of articles and scientific studies focused on cutting-edge developments in the field.

But the point of this section is not to tell you who I am not, but to tell you who I *am.*

I wrote 22 books on public speaking, effective communication, influence, rhetoric, eloquence, and other verbal skills. About half of them enjoyed best-seller status at one point in time. Search "Peter Andrei" in Amazon and you will find my catalogue.

I am grateful to have enjoyed a successful competitive public speaking career. I won national competitions, earned 32 awards as a competitive speaker and debater, and earned a seal of special distinction from the Massachusetts Speech and Debate League, leaving behind an unparalleled competitive record (or so I've been told – I never bothered to check for myself).

I coached hundreds of mentees in the art of effective speaking, including one of the country's top project managers, a Toastmasters national finalist, and a candidate for political office.

I have studied thousands of speeches in an attempt to unearth the secrets of language that changes the world. This is my profession. And my profession led me to rigorously study psychology. My study of psychology, in turn, led me to the subject of this book: what people want.

Now you know a little about who I am, where I came from, and what led me to writing a book – more of a manual, really – on human desires. Again, I am not a psychologist, but I believe I make a compelling case for these desires; a case I will outline shortly, resting on compelling evidence drawn from 38 different "categories" of the human experience. If you want to take my claims in the rest of the book at face value, feel free to skip the discussion of these 38 categories of evidence.

If you do not find the case credible or my credentials sufficient (I will say it again: I am not a psychologist), all you have to do is email me at *pandreibusiness@gmail.com* with the subject line "Refund Request." I will immediately pay you the price of the book, *and you can even keep the book.* Give it away, burn it, use it as a door-stop, whatever – I don't care. I just want to save you the time expense of having to repackage the book and send it back. I make this offer because I can't stand the thought of making money from someone who, in the end, isn't served by what they paid me for, and has to waste his precious time to get his money back. So far, I have not received a single request for refund. But should you choose to get your money back (and keep the book), it should take you about 30 seconds.

THE CASE FOR THESE DESIRES

I am making a bold claim in this book (or manual?). The burden of proof is on me. There is no doubt about that. Let me lay down the foundation of the case I am going to make in favor of the claims in this book; the claim that what you will shortly read about truly is what people want.

First, let's get "evidence versus proof" out of the way. In the strictest possible sense, I can only provide evidence, not proof. The only provable axiom of reality – provable beyond any doubt, that is – is Rene Descartes' famous "cogito ergo sum," or "I think therefore I am." Soren Kierkegaard, another renowned philosopher, argued that even Descartes' barebones axiom was too generous by assuming a "self" that is unsubstantiated, and that "something is thinking, therefore something exists" is the accurate formulation. If you demand *proof* to accept a statement as true, the only statement you can accept as true is "thinking is occurring, therefore something exists."

Good luck living life like that. Even in the most high-stakes legal proceedings, when a life or many lives are at stake, we settle for proof beyond a reasonable doubt, which is certainly different from proof.

So, I cannot possibly *prove* these desires. I can only provide *evidence* for them, just like we can only provide evidence for the guilt of a defendant in the highest courts of the land.

We all have our evidentiary thresholds: if you are gullible, you typically have low evidentiary thresholds, demanding little evidence to accept most statements as true, often accepting them simply because you heard them. If you are extremely gullible, you accept even *extreme* propositions in the same manner. Skeptics, on the other hand, demand a healthy amount of evidence. Extreme skeptics demand *proof,* failing to realize that nearly no statement can be proven, and failing to realize just how many propositions they already accept in the proper manner – on evidence or as assumed axioms – as opposed to on proof: statements such as "I exist," "there are other minds aside from my own," "my friends like me," "the world wasn't created two seconds ago with the appearance of age," "the physical world around me exists," "my sense experiences contain true information about the reality around me," and many others.

There's a spectrum here: the more gullible someone is, the less evidence they demand. The more skeptical someone is, the more evidence they demand. But this can lead to a trap: the "proof trap." And this isn't trapping *me* – the one making a case – as much as it is trapping you, the one listening to the case, in a bubble of undue and unreasonable doubt. So, I designed this case to be as compelling as possible; but what is possible is a *massive preponderance of evidence*, not *proof.* If you demand proof, you won't find it here, *or anywhere else.* But if you are appropriately skeptical – that is, as skeptical as you can be without condemning yourself to the desolate world of "thinking is occurring, therefore something exists" – then I wrote this section with you in mind. In other words, my attempt was to satisfy the highest possible evidentiary burden a skeptic could demand I satisfy before we get into the realm of demanding the impossible. I'll leave you with this quote: Alexander Vilenkin once said "It is said that an argument is what convinces reasonable men and a proof is what it takes to convince even an unreasonable man." That is what I provide to substantiate these desires: an argument based on a significant amount of evidence, more than enough to convince the rational skeptics of the world.

And remember, don't conflate the categories of evidence with "where the desires come from." Many of the categories of evidence happen to be *part* of where the desires come from; other categories of evidence are not. There is no necessary relationship between the two. For example, genetic evolution is both a category of evidence that gives us clues as to what humans want, but it also gives rise to human desires by shaping our brains over millions of years. We only care about it for the former reason, however. It both reveals what we are looking for and creates what we are looking for. On the other hand, the category "the world's top minds" describes a category of evidence which can reveal some of the desires, but isn't where they originated. The world's top minds didn't contribute to the creation of the desires the way evolution did (or at least not to the same extent): but they did *reveal* some of the desires.

So, let's begin unpacking that case by revealing the 38 categories of evidence upon which I base the remainder of the book.

THE WORLD'S TOP MINDS

There's a logical fallacy known as the argument from authority. What is this logical fallacy? It is trying to prove a claim on the basis of the authority and credentials of those supporting the claim. In a strictly logical sense, a claim is not true because authoritative figures support it. There is a similar fallacy known as the *ad hominem*, or "arguing at the person," which is typically attacking the source of the ideas in an attempt to discredit the ideas themselves. The basic truth is this: whoever states a claim has no bearing on the truth of that claim. If someone tells you to "not gamble with your life savings," but they go ahead and do it, are they suddenly wrong because they are hypocrites? Of course not.

So, am I committing the argument from authority fallacy by referencing "the world's top minds?" No. And why not? Because I'm not saying that claim X is *true* because person Y says it is; I'm saying that the vast majority of claims made by person Y are demonstrably true (which is an empirically provable – or rather sufficiently evidencable – claim), person Y makes claim X, therefore claim X is *probably* true. Or, formulated differently, I am saying this: authority figures tend to make correct statements on the subjects of their authority, an authority figure is making this claim, therefore this claim is *probably* true, and more believable (even though it is not proven) as a result, especially when combined and cross-referenced with other evidentiary categories. In short, I am not saying a claim is true because of the authority of those who agree with me, so I am clear of this fallacy. (By the way, this form of argumentation I present is used in courtrooms all the time. Why examine witnesses? Because credible people tend to state truths, and known liars tend to do the opposite. Why ask for expert testimony, and why ask the expert to elaborate on his credentials when you do? Because the judge knows that experts tend to be right on the subject of their expertise. If it's good enough for the Supreme Court, it should be good enough for us).

Who are the experts I am citing? There are too many to list. What are they experts on? Life. Can I tell you *anything* specific about them? Absolutely: they are the most renowned, astute, well-researched, compelling, incisive, piercing, and legendary writers since the invention of writing. Socrates, Plato, Aristotle, Shakespeare, Thomas Aquinas, Fyodor Dostoevsky – these are just some of the names on the long roster of history's brilliant minds; minds that produced a large body of "classic" work over thousands of years; a body of "classic" work which casts light on many innate human desires, which I then unpack for you today, in 2021 (as of this writing).

KEY INSIGHT:

Mindset Moves Mountains.

MULTIPLE SIGNS POINT TO THESE DESIRES

FIGURE 1: I use a methodological framework that draws upon multiple bodies of evidence to sufficiently prove the existence of a single desire.

THE WORLD'S GREATEST THINKERS HAD MUCH TO SAY

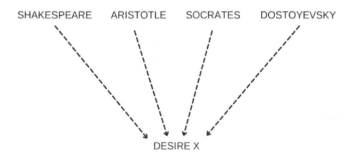

FIGURE 2: This is a simple body of evidence. The world's top thinkers – the brightest people who ever lived – left behind an extensive commentary on the human condition. Much of this alludes to or directly identifies human wants.

SCIENTIFIC STUDIES

There are fewer scientific studies on human desires than we would hope. However, we must not despair. First of all, although few studies hit upon human desires directly and explicitly, a mountain of studies – probably hundreds of thousands – *imply* human desires by studying human behavior under different conditions and constraints. Human desire is such a basic and foundational subject that hundreds of thousands of studies fall under its umbrella without the researchers even realizing or intending it. Second of all, there are still some classic, renowned studies on human desires we can draw from, even if the number is smaller than we would hope. There may not be many studies directly addressing this question, but those that have been conducted are typically very rigorous, very well-cited, and held in very high esteem by the academic community.

HOW WE REVERSE-ENGINEER SCIENTIFIC STUDIES

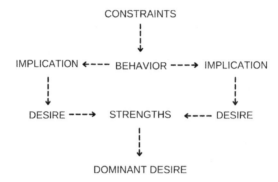

FIGURE 3: Many experiments impose constraints on people. The resulting behavior forks in two directions: one choice implicates one desire, and the other choice implicates another desire. The proportion of participants who made one choice versus the other reveals the strengths of the two desires and which one dominates.

BOOKS

Remember, these are just evidence *categories*: different places from which I draw evidence. I can't list all of the evidence under each category, simply because there is too much of it. I can't list all of the classical writers I've read over the past 20 years of my life who have touched on the subject of human desires. There are too many of them, and I can't possibly remember all of them, even if I was going to list them. I can't list all of the scientific studies that reference, in some fashion, either directly or indirectly, the subject of human desires. There are too many of them to list, and I can't possibly remember all of them, even if I was going to list them. However, I can turn my head 90 degrees to the right and list the books I have read that are part of the evidentiary body supporting the claims I make in this book. They are all sitting next to me on a shelf. You will find them cited in the references appendix, along with as much evidence as I can possibly cite from each category.

A LIFETIME OF READING REVEALED THESE DESIRES

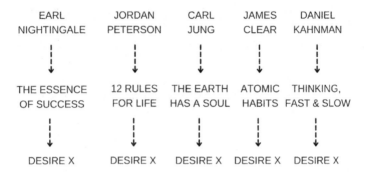

FIGURE 4: I have compiled these frameworks based, in part, on a lifetime of extensive reading across a wide scope of domains. Certain claims about human nature and human desire emerged time and time again by authorities on psychology. While I do not accept a desire-based claim if only one author presents it (unless they back it up with a high degree of evidence), I identify a desire if multiple authors across time point to it.

ESTABLISHED FRAMEWORKS

Luckily, I'm not starting from scratch. ERG theory, 16-need theory, Maslow's Hierarchy of Needs – these are just some of the many established frameworks revealing some of the human desires and psychological needs. This book elaborates upon these established frameworks, reveals their interrelations and disagreements, adds to them, provides examples of them, and proposes new ones, as well as illuminating human needs and desires that do not fall under any particular unifying framework, but that can be described by their type (fear needs, spiritual needs, etc.)

KEY INSIGHT:

Mindset Moves Mountains.

HOW WE FURTHER ELUCIDATE EXISTING FRAMEWORKS

MASLOW'S HIERARCHY OF NEEDS

↓

ESTEEM NEEDS

↓

CATEGORIZATION, ELUCIDATION, EXTRAPOLATION

↓

MORE SPECIFIC ESTEEM-BASED NEEDS AND FRAMEWORK

FIGURE 5: A level in Maslow's Hierarchy of Needs is the esteem needs category. We can further sub-categorize esteem, elucidating new "sub-desires" and extrapolating a broader and new framework.

PROPERLY BASIC BELIEFS

The following is an effective description of a properly basic belief drawn from a philosophy forum: "Typically properly basic beliefs are beliefs that are justified by experience. Suppose, for example, that I am in a classroom and see an apple on the teacher's desk in front of me. Suppose also that I form the belief that there is an apple on the desk in front of me and that belief is justified. In this case, my belief is not justified by other propositional beliefs but directly from the sense experience itself. One way to think about this example might be like this: the mental image of the apple on the table is doing the work of justifying my belief but notice that the image is not a propositional belief. It is just a mental image, or representation, we experience in 'our mind's eye.' The experiencing of the mental image is what supposedly justifies the belief, not an inference, or argument, from other more basic propositional beliefs. So, properly basic belief are beliefs that are justified but are not justified inferentially on the basis of other propositional beliefs but in some other, non-propositional, way." Another form of justification for these desires is that belief in them (or in most of them) is properly basic due to your inner witness of them.

KEY INSIGHT:

Mindset Moves Mountains.

WHAT IS A PROPERLY BASIC BELIEF?

DESIRE X

DESIRE X

FIGURE 6: You may consider these desires properly basic beliefs; claims you affirm on the basis of direct experience.

GENETIC EVOLUTION

If certain behaviors contribute to human survival and propagation, desiring to act out those behaviors is evolutionarily advantageous. This is true even if the desire is not evolutionarily advantageous in and of itself, but only because it motivates a human to pursue another behavior that is. Even if the desire is secondary to the evolutionary behavior it motivates, by motivating it, the desire becomes evolutionarily advantageous. For example, humans are uniquely cooperative creatures. We needed to cooperate hundreds of thousands of years ago to spear-hunt for big game. Thus, if a genetic mutation occurred (or, more likely, a series of genetic mutations) that made humans desire cooperation, the humans carrying that mutation would cooperate to a greater extent and thus survive to a greater extent, propagating until more and more of the human population inherited that same desire. This is a simplistic example but it illustrates the point: many of these desires are grounded in genetic evolution, and we find evidence for them in our genetic history by analyzing the behaviors that would have provided an advantage under the conditions of nature in which we evolved.

KEY INSIGHT:

Mindset Moves Mountains.

EVOLUTIONARY PSYCHOLOGY REVEALS THESE DESIRES

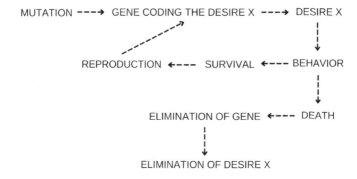

FIGURE 7: Our genetic evolution offers clues into the makeup of our slate of desires. By analyzing evolutionary need, we can often work backward and find a desire pushing us to perform an advantageous behavior.

CULTURAL EVOLUTION

Cultures evolve much like organisms do. A culture with effective core tenets, values, principles, and ways of life will typically outcompete a culture with less effective core tenets, values, principles, and ways of life. This is true even if it is not a zero-sum game of direct competition between cultures. The more effective culture will spread whether it is fighting the chaos of nature, another culture, or both. Note that "effective" in this context simply means "likely to lead to the longevity and propagation of the culture and the people in it."

What does this have to do with human desires? By viewing a particular desire through the lens of cultural evolution, we can support it or undermine it. How can we support the claim that X is a human desire by way of cultural evolution? We can extrapolate desires from the core tenets, values, principles, and ways of life of a culture, and we can do this in two directions. First, by determining what human desires would lead to the birth of a culture with a given set of core tenets, values, principles, and ways of life; second, by determining what desires a pre-existing set of core cultural tenets, values, principles, and ways of life would suggest to those living in the culture. Humans create culture, but culture also influences and creates subsequent humans, who then contribute to the culture. In summary, "what human desires would lead to the creation of a culture with this set of characteristics?" and "when a culture with these characteristics is in place, what kind of people does it create – or influence – and what are they likely to desire?"

HOW CULTURAL EVOLUTION CREATES THESE DESIRES

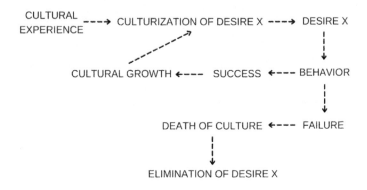

FIGURE 8: Cultural evolution is deeply impactful, shaping our psychological makeups on a fundamental level.

SOCIALIZATION

Political Socialization is described on Wikipedia as "the process by which individuals learn and frequently internalize a political lens framing their perceptions of how power is arranged and how the world around them is (and should be) organized; those perceptions, in turn, shape and define individuals' definitions of who they are and how they should behave in the political and economic institutions in which they live. Political socialization also encompasses the way in which people acquire values and opinions that shape their political stance and ideology: it is a study of the developmental processes by which people of all ages and adolescents acquire political cognition, attitudes, and behaviors. It refers to a learning process by which norms and behaviors acceptable to a well running political system are transmitted from one generation to another. It is through the performance of this function that individuals are inducted into the political culture and their orientations towards political objects are formed. Schools, media, and the state have a major influence in this process." How does political socialization reveal human desires? The answer is simple: political socialization is the process of an older generation (roughly speaking) instilling their values in the younger generation. Values can be reformulated as desires. The value of "individualism" gives rise to many particular desires, such as independence from excessive authoritarian forces, the desire for local autonomy, the desire for competition, etc. As with cultural evolution, we can apply a similar two-fold analysis: "what human desires would lead an older generation to socialize younger generations in this manner?" and "what kind of people does the socialization create – or influence – and what are they likely to desire?" This type of two-way analysis is a frequent tool in discerning human desires.

APPLYING THE TWO-WAY ANALYSIS TO SOCIALIZATION

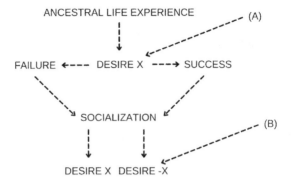

FIGURE 9: We can analyze what desires shaped the socialization itself (A), and then how that socialization influenced the desires of the recipient (B).

POLITICAL SCIENCE

Why do people cast their votes the way they do? Because they believe the party and candidate they vote for will better satisfy their desires than the alternative. Why do some candidates achieve impact with every word they utter, while others can't seem to captivate even a modicum of attention when they communicate? Because the successful candidates understand what people want, and how to present their candidacy as the way to attain it. The world of politics is the world of satisfying human desires by way of preexisting structures for allocating power. Who gets power in a democracy? The one who gets the most votes. Who gets the most votes? The one who convinces people that he will make their lives better. How is "better" measured? According to a set of desires acting as benchmarks. If you don't know what you want, you can't decide if the election of one candidate over another will make your life better or not. People vote for different candidates because they want different things, and the different candidates satisfy those different desires. A landslide election is an example of many people wanting the same thing – or rather, wanting it more than the other things they want – at the same time.

KEY INSIGHT:

Mindset Moves Mountains.

HOW POLITICS SHOWS US WHAT PEOPLE WANT

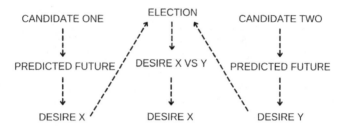

FIGURE 10: Success in politics is giving people what they want. It offers a tremendously illustrative window into human desires, showing us what predictive future wins people over. The voting behavior of independents is particularly illustrative, showing us which candidate better satisfied their desires totally removed from the lurking variable of party affiliation which, while satisfying desires of its own, may add uncertainty to this category of evidence.

HISTORY

The mass movements and revolutions of history clue us into latent human desires. The inflection points of history require many people acting in the same way at once, and people act to get what they want and avoid what they don't want. It is an easy exercise to examine a historical movement and extrapolate human desires from the movement. It is an easy exercise to examine mass movements and extrapolate mass motives.

KEY INSIGHT:

Mindset Moves Mountains.

HISTORY LEAVES CLUES TO HUMAN DESIRE

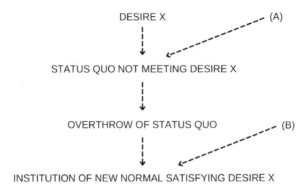

FIGURE 11: Analyze what the status quo was failing to provide (A) and what the new order sought to provide (B).

MUSIC

Music speaks to us on a deep level, and it can only speak to us on such a deep level by touching upon our desires. How else can music produce the emotional impact it produces? Popular music touches upon popular desires. Thus, we can analyze popular music and derive human desires from the words that clearly speak to the souls of millions, and we can even chart the ebb and flow of human desires over time by analyzing the changes in the subject matter of music over time. One of the most ubiquitous subjects? Love. It isn't a stretch of the imagination to look at the ubiquity of love as a subject of music and conclude that it is a similarly ubiquitous and foundational desire in humans. A similar two-fold analysis strikes again: people create music about what they want, and music that succeeds is music that speaks about what listeners want. Classical music or other forms of music without words might seem like a mystery according to this theory, but we will discover that it too touches upon human desires, albeit a slightly different set of human desires than music with words.

KEY INSIGHT:

Mindset Moves Mountains.

UNDERSTANDING THE DESIRES UNDERLYING MUSIC

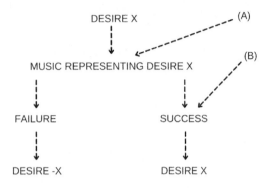

FIGURE 12: Analyze what desires the music expresses in the musician (A) and what desires successful music appeals to in listeners (B).

MARKETING

Marketing that works convinces people that buying a particular product will get them what they want, and to do so, marketing that works must speak to them about what they want. Thus, we can do the following: identify a marketing message that works (which is an empirical question); identify what it says, explicitly and implicitly; identify the human desires referenced therein. And this is becoming a scientific process. In the digital marketing world of today, testing is easier than it has ever been in the history of advertising. A process known as A/B testing allows marketers to test messaging with unparalleled precision. How does it work? For example, to determine which headline works best (which is more often than not the same as the headline that more effectively speaks to what people want), you don't have to guess (which would also mean guessing about what people want, undermining this as a viable evidentiary category). Instead, you can show 10,000 people the first headline, measure their response, show another 10,000 the second headline, measure their response, and determine which headline gets a better response before showing either one of them to 1,000,000 people. If the first headline touches upon one desire ("want to save time?") but maintains the overall form of the second headline which touches upon a different desire ("want to save money?"), this is essentially comparing the relative strengths of the desires, as well as confirming their individual realities. Such tests have probably been conducted tens of millions of times by companies around the world. Some sales pages have been sculpted in this fashion with extreme position. Looking at the words on those pages reveals what people want, because it reveals the messages that motivated people *en masse*, and have been meticulously proven to do so by a scientific process of rigorous and statistically significant testing by trained professionals.

SCIENTIFIC MARKETING REVEALS MOTIVATING FACTORS

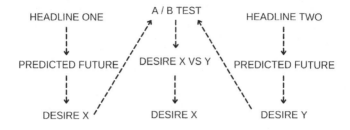

FIGURE 13: A/B testing is a methodologically bulletproof way to elucidate human desires and their priority-level.

MOVIES

Why do some movies speak to us? Much like music, there are three essential considerations to take into account when we consider movies as a body of evidence for what people want. First, what desires would push someone to create a movie like this? Second, what would viewing a movie like this inspire viewers to want, consciously or subconsciously? Third, what desires does seeing the movie satisfy? Or, in other words, what desires would push someone to see the movie? And analyzing one film in this manner is not nearly as instructive as analyzing multiple, abstracting major plot points, events, meta-narratives, and meta-concepts from the specific contents of the movies, and cross-referencing with other movies. As with music, this type of analysis allows us to examine the texture of human desires as they change over time.

KEY INSIGHT:

The Narratives That Captivate Us Are The Narratives We Want to Live in Our Own Lives.

THE TWO-WAY ANALYSIS APPLIES TO MOVIES

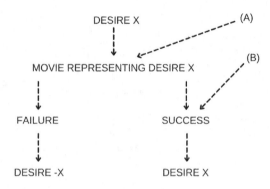

FIGURE 14: What desire does the making of the movie reveal (A) and what desires does it appeal to (B)?

ACCUMULATED EXPERIENCE

Information is passed down through generations: practical wisdom about how to interact with the world successfully is passed from parents to their children, and their children to their grandchildren, probably since the first man, albeit in an extremely and incomprehensibly rudimentary form. You are the recipient of such information, as were your parents and their parents. People tell each other things that they think will help them succeed. Part of the evidence for these desires comes from accumulated experience: the general understanding of what people want that has been refined and passed down over the generations, implicitly or explicitly. You already have a general understanding of what people want. Part of that general understanding – just part of it – comes from the accumulated experience of the human race; accumulated experience dealing, in part, with what humans want; accumulated experience of the human race in dealing with itself.

KEY INSIGHT:

What Has Been a Ubiquitous Part of the Environments In Which Humans Evolved? Other Humans.

ACCUMULATED HUMAN EXPERIENCE ABOUT HUMANS

ACCUMULATED EXPERIENCE

↓

EXPERIENCE ABOUT HUMANS

↓

SHARING THROUGH GENERATIONS

↓

GENERAL UNDERSTANDING OF HUMAN DESIRES

FIGURE 15: Humans accumulate experience about humans that they share onward through the generations, giving most people a general understanding about the slate of human desires and motivations.

SELF-OBSERVATION

Self-observation is not, on its own, an effective category of evidence. One cannot say "I want this, therefore everyone wants this." However, self-observation combined with multiple categories of evidence is much more instructive. Let's take a blatantly obvious example: the desire for adventure. You might say, if you are open and honest with yourself, "I want some sense of adventure in my life." You might even know this intuitively about yourself, without having to formulate it in words to understand it. This, on its own, cannot lead you to reasonably conclude that others want the same thing. But matching this self-observation – which can act as a starting point – with lessons about humans passed down through accumulated experience, the recurring plots in movies, the messages of popular songs, the stories of major figures throughout history, a basic understanding of genetic evolution (adventure can yield evolutionarily advantageous resources), scientific studies, books, and testimony from literary history's most incisive commentaries on human nature... then you can reasonably conclude that, "Yes, I want adventure, and most people do too."

KEY INSIGHT:

To Know Others, Know Thyself.

SELF-OBSERVATION ACTS AS A STARTING POINT

FIGURE 16: Do you observe a desire in yourself? Do you recognize what is motivating you? This is a perfect starting point, but it demands vindication from other categories of evidence. This allows you a sort of "staging ground" informing the direction of your forays into other areas.

OBSERVATION OF OTHERS

This is self-observation turned outward. Human desires are typically not hidden. Well, let me amend that: the more common, widespread, and strong human desires are typically not hidden. This might seem like a limitation, but isn't it an advantage? Is it not an advantage that the desires you will observe will be common, widespread, and strong? Observation of others, by untrained eyes analyzing them in passing, will not yield deep insights about their psychological states and deep, unadmitted desires. But it will tell you what most people want most of the time. See people all around you striving for more money? They want material comfort, peace, security. See people all around you taking hours out of their days to "hit the gym?" They want longevity, health, pride in themselves, and to be attractive to others. This might seem obvious. *Good.* It's supposed to be. The obviousness of (one of) the methods with which we can peer into what people want does not detract from the immense value of what the method discovers.

KEY INSIGHT:

To Know Thyself, Know Others.

OBSERVING THE ACTIONS OF OTHERS YIELDS INSIGHT

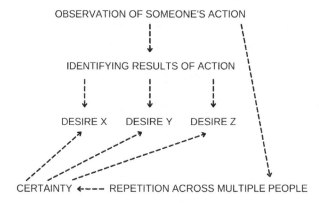

FIGURE 17: Direct observation of actions is an effective method. Make sure to note what the actors likely perceived the result of an action to be – this is what will inform your understanding of their desires, not actual results.

STORIES

Stories, like cultures and organisms, face a sort of "natural selection." If a story isn't interesting, it dies. Prior to written language, humans told stories verbally. The stories that captivated others, teaching them valuable lessons about the world and compelling their imaginations, spread; those that did not, died. And what makes a story compelling? A story is compelling if it bears some resemblance to reality. This is evolutionarily advantageous for organisms, cultures, and stories: a story bearing some semblance to reality teaches individual humans how to survive in the world, which strengthens their cultures and contributes to the cementing of the story in the collective psyche of the culture. And if a story resembles reality, the characters in it typically – more often than not, that is – must also resemble either reality or an idealized version of reality. So, to trace the argument thus far: stories that live instead of dying resemble reality; stories that resemble reality have characters in them that resemble people in real life; thus, by looking at what characters in the stories that survived wanted, we can extrapolate what people in real life want. The characters in the story resemble people in the world in some essential, fundamental manner. This is why the story is still around to be told. So, you can use this to vicariously peer into what people want.

KEY INSIGHT:

Stories Transport & Transform the Soul.

THE EVOLUTION OF STORIES REVEALS HUMAN DESIRES

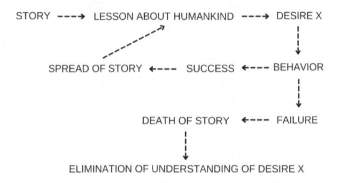

FIGURE 18: Stories that stand the tests of time resemble reality in some metaphorical, conceptual way. Reverse-engineer these stories to identify aspects of the human psyche. There is no such thing as a fiction story – every single story, while it may be literally false, conveys some metaphorical truth. Seek the metaphorical lessons of the foundational stories of your culture for insight into desire.

SOLUTIONS

What is a problem, in the purest sense of the word? A problem is an unsatisfied human desire. I cannot think of a more appropriate perspective from which we can determine the meaning of the word. And if a problem is an unsatisfied human desire, a solution, which is the inverse of a problem, must be a satisfied human desire. So, analyze the solutions of the world, reverse-engineering by looking at the problem they solve and determining what desire they satisfy in doing so. And they must satisfy a desire, or else they wouldn't be called a solution, and there wouldn't be a problem to solve in the first place.

KEY INSIGHT:

It's Not a Problem If It Doesn't Cause Pain Now or In the Future. Pain Is the Fundamental Problem.

WHAT MAKES SOMETHING A PROBLEM? THIS IS A CLUE

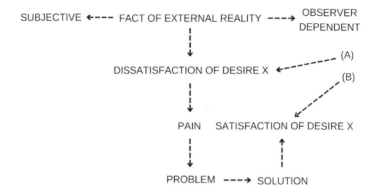

FIGURE 19: Facts of reality are not by themselves problems. The fact that your car broke is not a problem – whether it is a problem is a subjective, observer-dependent experience. And it becomes a problem if it dissatisfies a desire. This causes pain – the pain is the problem – motivating a solution which satisfies the desire. Find what the fact of reality that became a problem dissatisfied (A) and what the solution changed to create satisfaction (B).

SPEECHES

Legendary speeches became legendary by producing unparalleled emotional impact on listeners and, decades or centuries later, on readers. Emotional impact can be defined according to two broad categories: "good" emotion and "bad" emotion; emotion signaling "approach" to a novel stimulus or "escape" from a novel stimulus. This is an ancient radar system in our minds that helps us avoid pain and achieve pleasure. And what is pain – at least, most pain – if not the dissatisfaction of a human desire? What is pleasure if not the satisfaction of a human desire? To trace the argument, legendary speeches achieve emotional impact; emotion is either "bad" or "good," with bad emotions (typically) acting as predictors of pain and good emotions (typically) acting as predictors of pleasure; pleasure and pain are, respectively, the satisfaction and dissatisfaction of human desires. Thus, by looking at the nature of the emotional impact of a legendary speech, we can discern the nature of the human desires at the base of the emotional impact. This is a process I am quite familiar with, having done it time and again in my catalogue of books on public speaking, particularly those centered on how legendary leaders speak.

REVERSE-ENGINEERING SUCCESSFUL SPEECHES

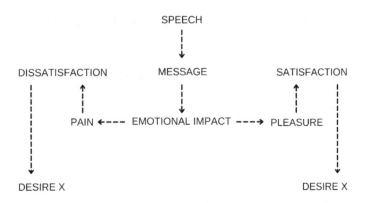

FIGURE 20: Successful speeches appeal to emotion. Emotion is intrinsically tied to desire.

LEADERS

Leaders get people to do things. People do things, more often than not, because they believe doing the thing will cause them more pleasure than pain, and will have the biggest pleasure-payoff out of all the available options. Pleasure and pain are the satisfaction and dissatisfaction of human desires. Thus, we can trace a line from the leadership of legendary leaders all the way to the desires motivating those they lead. I have also conducted this type of analysis time and again in my books on how the most impactful leaders of human history spoke. The remainder of this book, when we begin discussing the desires, centers on this body of evidence. Why? Because I think the most practical and instructive way of presenting the human desires is by showing you how effective leaders throughout human history have appealed to the desires in their communication, so that you can learn how to do the same in your communication.

KEY INSIGHT:

Effective Leaders Motivate. And Motivating Demands Appealing to Motives. Motives Shape Desires.

SUCCESSFUL LEADERS APPEAL TO DESIRES

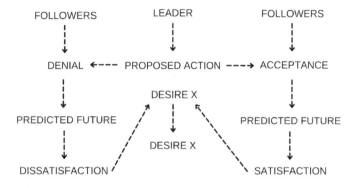

FIGURE 21: Successful leaders motivate action. People act because they predict that acting will satisfy one or more of their desires. Thus, analyze the proposals of successful leaders to identify the desires embedded therein.

CHOICES

Gathering evidence from the choices people make is a particularly compelling strategy because it stacks desires against each other. If one choice yields satisfaction of desire X, and the other yields satisfaction of desire Y, and they are mutually exclusive, we can analyze behavior of large groups of people when presented with the choice, and determine which desire is more compelling to them while also validating each desire individually. Further, we can invert the process: if one choice yields dissatisfaction of desire X, and the other yields dissatisfaction of desire Y, we can discern just as much about human desires from this scenario.

KEY INSIGHT:

If You Are Questioning What Someone Is Hoping to Achieve, Imagine the Predicted Consequences of Their Actions.

CHOICES ILLUMINATE UTILITY; UTILITY INDICATES DESIRE

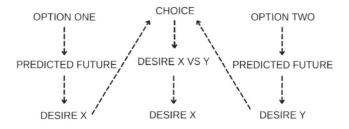

FIGURE 22: People choose the option that they predict will satisfy more of their desires than the others.

CHOICES HIERACHIES REVEAL RELATIVE DESIRE

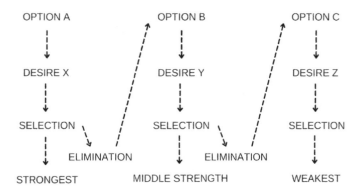

FIGURE 23: With choice-hierarchies, we can find the relative strengths of every desire in a set of options. Eliminate the first selection, and observe the next best choice. Eliminate that one, and observe what they do then.

EXTRAPOLATION

Human desires implicate other desires. Words are not desires; they are just symbols that describe desires. Applying a word to an abstract concept defines it rigidly but doesn't remove the abstraction; there is always another word, or clump of words, that works, and these new words, to our linguistic minds, appear to be slightly different desires. We can extrapolate unknown desires purely from known desires. I believe there is an upper limit to the extent of this process, but I haven't pushed the process there yet, preferring to be more conservative in my extrapolation of unknown desires from known desires. People want adventure. Adventure demands an appropriate amount of danger. Adventure demands a little chaos mixed in with order. Adventure demands challenge. Adventure demands novelty. Adventure demands all sorts of things. If adventure is inextricably linked with other desires, and people desire adventure, does it not follow that they want those other desires as well? This is the principal method of extrapolating unknown desires from known desires.

HUMAN DESIRES LINK IN AN INTERRELATED WEB

DESIRE X

DESIRE Y

DESIRE Z

DESIRE J

FIGURE 24: Every desire implicates a broader web of interrelated and intercausal desires.

GOOGLE

Every single Google search is compiled in a database. We can access reports revealing how many times a particular set of keywords was searched. This is an extremely effective way of researching what people want for four reasons: first, it is quick; second, it is empirical evidence; third, it allows for empirical comparison between desires; and third, it reveals what people are willing to admit they want when they know nobody is watching. If 10,000,000 people every month are searching for "how to be at peace," this vindicates the claim that people want peace. If 10,000,000 people every month are searching for "how to have adventure in life," this vindicates the claim that people want adventure. Are peace and adventure necessarily contradictory? No, but even if they were, it wouldn't matter. This is an exploration of what most people want most of the time, not what all people want all of the time. Contradiction between desires is not a foundational self-contradiction within the premise of the book, because the premise was never "all people want all of these desires all of the time."

COMPARING SEARCH VOLUMES YIELDS INSIGHT

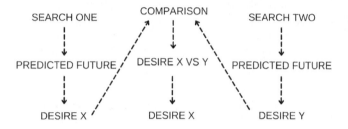

FIGURE 25: Use search volumes to identify desires.

SALES

People buy things they want. They want the products they want because the products they want typically satisfy some fundamental desires. Analyzing commercial behavior clues us in to human desires because of the immediate "want" presented by buying behavior, but also because of the other "wants" implicated by this initial want.

CONSUMER ACTIVITY YIELDS SECOND-ORDER DESIRES

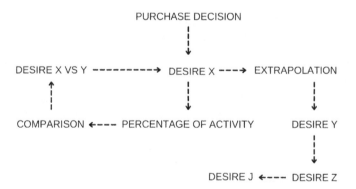

FIGURE 26: Identify a particular purchase decision. Identify what desire it fulfills. Identify the percentage of economic activity these purchase decisions comprise. Compare the different percentages of purchase decisions linked to different desires to compare the

strengths of the desires. And while this is true with all of these methods, you can then extrapolate from the identified desire.

PSYCHOLOGY

Psychology is perhaps too broad a term to describe this particular category of evidence correctly. This category of evidence is more appropriately described as a subset of psychology; as the testimonies and stories of clinical psychologists, therapists, and psychiatrists. There is a massive body of evidence taking the form of particular stories of particular clinical sessions with particular patients of particular psychologists that reveal particular desires in those patients. But all this particularism can limit evidence of this category – and all similarly particular categories – if you limit analysis to just one testimony. However, this is an extremely viable method if we explore patterns emerging over a large number of these testimonies.

EMERGENT PATTERNS OF CLINICAL TESTIMONIES

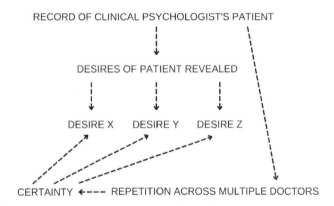

FIGURE 27: Anonymous but detailed clinical reports provide insight into human desires with a level of depth that exceeds nearly any other category of evidence.

COPYWRITING

Copywriting is the art of writing to get people to take action. Much like general accumulated experience, the field of copywriting is a close-knit community of people with specific accumulated experience. Since the advent of the field, perhaps a few centuries ago, effective copywriters seem to have made a habit of writing books. This hasn't stopped. Imagine this: 300 years ago, one of the first copywriters spends 40 years getting people to buy things with extreme efficacy. He writes a book. This book references how to touch upon human desires in copywriting. The next guy, starting his career 40 years after the first, reads the first copywriter's book, and spends 40 years applying similar methodologies. He writes his own book, which testifies again to the power of a particular set of human desires. This process carries on to the present day, yielding an extremely thorough and time-tested body of "accumulated experience" about what people want.

THE EVOLUTION OF PERSUASIVE WRITING

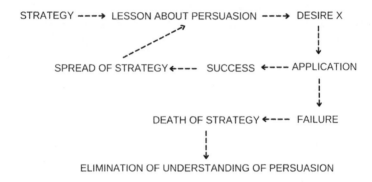

FIGURE 28: Copywriting has undergone a process of ongoing "cultural evolution." Copywriting professionals have amassed an impressive array of knowledge about what kind of writing persuades – and what desires it must play upon to generate an emotional pull to the product.

BEHAVIORAL ECONOMICS

Behavioral economics is a brilliant new field that, according to Wikipedia, "studies the effects of psychological, cognitive, emotional, cultural and social factors on the decisions of individuals and institutions and how those decisions vary from those implied by classical economic theory." It sits at the intersection of economics and psychology. And there is a massive body of scientific studies examining human behavior when presented with different choices. These studies, while not directly touching upon the human desires, can imply them. For example, the "present bias" indicates, through empirical evidence, that humans are biased toward short-term gains, even though the short-term gains or pleasures are significantly smaller than long-term gains presented in the choice architecture of the scenario. This indicates an innate, subtle, and often subconscious desire for speed; immediacy; nowness. This is just one of countless examples.

BEHAVIORAL ECONOMICS PULLS BACK THE VEIL

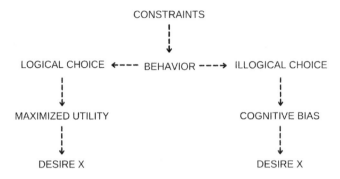

FIGURE 29: Behavioral economics studies illogical decision-making. If constraints produce behavior that represents a logical choice that maximizes utility, you can identify this maximization of utility as the maximal satisfaction of a given desire. On the other hand, the illogical choice represents the biasing influence of a "lurking desire," such as immediacy in the case of the present bias.

CROSS-CULTURAL OBSERVATION

Just like we can't make a compelling case for a desire based on one data point in one category of evidence, like extrapolating a broad-based human desire based on your self-observation at one point in time without cross-referencing with external observation or some other corroborating evidence, our analysis becomes significantly stronger when we perform cross-cultural observation or, more generally, cross-variable observation. If we compare two groups of 10,000 people living in drastically and dramatically different circumstances, and they still appear to exhibit some of the same core desires, we can postulate the existence of those desires with much more certainty.

KEY INSIGHT:

The Similarities Between Vastly Different People Speak to What Is Innate and Essential In the Psyche.

IDENTIFYING SHARED CULTURAL COMPONENTS

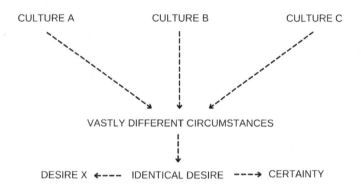

FIGURE 30: Desires manifest themselves at a cultural level, not only at an individual. If multiple cultures in vastly different circumstances express an identical desire, you can identify this desire with a high degree of certainty.

THE BUSINESS WORLD

I once heard a free-market economy described as "the most moral economic system, because for you to get what you want, you have to give me something I want." Well, based on this seemingly self-evident principle, businesses exist to give people what they want. Entire industries crop up to give people what they want. Different industries command different levels of demand. So we can see what people want according to the businesses and industries that exist to satisfy those desires, and we can also compare the strength of different desires according to the levels of demand commanded by different industries, roughly speaking.

KEY INSIGHT:

Behind Every Business Is an Unsatisfied Desire. Behind Every Product, a More Specific Unsatisfied Desire.

HOW THE ECONOMIC LANDSCAPE REVEALS PSYCHOLOGY

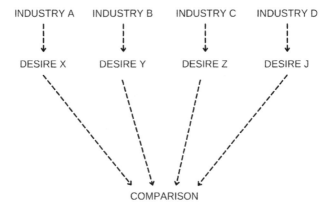

FIGURE 31: Different industries satisfy different desires. There is an economic theory stating that when a new desire emerges – no matter how specific or niche – a new business or industry emerges to meet it. Compare the demand commanded by different industries to compare the relative strengths of the desires they satisfy.

THE SELF-HELP BOOK MARKET

Self-help books exist to help people get what they want. This is an extremely specific form of evidence. You bought this book on what people want because you want to know what people want, which tells you at least what some people want: to know what people want. Are books on leadership exploding up the bestseller charts? People want to lead, and they want the secondary desires implicated in the desire to lead, which may be more fundamental, more widespread, or less so. Are people reading books on saving money? They want financial security. Trend analysis in the self-help book market reveals what a subset of people wants, and how these wants change over time.

KEY INSIGHT:

People Read What They Read to Get What They Want. This Is a Highly Specific Form of Analysis.

USING THE BOOK MARKET TO IDENTIFY DESIRE SHIFTS

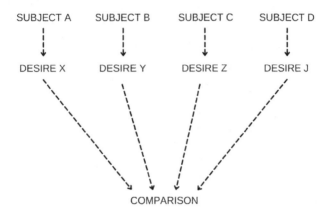

FIGURE 32: Apply the same analysis you applied for the economic landscape to the self-help book market.

ACTION

This is perhaps the most fundamental category of evidence. What do people do? If you want to look at motives, look at the consequences of actions – or, more accurately, on what a reasonable person would have expected the consequences of an action to be. Why? Because, if they took the action, then that's what they wanted. And if multitudes perform the same action, it is what multitudes want.

LOOK NOT AT STATED INTENTIONS, BUT RESULTS

FIGURE 33: Analyze the predicted results of actions.

EFFECTIVE PERSUASION

Effective persuasion almost always appeals to the self-interest of the audience. Analyze the content of a successful persuasive message and you will discover the content of people's self-interest.

PERSUASIVE SUCCESS REVEALS MOTIVATING FACTORS

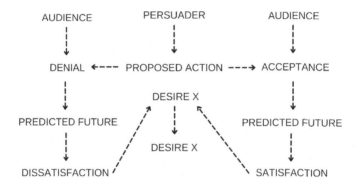

FIGURE 34: Reverse-engineer successful persuasion.

SPIRITUAL EXPLORATION

Some of these desires emerged as unifying threads across spiritual exploration conducted by maximally diverse groups of people in maximally diverse places under maximally diverse circumstances over 5,000 years of time – since the advent of writing, and possibly even before that. This category of evidence is not itself conclusive, but it is a starting hint, a nudge telling us that "there's probably something to this – check it out further."

KEY INSIGHT:

Some Human Desires, Some Human Needs, Can Appropriately Be Described as Spiritual.

THE COMMON DENOMINATOR OF SPIRITUAL EXPLORATION

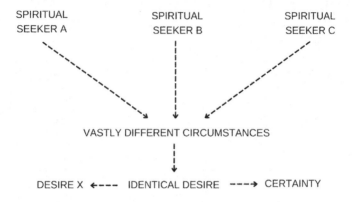

FIGURE 35: If spiritual seekers across space and time and in vastly different circumstances presented an identical desire, you can identify this desire with near-certainty.

UNSUBSTANTIATED BELIEFS

People believe what they want to believe: If people believe something without any evidence and even in the presence of disconfirming evidence, it often means they want to. From this, we can extrapolate what they want more generally – what psychological payoff (or desire satisfaction) belief in the unwarranted claim delivers.

REVERSE-ENGNEERING MOTIVATED BIASES

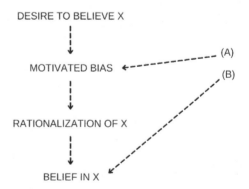

FIGURE 36: People with a desire to believe something will experience a motivated bias to believe it, leading to a rationalization of that belief. Analyze why they are motivated to

believe it – what desires compel them to believe it (A) – and what desires belief in the proposition satisfies (B).

ART

This one is tricky. Art is abstract. But, in its abstraction, it speaks to our intuitive, unconscious minds, revealing meaning to us – or reminding us of meaning we already encountered – that we don't know we know and don't know we encountered; meaning conceptualized on the most intuitive and pre-verbal levels of our cognition. I don't rely on art as evidence for these desires, unless the art is extremely clear-cut. But it is certainly a potential ground of evidence for someone with a more trained eye. And I can also listen to people with trained eyes unpack art, and use this as a category of evidence through them.

ARTISTIC EXPLORATION REVEALS OUR PSYCHE

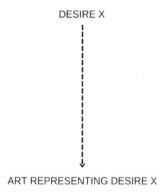

DESIRE X

ART REPRESENTING DESIRE X

FIGURE 37: People with a trained eye can reverse-engineer art to peer into the psyche of the artist, as well as the claim the artist was seeking to intuitively present about the human condition. This is not true with all types of art, and I am certainly not equipped to perform this type of analysis, but I have seen many people who understand art and symbology derive meaningful and (eventually) well-evidenced propositions about human nature from art.

THE COLLECTIVE UNCONSCIOUS

Carl Jung, one of history's most brilliant psychologists, posited the existence of a collective unconscious: "the part of the unconscious mind which is derived from ancestral memory and experience and is common to all humankind, as distinct from the individual's unconscious." What is in the collective unconscious? It's a big question, but we have some preliminary answers: primordial, archetypal imagery. Some of this imagery takes the form of ideals toward which we ought to strive; of positive goods we want to maximize. These are human desires, and human desires humans are born with and nearly all humans share.

THE FOUR LAYERS OF THE HUMAN PSYCHE

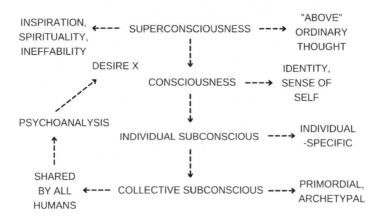

FIGURE 38: I propose four basic levels to the human psyche: super-consciousness, which is the seat of our spiritual and transcendent experiences, ordinary consciousness, which is our day-to-day experience and the seat of our self-identity, the individual subconscious which is unique to us, and the collective subconscious, which is the part of our subconscious that all humans share. Archetypes and primordial images – images and symbols that we are born with a propensity to understand – are housed in the collective subconscious. It is shared by all humans, and desires housed in it are too.

HUMAN COMMONALITY

Humans, despite their differences, tend to have a ground of commonality. We tend to want to live, reproduce, protect our families, improve our material situations, avoid intense pain, avoid boredom and monotony, tell and hear stories, socialize, form bonds, experience friendships, enjoy our social circles, love, and much more. Many desires are embedded in this ground of commonality. Because of this commonality, extrapolating that most people have a particular desire from a study of evidence referring to a small subset of people (assuming they aren't an especially weird subset) is not an undue leap, though it may not be thoroughly conclusive.

APPEALING TO COMMONALITY LETS US EXTRPOLATE

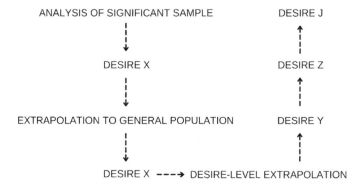

FIGURE 39: Humans are both shockingly similar and shockingly unique. We share a great deal of our desires.

SELF-EVIDENCE

You might regard many of the claims that follow about what humans want as self-evident. I would never make a claim on the basis of its self-evident nature; few claims have such a nature. However, you are free to regard many of these claims, and you probably will, as practically self-evident. It's not why I make the claims or how I support them, but it can, and likely will be, a reason you believe them.

VISUALIZING SELF-EVIDENCE

DESIRE X

DESIRE X

FIGURE 40: You may or may not regard the frameworks in the book as self-evident.

THERE YOU HAVE IT

Now you understand the body of evidence upon which I base the propositions in this book. Next, we will discuss some foundational meta-theories of human desires before beginning to explore the specific desires themselves. This groundwork is necessary to properly understand the desires and how to use them effectively in your life.

38 CATEGORIES OF COMPELLING EVIDENCE

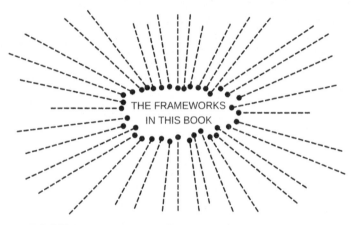

FIGURE 41: 38 evidentiary bodies support these claims.

ABSTRACTION

If we identify specific manifestations of a desire, we can apply "upward abstraction," finding the common denominator of the specific manifestations to discover more general levels of desire.

KEY INSIGHT:

The Forces of the Psyche Can be Characterized by Specific Manifestation or by Abstract Source. Both Are Useful.

VISUALIZING CONCEPTUAL ABSTRACTION

FIGURE 42: This reveals the process of abstraction with inhibitions. Abstracting desires works in the same way.

WHY ARE THEY WORTHWHILE?

Briefly, we must answer this question: why are the human desires worthwhile? Or, more accurately, why is knowing them worthwhile? They are worthwhile because they are the key to human motivation, influence, persuasion, and effective communication. They help you predict how people will act. They allow you to understand a plethora of potential persuasive approaches, and discover countless directions from which you can appeal to the self-interest of your listeners. They help you understand history, politics, and the great literary and artistic accomplishments of humanity. I could continue, but you bought this book, which tells me you already know they are worthwhile.

THE FOUNDATIONAL THEORIES

I know you are itching to get straight into the desires, but these foundational theories are insurmountably valuable for unlocking the full potential of the information disclosed further in the book. I present these foundational theories through the lens of presenting a message to a group of people (perhaps one of the most fundamentally human actions one could take) as I believe this lens offers you the most utility.

CONE OF ATTENTION

Every single audience has a set of subjects that, if you communicate about these subjects, results in them narrowing their attention to only focus on you. This is "top of cone" communication, near the vertex of the cone, where its volume is smaller; where it is narrower. If you speak about these "top of cone" subjects, your audience will narrowly focus on you. Think about it: A cone is narrower at the top. It includes fewer things, and if you're lucky, the cone of attention will be so narrow it only includes you and your message. Of course, it has nothing to do with luck, and everything to do with deliberately choosing the correct inputs.

On the flip side, every single audience has a set of subjects that, if you speak about them, will completely dilute their attention away from you. These are "bottom of cone," where its volume is larger; where it includes more things – distractions – and not only you.

Here's where it gets tricky: There is no universal cone.

Here's where it gets simpler: There is a sort of universal vertex.

Imagine a bunch of different cones overlapping only at the top, flaring out in different directions but meeting in a shared vertex.

You are probably wishing there was some sort of universal cone; that there was some sort of universal key unlocking every single person equally, and grabbing everyone's attention to the same degree. The core psychological human desires are that key. If you speak about the core human desires, you will almost always be "top of cone," and your audience – and almost any audience – will give you their narrow attention. If you speak without invoking the core human desires, that's a problem. You'll be "bottom of cone," and you won't earn undivided attention.

That said, every single audience has a different cone. In other words, they want different external things, but they want those different external things (the body of the cone) because they satisfy the same core desires (the overlapping vertex of the cone). A financier on Wallstreet wants to hit the next hot stock to satisfy the same desires as a fisherman in East Asia seeking a full net of fish. Sure, these are drastically different means, but to the same primordial psychological ends.

HOW TO ENSURE PEOPLE PAY ATTENTION

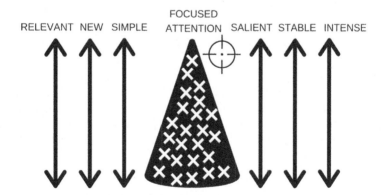

FIGURE 43: At the top of the cone, you bring your audience to a state of focused attention, including only one item: you. As the cone broadens toward the bottom, it includes more items: you, their car repairs, their weekend plans, the price of tea in China,

etc. Aim to bring your audience to the top of the cone by applying the new, relevant, simple triad and achieving saliency, intensity, and stability. These qualities generally bring you "top of cone."

Let me put it this way: Many of us want the same things, but we go about achieving those things in different ways. There are means (what we want to achieve) and ends (why we want to achieve those things). While the means differ wildly, the ends are often very similar. They are a set of core human desires and needs.

Why am I telling you this? Because of the cone of audience attention, of course. If you know your audience's means and ends, invoke them both. You'll be right there near the vertex of the cone. If you don't know the means, then identify the ends and invoke those. That will get you very close, and because most of these core desires are widely shared, they are the unifying point for diverse cones of attention; they are where different cones of attention, flaring out in different directions and belonging to wildly different people, meet.

How do you identify the core desires at play? Use the "many-fold-why."

A financier wants to hit the next hot stock. Why? To make money. Why do they want more money? To afford nicer things, and to feel financial security. Here, we branch.

The "nicer-things" branch: Why do they want to afford nicer things? To have a more attractive outward appearance. Why do they want that? For social status and prestige. You have isolated two core motivating desires of that financier.

The "financial security" branch: Why do they want financial security? To be safe no matter what happens. Why do they want that? To be free to do whatever they want, and free from fear. You have isolated two more.

Now we know the exact motivating factors that will make an audience of financiers (and probably fishermen too) listen in. We have the exact, core, psychological human desires that will immediately take you to the "top of cone," where effective communication happens because you met its prerequisite: attaining attention.

Remember this: Social status, prestige, freedom to act, and freedom from fear are all key motivating desires that describe why the fisherman wants a full net. What is inherently valuable about a bunch of flopping fish trapped in a rope net in the middle of the ocean? Nothing. It is only valuable because it fulfills the deeper desires of the fisherman. Want to know why someone does something? Look at the impacts of their action. You will find that the wide and infinite array of diverse human action often boils down to satisfying the same core desires, which is where disparate and diverse cones of attention belonging to disparate and diverse people unite.

KEY INSIGHT:

Core Motives Create Disparate Actions.

UNDERSTANDING THE TWO DIFFERENT KINDS OF AUDIENCES

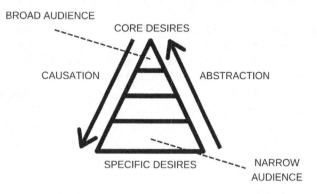

FIGURE 44: A broad audience with no clear-cut defining characteristics share their core desires, while a narrow audience with clear-cut commonalities (like sharing a profession) are much more likely to share specific desires.

THE PYRAMID OF DESIRE AND THE PYRAMID OF SCOPE

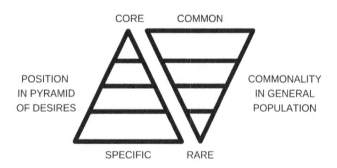

FIGURE 45: The core desires are more common, and any particular specific desire is less common. The closer you are to core desires – the higher the level of abstraction at which you define a desire – the more common it is.

You bought (or borrowed or stole) this book because you want to be more influential. What could give you more influence in communication than what I just told you?

THE HUMAN DESIRE PYRAMID

All humans have a set of core, innate desires; we desire other desires to satisfy our core desires; we desire other desires to satisfy the desires that satisfy our core desires; we desire other desires to... continued endlessly.

We have thousands of desires. Some of those desires are core, and other desires are manifestations of those core desires.

We have desire X, and then because of desire X, we have desire Y, because desire Y satisfies desire X. And then because desire Z satisfies desire Y, we want that too. And so on and so forth.

In summary: We have a set of core desires, and from those core desires emanates a massive pyramid of desires which are all linked because they satisfy other desires. Let's revisit our financier who wants the next hot stock: A financier wants to hit the next hot stock. Why? To make money. Why do they want more money? To afford nicer things, and to feel financial security. Here, we branch.

The "nicer-things" branch: Why do they want to afford nicer things? To have a more attractive outward appearance. Why do they want that? For social status and prestige. You have isolated two core motivating desires of that financier.

The "financial security" branch: Why do they want financial security? To be safe no matter what happens. Why do they want that? To be free to do whatever they want, and free from fear. You have isolated two more.

Core desires: Social status and freedom.

Level one derived desires: A more attractive outward appearance, and to be safe no matter what happens.

Level two derived desires: Affording nicer things, and financial security.

Level three derived desires: More money.

Level four derived desires: Hitting the next hot stock.

The core desires at the top of the pyramid are more likely to be shared by others. Almost everyone shares the desires of high social status and freedom. Not everyone shares the desires of hitting the next hot stock. As you move further down the pyramid, into tertiary desires (and even further), you begin to reach a place where the set of desires is more and more unique to your audience.

And we branch into "affording nicer things," and "financial security" at level two of the desire pyramid. The more you satisfy the "nicer things" desire, the less you can satisfy the "financial security" desire. A great deal of human indecision and internal conflict has to do with having two conflicting desires (as this financier does) and not knowing the degree to which to satisfy each. Further, much human motivation derives from having conflicting desires and seeking to reach a point of abundance where the sheer magnitude of resources renders the conflict meaningless.

And here's a key lesson: Every person has different derived desires, similar core desires, and a different value hierarchy; in other words, they place their desires in different hierarchies of value. This flows directly into the next few theories of persuasive communication.

SALIENCY, INTENSITY, AND STABILITY

Here's how this theory connects to audience uniqueness and the idea of audience personas: first, build an audience persona; second, identify the subjects that are salient, intense, and stable to that audience persona; third, speak in terms of those subjects.

Every single statement has three qualities: saliency, intensity, and stability. Every statement has these qualities in varying amounts, and the most compelling statements have the most of all of them.

Saliency: How many people care about a given subject, or in other words, how important a given subject is. It is the portion of the population that cares about something.

Intensity: How strongly people care about a subject; a measure of how much energy people are willing to devote to the subject.

Stability: How long people are willing to continue caring about a given subject, or how easy it is to switch the opinions of those who do care about a given subject.

ENSURING YOUR MESSAGE ENGAGES THE AUDIENCE

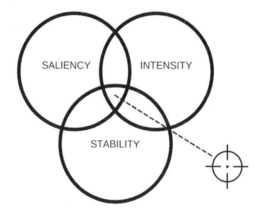

FIGURE 46: Conceive of saliency, intensity, and stability as a three-way Venn-diagram. Ensure your message is salient, intense, and stable; ensure it occupies the central position of the diagram.

KEY INSIGHT:

Common, Strong, and Long-Standing Hopes Unite Us.

HOW TO HOOK AND KEEP AUDIENCE ATTENTION

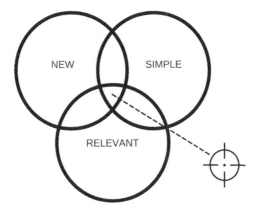

FIGURE 47: Conceive of the new, simple, and relevant triad as a three-way Venn-diagram. Ensure your message is new, simple, and relevant; ensure it occupies the central position of the diagram.

NEW, SIMPLE, RELEVANT; SALIENT, INTENSE, STABLE

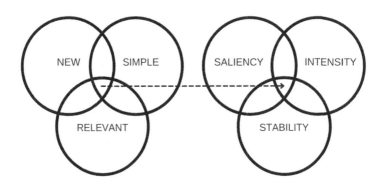

FIGURE 48: Satisfying the new, simple, relevant triad significantly improves your likelihood of achieving saliency, intensity, and stability.

In summary, saliency is how many people care, intensity is how much they care, and stability is for how long they will care.

Because saliency, intensity, and stability are not intuitive concepts, here's another helpful way to think about them: saliency is how important a topic is, intensity is how important it is to those who think it's important, and stability is for how long it will be important to those who think it's important.

Every compelling subject or statement is salient, intense, and stable: by combining these three qualities, you can maximize the chance that what you're saying will have an impact on your audience and that they will tune in. In many cases, however, your topic might not be salient, intense, or stable. In this case, the best strategy is to find the most salient, intense, and stable consequences of what you're speaking about and deliberately connect them to your subject.

Everything of impact occurring in the real world has consequences and is connected to other occurrences. Many topics are part of an interconnected consequence web of second, third, and fourth order effects, in which everything impacts everything else in one way or another.

By tapping into and connecting your subject to another one which is more salient, intense, and stable, you gain the very useful benefit of speaking in terms of something which most people in your audience will care about, which they will care about strongly, and which they will continue caring about long after you finish your speech. Stability is particularly important: stability is essentially the longevity of concern, interest, or relevance your ideas have to your audience. If they only care about what you're saying when you're saying it, and not after or even before you've said it, that's obviously not a good situation. Avoid this by connecting your idea to something you know your audience will care about in the long run.

As any career politician will vehemently assert, the economy is the most salient, intense, and stable issue. People will vote for a candidate who has a disappointing personal track record if they believe that he or she will lower their taxes. People love money. It's that simple. In order for our climatologist to tap into the salient, intense, and stable nature of how the general population thinks about the economy, money, and personal finance, they can say something like this: 'To my understanding, people usually don't realize how expensive climate change will be. It's not their fault, of course, but let me illuminate some numbers. The federal government, as well as state governments across the country, will have to increase taxes in order to deal with the consequences of climate change, so the average increase in taxes per person can be up to $1,000 annually. Similarly, if you live close to a coast, lake, or major river, you might have to pay up to $10,000 to protect your house from flooding caused by climate change.'

It might make you cynical to think that money is high on the list of what people care about, but it shouldn't. It makes sense that it is, so use it to your advantage.

Think of these three qualities as a three-way Venn diagram. In other words, think of them as three circles that each overlap each other. Something can be in only one circle, in two circles, or in the center where they all overlap, and it is enclosed by all three circles. The more circles your subject and theme are enclosed by, the more interested in your speech your audience will be. If your subject either ends up in the middle of that diagram, or you can find a logical connection that brings it there, then your persuasive power will be maximized."

This strategy of aligning your subject to something your audience cares about – something salient, intense, and stable to them – is the essence of backing the entire process with a powerful motive.

PERCEIVED MARGINAL BENEFITS, PERCEIVED MARGINAL COSTS

If you ever took a Microeconomics course, you're familiar with the marginal benefits versus marginal costs equation. The adage of "energy in, energy out" is the same as marginal benefits versus marginal costs. If someone perceives the marginal benefits of an activity to be greater than the marginal cost (including the value of the alternative activity forgone), all else equal, they will do that activity until the marginal benefits begin to be eclipsed by the marginal costs. If the costs exceed the benefits, they won't engage.

Energy in, energy out: If the energy someone has to put into an activity is greater than the rewards they get out of that activity, they won't engage in it.

Marginal benefits > marginal costs = activity engaged in until marginal costs > marginal benefits.

Marginal benefits < marginal costs = activity not engaged in until marginal costs < marginal benefits.

THE CRUCIAL ACTION-SELECTING COGNITIVE ALGORITHM

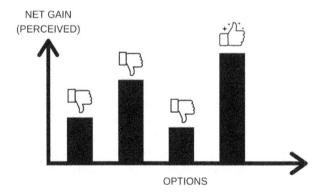

FIGURE 49: If an option has the highest perceived net gain of all the other options available, people select that option. Thus, a major sub-goal of your persuasive effort is to raise the perception of net gain associated with your proposal.

Keep in mind the essential key of applying this theory: This has nothing to do with actual benefits and actual costs, and everything to do with perceived benefits and perceived costs.

And this is exactly how this theory links to self-interest and WIIFM. When you speak in terms of self-interest – and answer the question "what's in it for me?" – perceived marginal benefits (or energy out) seem higher than perceived marginal costs (or energy in).

Now, you might be asking "What activity are they engaging in? What does this have to do with persuasive communication and applying persuasive communication patterns?" The activity they are engaging in (if you properly balance this equation by addressing self-interest and WIIFM) is listening to you; it is opting-in to give you their attention and mental space. Those are resources – scarce resources – that you are implicitly asking them to give up to you. You must ensure they think what they get by giving up the resources to you is greater in value than the resources themselves.

As for question number two – "what does this have to do with persuasive communication and persuasive communication patterns?" – the answer is *everything*. If you don't get them to opt-in to receiving your communication with enthusiasm by showing them, implicitly and explicitly, that marginal benefits far exceed marginal costs, then you don't get their attention, which means you can't persuade, because you can't truly communicate. Sure, you can try, but nobody will really be there to receive your message. They will be running through a to-do list, day-dreaming, or thinking about a totally unrelated subject, all while pretending to listen to you.

And this links perfectly to our next theory of eight seconds and the mental checklist, which then links to structure theory.

Before we get into that, know this: The further benefits exceed costs, the more enthused and attentive your audience will be. On the contrary, the further costs exceed benefits, the less enthused and attentive your audience will be. Yes, there is a threshold where marginal benefits are greater than marginal costs, but there is also a spectrum: The more marginal benefits exceed marginal costs, the more attention you get.

THE TIP OF THE ICEBERG

The universe is massive. It is roughly six trillion, that is 6,000,000,000,000, miles long, or 3.168 feet multiplied with ten to the power of 16. In this span of space, we know of nothing more complex than human beings. (And if you still feel small, remember that there are particles inside of you that are roughly as small relative to you as you are relative to the universe). Now, absence of evidence is not evidence of absence; our ignorance of something more complex than the human brain does not prove its nonexistence. But insofar as we understand the universe, we're it: the single most complex entity. We are incomprehensibly complex. Every single human being has depths to his personality we cannot even begin to fathom. We can't even begin to fathom or understand our own complexity, let alone that of others. Why am I telling you this? Because I want you to understand that these desires are just the tip *of the tip* of the human iceberg. And it's an incomprehensibly large iceberg.

HUMAN BEINGS ARE INFINITELY COMPLEX AND DEEP

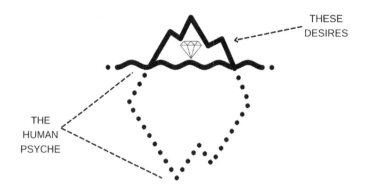

FIGURE 50: These desires – while they are deeply comprehensive and essential to psychology – only represent the tip of the iceberg of psychology.

FIVE-FOLD-WHY

So, we now turn to the final of the foundational theories: the benefit-extrapolating five-fold-why. This does something incredible. It is so unprecedented in my studies of communication theory. It is an algorithm based on a bedrock principle of human psychology that we can easily, effortlessly, and quickly apply to a benefit-driven statement (that is, a desire-driven statement) to drive yet deeper. Let me give you an example. Let's say you are debating your contender for the presidency leading up to election day. Let's say a major goal of your agenda is to raise gross domestic product (GDP). The truth is this: that's not a very compelling goal; it is, in fact, a superficial benefit, that is not inherently worthwhile. So, apply the benefit-extrapolating five-fold why. Why one: "Why do we want higher GDP?" Answer one: "We want higher GDP because it's not just a vanity-number; it correlates with valuable things." Why two: "Why do we want those valuable things?" Answer two: "We want those valuable things because they include higher life expectancy, lower infant mortality rate, and greater access to education." Why three: "Why do we want those things?" Answer three: "Because people will live longer; they will spend more time with their families on this Earth, and there will be less human sorrow; because fewer mothers will experience the greatest, most heart-wrenching tragedy that can ever befall them; because, as we expand educational access, people will reach ever-higher towards fulfilling their newfound potential." Why four: "Why do we want those things?" Answer four: "Because they are inherently valuable."

This does something wonderful: it gives your benefits drastically more power by digging down to the benefit of the benefit of the benefit of the benefit, so on and so forth, until you reach the inherently valuable benefits (which are inherently valuable because they hit upon the inherently valuable desires).

And that's what it's all about. It's about diving deeper and deeper, until you find the inherently valuable benefits, and then using them as the starting point of your benefit-driven language. In other words, instead of leaving your audience members confused, wondering "why is this person obsessed with GDP?" you break down the benefits of that benefit, in extremely impactful, compelling, human terms.

HOW TO FIND INHERENTLY WORTHWHILE MOTIVATORS

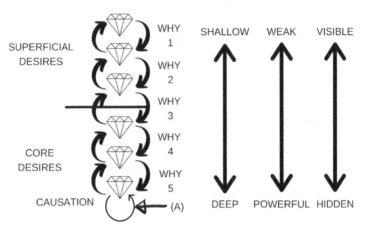

FIGURE 51: With every "why" you go from more superficial desires to more core desires. At the very bottom of the chain is the self-contained motivator: the thing for which the answer to the question "why" is "for its own sake" (A).

THE BASICS OF THE HUMAN DESIRES AND NEEDS

Let us begin at the beginning.

WHAT ARE HUMAN DESIRES?

Human desires are basic wants. They are engineered into every single person, in part, by evolution. Through psychological research, the human desires emerge to us. They are then organized into theories, but still exist on their own. In other words: while the human desires are categorized into theories (with some overlap between them), they still act on their own, as independent drivers of human action. And, depending on the person, some basic human need or human desire might be more dominant than others. So, if you're thinking "this seems nothing like me, and I'm human!" then I want to remind you of two things: maybe you aren't looking deep enough, and need to search harder for the basic human need or human desire manifesting in your life. Or, maybe this particular need or desire is not a dominant force in your life (but is in the lives of certain others).

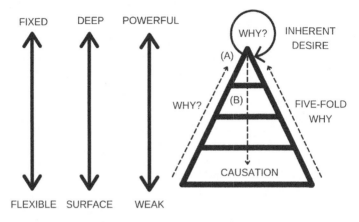

FIGURE 52: While desires technically sit at the top of the pyramid (A) and motives make up the pyramid(B), I use the two terms interchangeably in this book.

WHAT IS THE CAUSE OF INTERNAL CONFLICT?

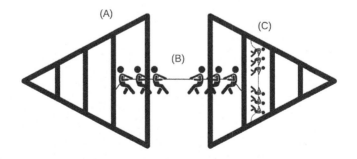

FIGURE 53: Two competing desire hierarchies that are not integrated into one well-organized hierarchy leads to a tug of war that creates internal conflict (B) – "serving two masters" or "chasing two rabbits." The conflict is often between what we want to do and what we should do. There can also be internal conflict within hierarchies (C).

STRONG AND STABLE HIERARCHIES OF DESIRE

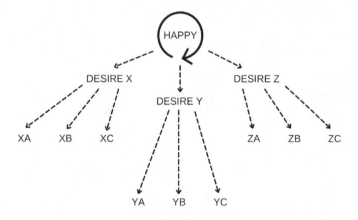

FIGURE 54: Strong desire hierarchies are flexible, with multiple ways of achieving the essential, core, overarching desire. If one fails, you have many alternatives.

WEAK HIERARCHIES OF DESIRE

FIGURE 55: Weak desire hierarchies are not broad-based. They are narrow. If you have only one way to be happy and only one way to achieve that, one point of failure ruins your chances of achieving happiness. The broad hierarchy can withstand multiple points of failure.

WHAT ARE HUMAN MOTIVES?

Human motives are manifestations of human desires. A human desire is clean surroundings. A human motive might then be a clean, pearly white kitchen remodel.

Human motives are what people seek to satisfy desires. In other words: human motives are different actions and goals people seek. Human motives differ between people. On the other hand, human desires are what human motives satisfy. Human desires are largely the same between people.

HUMAN MOTIVES VERSUS HUMAN DESIRES

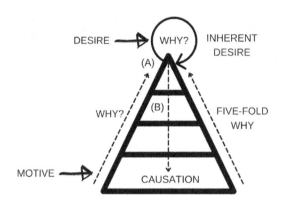

FIGURE 56: I propose terming the core, inherent motivating factors as "desires," and the things desired only or primarily to satisfy the inner desire as "motives." For our purposes, it is okay to use the terms interchangeably.

WHY DO BASIC HUMAN NEEDS AND HUMAN DESIRES MATTER?

You probably want to succeed in life, be it as a leader, in business, in politics, or at *anything involving other people.* To do that, you need to motivate people. You need to drive people. You need to inspire people to take action.

But how? Here's how: with the basic human needs and desires. Think of it this way: if you understand the basic human needs and human desire, you have a simple manual to the human brain. By using the basic human needs and human desires (like I'll show you how), you can become infinitely more persuasive, influential, and successful.

KEY INSIGHT:

Mindset Moves Mountains.

INFLUENCE PRODUCES SUCCESS

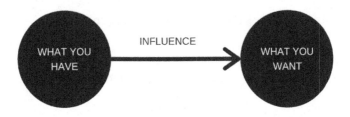

FIGURE 57: Influence produces success by giving you the power to turn what you have into what you want.

THIS KNOWLEDGE PRODUCES SUCCESS

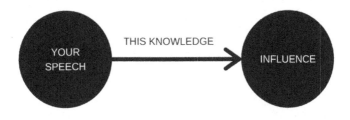

FIGURE 58: This knowledge produces success by giving you the power to produce influence with your speech.

HOW CAN YOU USE THE BASIC HUMAN NEEDS AND HUMAN DESIRES IN COMMUNICATION?

I'll cut right to the big answer: you can use the basic human needs and human desires in leadership, to motivate your team, in writing, to write with power, in public speaking, to speak with power and persuasion, in everyday conversations, to inspire other people, and in meetings, to get what you want. In other words: you can use the basic human needs and human desires any time you are communicating to a human with the desire to receive a specific action (even if you just want some undivided attention). And here's a hint: that's a lot of the time.

In this chapter, you'll learn the dominant theories of the basic human needs, human desires, and human drives. But more importantly, you'll learn how to use each one in your communication. How? With examples for applying each and every basic human need and human desire in your communication.

At its core, using the basic human needs and human desires in communication is presenting the action you want people to take as the way to fulfill one of the desires.

But this raises the question: is it ethical? Yes. And here's why: you're not lying to anyone. You're not manipulating anyone. You're not harming, swindling, or using anyone.

Instead, here's what you are doing: engineering your communication to focus on the fundamental, genetically-wired things people care about.

In fact, one might argue (and I do) that it is unethical to *not* speak in terms of the basic human needs and human desires. Why? Because you are trying to force your communication on someone without paying proper respect to the evolutionary, *drilled-in-their-head desires* they seek to fulfill.

A NOTE ON THE EXAMPLES

The examples of the desires are drawn mostly from the inaugural addresses of United States presidents. They are segments of the speech that show how the president invokes the desire to get action. They are drawn with no ideological inclination: I pick the best examples I know of based on my knowledge of almost every single inaugural address delivered in American history. I try and succeed (with maybe two or three exceptions) not to repeat any examples. So, if example A is an example of invoking both desires X and Y maximally effectively, and I already used example A to exemplify desire X, I will use example B to express desire Y, even if example A is a better fit. The examples are not endorsements of any particular political ideology or political figure. Ronald Reagan, Bill Clinton, and Barack Obama appear frequently. Chances are, if you like Clinton and Obama, you are not a big Reagan fan, and vice-versa. Remember, the examples are an analysis, not a positive or negative judgement of the message, individual, or ideology. In this book, I act as an investigator, not a judge. I ask you to do the same. Now, why do I use inaugural addresses? Aside from their inherent intrigue, aside from my extensive knowledge of their intricacies, I use inaugural addresses because of their intentionality. I cannot think of another kind of message crafted so meticulously by expert speech-writers, psychologists, and... geniuses. And they must be crafted meticulously, because their stakes are incomprehensibly high. Every single word, intonation, and unit of meaning is deeply deliberate: and yes, every single desire-invocation, whether it be implicit or explicit, is in all likelihood deeply deliberate too.

A NOTE ON OVERLAP

I referenced it briefly, but allow me to restate it: some examples exemplify more desires than the one it is tied to in the book. The desires are inextricably interlinked with one another: where there is one, there is likely another one or another ten closely following. If you can identify multiple desires overlapping in one example, good on you: it reveals your intuitive grasp of the subject matter. There is another form of overlap to keep in mind: different frameworks of human desires occasionally overlap with one another.

THE OVERLAPPING NATURE OF THESE FRAMEWORKS

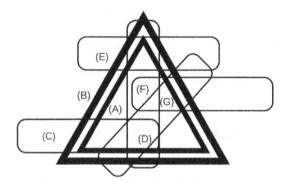

FIGURE 59: This is just an example of the overlap, and does not include all the frameworks in the framework of frameworks. Maslow's Hierarchy of Needs (A) defines three levels of needs that ERG theory layers upon (B). The life-force eight overlap with the basic needs of Maslow's Hierarchy (C) and with the economic values (D) that overlap with all of the theories pictured. The spiritual needs (E) overlap with Maslow's Self-Actualization need and the growth level of ERG theory. The esteem needs (F) overlap with the esteem level of Maslow's hierarchy, as well as parts of the economic values and ERG theory. They also overlap with 16-need theory (G) which also overlaps with the economic values, Maslow's Hierarchy, and ERG theory. This includes seven of the 16 frameworks of human desire revealed in the book.

A NOTE ON THE VALUE OF OVERLAP

The overlap between frameworks is beneficial. We can assume with a relatively high degree of certainty that if a particular desire occurs over and over again across different frameworks, it is a more powerful and ubiquitous desire. This is crucial information.

HOW DO THESE FRAMEWORKS CONNECT?

THE DESIRE FRAMEWORKS
DO NOT CONNECT LINEARLY

THE DESIRE FRAMEWORKS
ARE ALL INTERCONNECTED

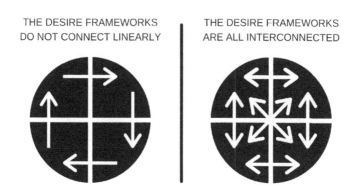

FIGURE 60: A more intuitive way of conceiving the relationships between the theories is to say "they connect nonlinearly; they are interconnected" and to leave it at that. You don't need to understand the full extent of the overlap.

OVERLAP SHOWS US RELATIVE STRENGTH OF DESIRES

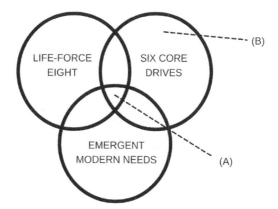

FIGURE 61: You can conclude that a desire appearing in the framework of the emergent modern needs, the life-force eight, and the six core drives is more fundamental and powerful than one appearing only in the six core drives. This is not a hard-and-fast rule, but it is a powerful and generally accurate heuristic.

SUBTEXT

The examples do not explicitly hit upon the desires. For some of the desires, that is unwieldy and awkward, if not outright offensive. They hit upon the desire in subtext and implication: gently, intuitively; sending the desire-driven message to the subconscious minds of the audience members, not beating them over the head with it. Make sure to keep this in mind as you read the examples. It's not always supposed to be obvious: that is intentional. Train your eye to read into the subtext of the message, for that is often where you will find the desire invocation.

COMMUNICATION STRATEGIES APPEAL TO TWO MINDS

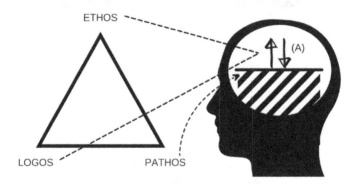

FIGURE 62: Aristotle's timeless persuasive model is ethos (evidence), logos (logic), and pathos (emotion). Emotion primarily targets the subconscious mind. Ethos and logos primarily target the conscious mind. Appealing to human desires can target both – it depends on the nature of the appeal. Subtextual and subtle appeals target the subconscious. The two minds influence each other. Conscious thought habits shape subconscious habits (A).

KEY INSIGHT:

There Is a Universe of Implicit Meaning Living Under the Literal Meaning of Spoken Words.

YOU CAN SPEAK UNSPOKEN WORDS

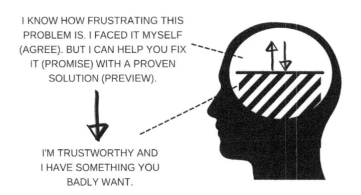

FIGURE 63: Some meaning demands subtlety. Some words cannot be spoken, but you need to convey their meaning nonetheless. How is this possible? By embedding the meaning in subtext. For many of these desires, you must embed your appeals in subtext. Many of the examples do.

A NOTE ON POSITIVE AND NEGATIVE EVIDENCE

In this context, I regard an example as providing positive evidence for a desire if it invokes it in a positive way; that is, in a way that approves, intensifies, and channels the desire. I regard an example as providing negative evidence for a desire if it advocates abandonment of the desire. In short, positive evidence is "we will do X... we want Y... we deserve Z..." while negative evidence is "we must set aside X... we must stop demanding Y... we must leave behind Z..." Both models are instructive, although you will find mostly positive evidence in the examples as I believe it offers more utility.

ARE THERE MORE?

Are there more desires than the ones I present in the book? Are there more examples? With certainty. I had to stop somewhere near 200.

...............................Chapter Summary...............................

- Understanding what people want allows you to speak with drastically more impact and influence.
- I draw the desires in this book from 38 different categories of the human experience. The evidence is strong.
- The desires in this book are not exhaustive. I have selected the 200-odd desires that are most compelling to use.

- I organize the desires by the psychological frameworks that contain them. There may be some overlap.
- Each desire includes a historic example from a leader – usually a U.S. President – using it in his speech.
- The examples are often subtextual and subtle. They do not hit you over the head with the desires. They often imply them.

KEY INSIGHT:

It Is Deeply Selfish to Communicate to People Without Speaking to Their Interests and To Expect Undivided Attention as You Do So.

The Further Removed From Their Interests Your Message Is, the Less Attention You Should Expect By Default. This, Of Course, Doesn't Mean You Can't Generate Interest.

Claim These Free Resources that Will Help You Unleash the Power of Your Words and Speak with Confidence. Visit www.speakforsuccesshub.com/toolkit for Access.

18 Free PDF Resources

12 Iron Rules for Captivating Story, 21 Speeches that Changed the World, 341-Point Influence Checklist, 143 Persuasive Cognitive Biases, 17 Ways to Think On Your Feet, 18 Lies About Speaking Well, 137 Deadly Logical Fallacies, 12 Iron Rules For Captivating Slides, 371 Words that Persuade, 63 Truths of Speaking Well, 27 Laws of Empathy, 21 Secrets of Legendary Speeches, 19 Scripts that Persuade, 12 Iron Rules For Captivating Speech, 33 Laws of Charisma, 11 Influence Formulas, 219-Point Speech-Writing Checklist, 21 Eloquence Formulas

SPEAK FOR SUCCESS COLLECTION BOOK

VIII

DECODING HUMAN NATURE CHAPTER

II

THE WAR OF ALL:

Desire, Conflict, Communities, Productivity, and Leadership

THE IMPACT OF DESIRE HIERARCHIES

T HIS SECTION BREAKS DOWN THE IMPACT of the frameworks that follow in the remainder of the book, revealing how the components of desire hierarchies influence the behavior of organizations, individuals, and societies. It also illuminates the role of leaders in organizations and societies through the lens of human desire. It touches on the meaning of an integrated psyche, an integrated organization, the "war of all against all," how to break vicious cycles of conflict, how to sustain virtuous cycles of progress, how progress reduces the need for conflict, and the crucial function of leaders.

RECOGNIZING THE PSYCHOLOGY OF AN INTERNAL WAR

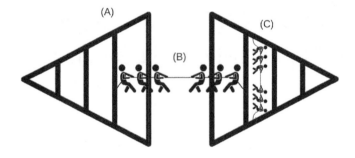

FIGURE 64: People can be pulled in two directions at once by two competing desire hierarchies (A). This creates conflict, confusion, an "unintegrated being," and uncertainty (B). Two parts of one person are fighting. This can occur within a hierarchy (C) geared toward an integrated and consistent set of core desires (inherent desires). It can also occur between two separate hierarchies. This is an internal conflict between warring inherent desires and their respective desire pyramids. This is dangerous territory. Ancient Greek philosophers apply a similar model to "our passions" and "our reason." Eastern ethicists warn us of "two wolves" inside of us, one feral and evil and one noble and good. Which one wins? "The one you feed more." And this is not purely an individual condition. It occurs in relationships, between inanimate objects designed by humans (like technological algorithms designed to meet the goals of a social media company) and users, in companies, between companies, and everywhere else you can possibly imagine. This is why the best societal systems create a balance in which the best way for someone to reach their desires is to help someone else reach theirs. This turns the tension inherent in a conflict-ridden system into productive energy. The individuals at large litigate how best to exchange desires.

THE HUMAN CONDITION (OR A KEY PART OF IT)

FIGURE 65: In our base state, in the absence of an overarching common hierarchy of desires and values, we each have warring desire hierarchies that come into conflict with the others. Now, make no mistake: most core human desires are shared, but the manifestations of these shared desires can often be exclusive ("I want to have this land" versus "you want to have this land" – the desire for land is common, but its practical manifestations conflict).

THE WAR OF ALL AGAINST ALL

EXTENT OF WAR OF ALL AGAINST ALL

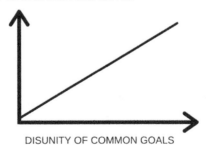

DISUNITY OF COMMON GOALS

FIGURE 66: Philosopher Thomas Hobbes called this state of affairs the war of all against all.

DISUNITY OF COMMON GOALS INHIBITS PROGRESS

HOW THE WAR OF ALL AGAINST ALL IMPACTS PROGESS

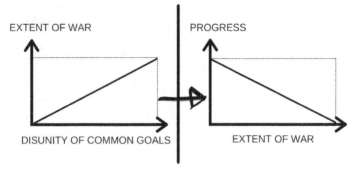

FIGURE 67: As the disunity of common goals rises, the extent of the war of all against all rises. As the extent of the war of all against all rises, progress (or the potential for progress) drops. Note that what we mean by progress in this context does not necessarily mean progress toward the right set of ideals (we will get to that shortly) but progress toward any set of ideals and desires.

AN AUTOCATALYTIC PROCESS OF CONFLICT

HOW PROGRESS IMPACTS THE WAR OF ALL AGAINST ALL

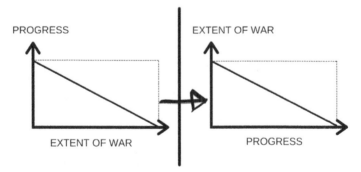

FIGURE 68: Conflict creates conflict. As conflict rises, progress (or the potential for progress) falls. As progress falls, conflict rises. As conflict rises, conflict tends to rise.

A VICIOUS CYCLE OF CONFLICT EMERGES

INCREASE IN CONFLICT   *REDUCTION IN PROGRESS*

FIGURE 69: This is a more straightforward representation of the vicious cycle of conflict revealed previously. As conflict rises, progress falls; as progress falls, conflict rises.

HOW THE STATUS QUO EMERGES OUT OF THE CONFLICT

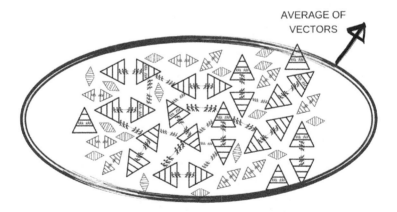

AVERAGE OF VECTORS

FIGURE 70: Movement toward any set of ideals – whether of individuals, organizations, societies, or civilizations – can be conceptualized as the result of the average of vectors of desire. Two equally strong groups pulling in two exact opposite directions produce exactly no movement toward any set of ideals. The vectors of desire cancel out. One individual with an extremely strong desire can pull many people with weak desires toward his preferred ideal. The key idea is that disunity inhibits progress toward any set of ideals because the vectors of desire cancel out. Consider political disunity in the United States. Why can Congress hardly pass a bill? Why can Congress hardly move toward a set of ideals? Because two almost equally strong groups are pulling in two almost opposite directions. The result? Exactly what we observe: slow movement toward the average of the desire vectors (which are adjusted to account for strength of desire and the capability of the group to effectuate change), as well as fits and spurts of faster movement tilted in one direction or the other when one group temporarily gains the upper hand over the other. This is by design. James Madison, one of the most influential framers of the United States Constitution, said that "ambition must be made to counteract ambition." This vector model is highly predictive, explaining the current state of affairs perfectly.

THE STATUS QUO: A POLITICAL ANALOGY

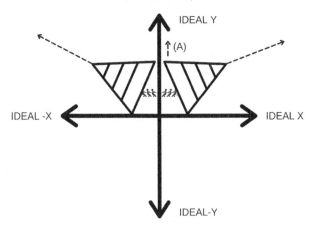

FIGURE 71: This represents two groups of equal strength with two almost opposite desire hierarchies of equal strength. They both pull with equal strength in two almost opposite directions. The vectors almost entirely cancel out, resulting in slight movement toward their average (A). This is a political model in the broader sense of the word: "the debate or conflict among individuals or parties having or hoping to achieve power." This applies to almost all decisions made in almost all groups. It also applies to individuals with desire-hierarchies war.

KEY INSIGHT:

Strong Opposing Views Produce Gradual Movement. Good.

RAPID CHANGE IN ONE DIRECTION

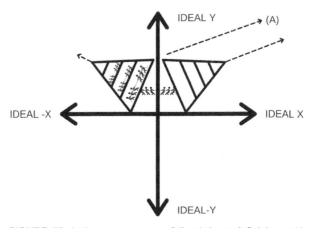

FIGURE 72: Let's say one group falls victim to infighting, with conflicts between desires that are subordinate to the core desire of that group (and analogous conflicts between subgroups of the group itself, corresponding to the warring desires). The other group gains relative strength. A weak pull to the left and a strong pull to the right results in movement that mostly pushes to the right (A). This is why unity, inner-group compromise, and the ability to "set aside differences to fight for the highest common goal" is essential. So is the ability to settle for getting "a lot of what I want but not everything" as opposed to "stubbornly holding out for everything I want within the group," which can sometimes influence the group but risks weakening the group as a whole and "getting much less of what we all want." This is the wisdom of the adage that you should "pick your battles." In the absence of these characteristics, a group falls to infighting, and its vector weakens, allowing it to be pulled in other directions by other groups, or in the absence of other groups, to move less in the direction it would like to move than it otherwise could. This is why it is also essential for a group to be crystal-clear on the highest ideal, and not to let squabbles over lesser ideals preclude the group from attaining its highest ideal.

KEY INSIGHT:

Infighting Often Sacrifices the Lesser Ideals to the Highest.

RAPID CHANGE IN THE OTHER DIRECTION

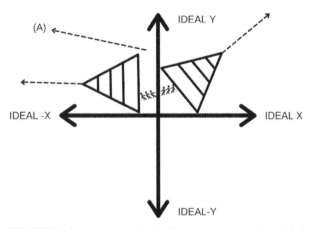

FIGURE 73: One group orients itself toward a more extreme ideal and the other maintains orientation. The vector shifts in the corresponding direction (A). Extreme positions motivate other groups to take extreme positions to keep the vectors in balance and maintain equilibrium.

WHAT POLITICAL HISTORY SAYS ABOUT HUMAN DESIRES

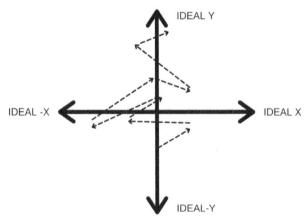

FIGURE 74: This is what human history looks like through this lens. Hopefully the arc bends toward justice.

HOW DO CYCLES OF RAPID CHANGE OCCUR?

HOW DOES ANY CHANGE OCCUR?

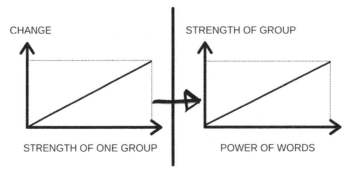

FIGURE 75: Part of the role of leadership is to effectuate change (when change appears necessary in light of the best possible desire hierarchy). When the relative strength of one group rises, change happens. When the power of one group's (or individual's) words rises, its strength does. So, when the power of your words rises, change does too.

WHY IS HISTORY AND PROGRESS A BACK-AND-FORTH?

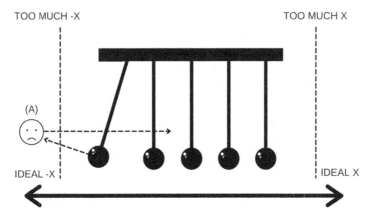

FIGURE 76: An extreme movement in one direction creates the consequences of extremism. This results in "unhappiness," motivating a push back in the other direction (A). When one group gains immense and rapid power and uses it to pull in an extreme direction quickly, this is how the now-subordinate group regains strength; due to the consequences of the powerful group's extremism. This may also be why, in a closed system, political change seems to slow down over time. The back-and-forth

pendulum swings gradually lose momentum, zeroing in on a balance. This may explain the position that "history has ended." Remember, by "political," we refer to the broad definition of the word: "the debate or conflict among individuals or parties having or hoping to achieve power." All leadership deals with politics by this definition. These models are not abstract theories dealing with a kind of leadership you may not need to exercise. They are universal models with broad-based applications. They explain fundamental psychological realities of organizational change and progress over time.

HOW THE PERPETUAL POWER STRUGGLE ENDS

EXTENT OF WAR OF ALL AGAINST ALL

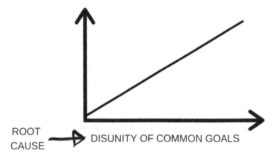

ROOT CAUSE ➔ DISUNITY OF COMMON GOALS

FIGURE 77: The extent of the war of all against all is caused by a disunity of common goals. This is the root cause. Authoritarianism seeks to instill unity by forcefully clamping down on disagreement and political conflict, which is only a symptom of the root cause. This is fairly universal. This is what the "office tyrant middle-manager" is all about. On the contrary, a more democratic approach seeks to eliminate the root cause in the first place by using freedom of speech and thought to persuade people to adopt the same hierarchy of ideals. This is an unimaginably more effective process of organizing human interaction.

KEY INSIGHT:

Consensus On What Constitutes "Good" Is Essential For Unity.

WHAT HAS TO HAPPEN TO END THE VICIOUS CYCLE

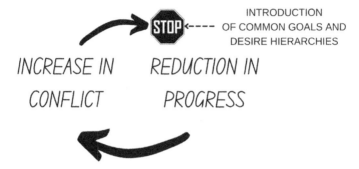

FIGURE 78: Simply put, the vicious cycles we discussed thus far end with the introduction of common goal and desire hierarchies. This doesn't mean that everyone has to agree on everything – only on the big things and values.

HOW LEADERSHIP IS SUPPOSED TO END THE CYCLE

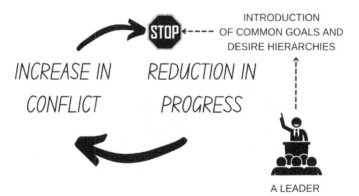

FIGURE 79: How are common goal and desire hierarchies developed? By the persuasive words of leaders, in part.

KEY INSIGHT:

True Leaders Strive For Unity.

WHERE THE INSTINCT TO FORM HIERARCHIES COMES FROM

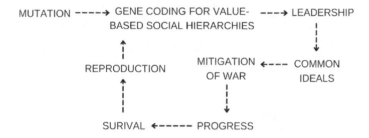

FIGURE 80: The human instinct to form hierarchies and defer to leaders and authority figures may be evolutionarily ingrained in part because leaders and authority figures are catalysts for the introduction and propagation of common ideals. Why does this help an organism survive and reproduce? Because it mitigates the war of all against all.

AN FRAGMENTED PERSON AND AN INTEGRATED ONE

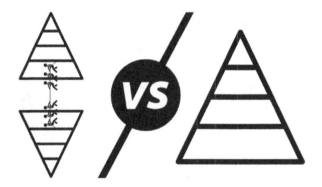

FIGURE 81: A fragmented person is pulled in two directions by two different hierarches of desires and two different "highest ideals," which really means no highest ideal. What happens between different groups with different desire hierarchies happens within individuals with different desire hierarchies: the warring hierarchies cancel out. Imagine a ship trying equally hard to go to two ports. It will land exactly in between the two ports – the vectors will average. And that probably means it will crash into a shore

somewhere, arriving nowhere but destroying itself. Bestselling author Jordan Peterson says he ensures he is 100% on-board with a goal before working toward it. If 30% of him is not on-board, that means that another 30% of him must cancel out the initial 30%, meaning that he is only 40% as effective as he otherwise could have been. This is true of individuals, organizations, societies, and civilizations. An integrated person is a person who is pulling toward one highest ideal, ticking off sub-goals and sub-values along the way. An integrated person is, or will be, a successful person. That is almost certain. And again, the same holds true for organizations and groups.

A FRAGMENTED ORGANIZATION AND AN INTEGRATED ONE

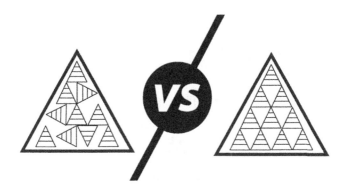

FIGURE 82: On the left is a fragmented, non-integrated organization. Four people within the organizational hierarchy do not have hierarchies of desires and values that align with that of the organization. On the right is an integrated organization. Which one will win? Which one will outthink? Outproduce? Outwit? Outlast? Which one will be more pleasant to be a part of? Which one will be a success, and which one will fall apart?

KEY INSIGHT:

A Disunified Organization Is a Disempowered One. Division Can Be Productive, But Primarily In the Context of a Common Highest Ideal.

AN ORGANIZATION IN THE SOCIAL ENVIRONEMNT

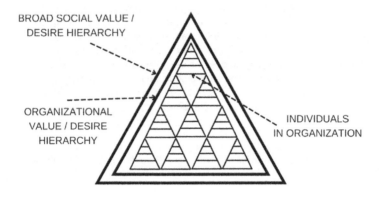

BROAD SOCIAL VALUE /
DESIRE HIERARCHY

ORGANIZATIONAL
VALUE / DESIRE
HIERARCHY

INDIVIDUALS
IN ORGANIZATION

FIGURE 83: This is an organization in which everyone is aligned with the goals of the organization, and the goals of the organization are aligned with the goals of the society at large.

A WEB OF ORGANIZATIONS POINTED AT COMMON IDEALS

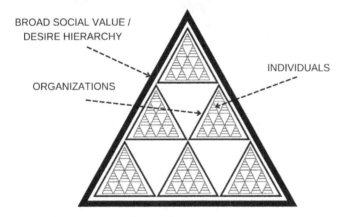

BROAD SOCIAL VALUE /
DESIRE HIERARCHY

ORGANIZATIONS

INDIVIDUALS

FIGURE 84: This is a web of organizations pointed toward an agreed-upon societally-recognized highest ideal. The introduction of a common enemy can cause this type of unity within an in-group. During World War II, American liberals and conservatives shared the common ideal of winning the war and defeating their common enemy, and this common ideal created this type of unity because it temporarily took the place of the disunified ideals.

WHY PROGRESS TOWARD GOALS IS NOT ALWAYS GOOD

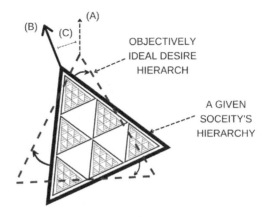

FIGURE 85: Getting closer to a set of goals is only good if the goals are good. So far, we haven't discussed good goals and bad goals – only goals. Just because a society is entirely united does not mean it is united in the right ideals. The objectively ideal desire hierarchy (A) may differ from a society's hierarchy (B). In this case, the best thing to do is to close the gap (C).

A UNITED WEB OF ORGANIZATIONS AIMED AT WRONG IDEALS

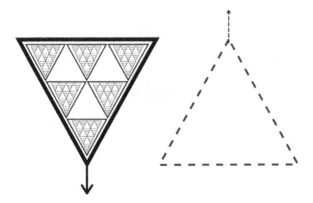

FIGURE 86: Many evil groups throughout history have been deeply united. Unity in the name of the wrong ideals is even more vicious than the war of all against all. It is rapid progress in the absolute worst direction.

WHAT SHOULD A GOOD LEADER DO IN A SICK SOCIETY?

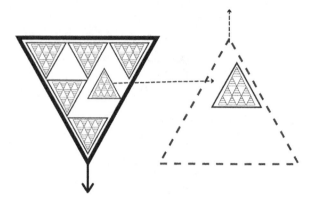

FIGURE 87: In a sick society, a good leader should guide the organization toward the best possible goal-hierarchy, even if that means going against or completely reversing the goal-hierarchy under which the society at large is organized. This is what it means to be a moral visionary.

THE FUNDAMENTAL FUNCTION OF LEADERSHIP

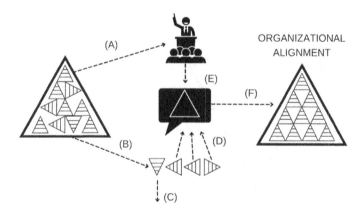

FIGURE 88: A major role of a leader – who sits at the top of an organization or sub-group's hierarchy (A) – is to identify those who are not in alignment with the organization's desire-hierarchy (B), send off those who are completely at odds with it (C), and speak to those who are partially at odds with it (D), using persuasive words to convince them to adopt the appropriate hierarchy of values and desires (E), creating an aligned organization (F).

A LEADER'S GREATEST CONTRIBUTION TO SOCIETY

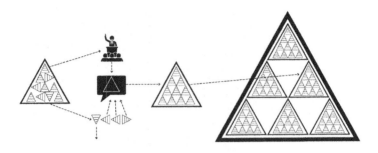

FIGURE 89: A leader's greatest contribution to society is an organization aligned to the ideals of the society insofar as those ideals are the proper ideals. When attempting to persuade unaligned people, the leader must be open to being persuaded. In this case, the leader learns from those with unaligned hierarchies and, if they convince him that their ideals and goals (and the emerging actions) are superior, the leader moves the organization that way.

DISPARATE VALUE HIERARCHIES CREATE FRAGMENTATION

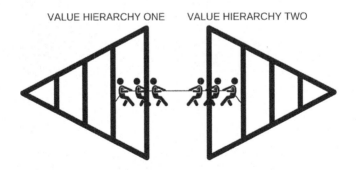

FIGURE 90: Let's revisit warring value hierarchies once more in light of the social environment.

A SOCIETY AT WAR WITH ITSELF GOES NOWHERE

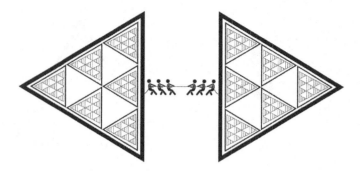

FIGURE 91: Disparate desire hierarchies may, over time, produce social stratification by gradually aligning individuals and organizations in opposite directions such that the end result is, in effect, two societies coexisting.

THIS IS A THEORETICAL AND ABSTRACT MODEL

REALITY   THESE MODELS

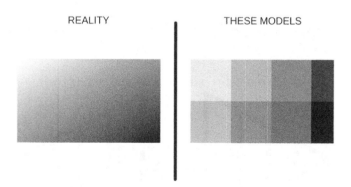

FIGURE 92: Reality is infinitely complex. These models, high-resolution as they may be, are still just models. There are exceptions and contingencies.

THIS MODEL OFFERS YOU GRANULAR INSIGHT

HOW MOST PEOPLE SEE
COMMUNICATION

HOW THESE MODELS
ALLOW YOU TO SEE IT

 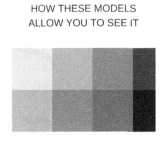

FIGURE 93: These models of communication, human desire, psychology, organizational change, and leadership are drastically more granular and high-resolution than the mental models most people use to approach these subjects. Thus, they give you higher predictive power.

REVISITING THE VICIOUS CYCLE IN ITS SIMPLEST FORM

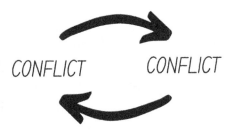

CONFLICT   *CONFLICT*

FIGURE 94: Briefly reconsider this cycle. Conflict creates conflict. We will shortly break down exactly why more deeply, giving you a greater understanding of the cycle.

THE VIRTUOUS UPWARD CYCLE OF SUCCESS

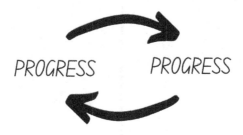

FIGURE 95: We will also break down exactly why progress produces progress. Briefly reconsider this cycle as well.

HOW SUCCESS TURNS INTO FAILURE AND CONFLICT

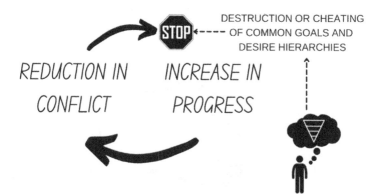

FIGURE 96: An increase in progress strengthens desire-hierarchies by increasing the amount of options available to individuals or by raising the accessibility of suitable options that satisfy core desires. This, in turn, reduces the need for conflict. We know how you, as a leader, can break the negative cycle. How does the positive cycle break? When someone with a disparate value / desire hierarchy destroys, cheats, cheapens, or weakens common ideals.

WHY THE VIRTUOUS CYCLE PERPETUATES ITSELF

WHY PROGRESS CREATES PEACE

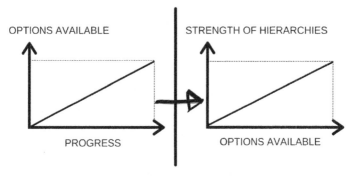

FIGURE 97: Progress increases the number of available options (or "the number of things I can do that will allow me to satisfy my most important desires and values.") As the number of satisfactory options available rises (or the accessibility of preexisting options rises), the strength of desire hierarchies increases.

HOW STRONG DESIRE HIERARCHIES STOP CONFLICT

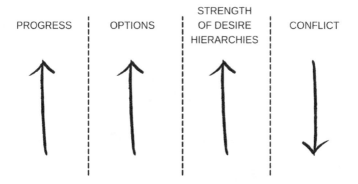

FIGURE 98: As progress rises, the number of satisfactory options rises, which raises the strength of desire hierarchies. This reduces conflict over limited options, which cycles back into allowing for more progress.

HOW WEAK DESIRE HIERARCHIES CREATE CONFLICT

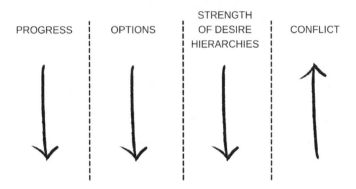

FIGURE 99: As progress falls, the number of satisfactory options falls, which decreases the strength of desire hierarches (in fact, this is axiomatic, as the number of satisfactory options and the strength of desire hierarchies are equivalent). This, in turn, creates an impetus for conflict over the limited supply of satisfactory options. The resulting conflict then reduces progress (or the potential for progress). This is the vicious cycle.

WHY HAVING LOTS OF OPTIONS ELIMINATES CONFLICT

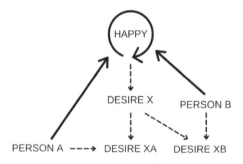

FIGURE 100: Let's say that person A and person B share the core, singular, and self-contained desire of being happy. They both want to be happy for the sake of being happy. Let's say that, to be happy, they both want "desire X." They want X because X allows them to be happy. Let's say that, to get X, which will allow them to be happy, they can either get XA or XB. Both are equally effective at satisfying desire X and, in turn, making them happy. Let's also

assume that only one person can enjoy XA and XB at once – that XA and XB have limited accessibility, only allowing for one user at once. Person A can get XA to satisfy X and be happy; person B can get XB to satisfy X to be happy. The number of available satisfactory options – which progress creates – has eliminated a major impetus to conflict in the form of competition over limited satisfactory options, allowing both person A and person B to be happy.

THIS IS A FUNDAMENTAL CAUSE OF HUMAN CONFLICT

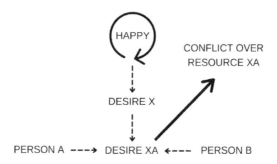

FIGURE 101: Let's reconsider the same scenario, except this time, there is no desire XB because the option doesn't exist. There hasn't been enough progress to create it yet. To be happy, both person A and B need to get X. To get X, they both need XA. This is the only option available to them. It permits only one user at once. In this case, the dearth of available options forces person A and person B into conflict over option XA. Sadly, because person A and person B are now busy squabbling (or killing each other, depending on the historical era), they are no longer being productive. The conflict is wasting their time, energy, and resources (or even ending their lives), hindering or eliminating their ability to be productive and create progress that allows for more options which mitigates the need for conflict. The conflict, caused by a lack of options, caused by a lack of progress, is now reducing progress and reducing options, leading to more conflict. Some historians believe it is a miracle that we – and by we, I mean humanity – have escaped this sorry state of affairs at all. One clever way to circumvent this process is to enforce rules that redefine the terms of conflict, forcing a situation in which the only permissible type of conflict is one in which "we decide who gets XA by seeing who can be more productive." This is the wisdom of free markets. Instead of conflict eliminating progress, this type of system turns conflict into progress. Another brief note is that, as

discussed previously, external enemies create inner-group unity. As a result, conflict between groups, while almost always creating a net decrease in progress (unless conflict has been bent into motivating productivity), can create localized increase in productivity by unifying groups.

WHY ORGANIZATIONAL FAILURE IS CONTAGIOUS

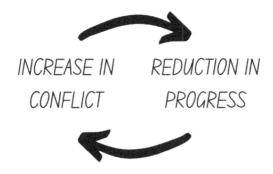

INCREASE IN CONFLICT   *REDUCTION IN PROGRESS*

FIGURE 102: In the absence of the constraints discussed previously, organizational failure becomes contagious.

YET ANOTHER CRUCIAL FUNCTION OF GOOD LEADERSHIP

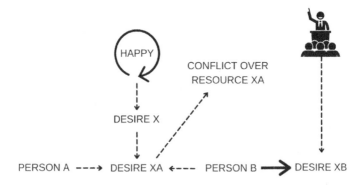

FIGURE 103: How can leaders prevent conflict and, as a result, create progress? By introducing people to more options that allow them to be happy, either by creating these options or revealing them to people who otherwise would have squabbled over the same resource. In this case, person A and person B would have

squabbled over XA, but a wise and observant leader showed person B that they can use XB to become just as happy.

HOW PROGRESS IMPACTS DESIRE AND OPTION HIERARCHIES

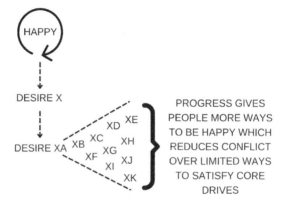

FIGURE 104: Simply put, progress creates options. Options produce progress and eliminate conflict.

THE FRACTAL MODEL OF THE HUMAN PSYCHE

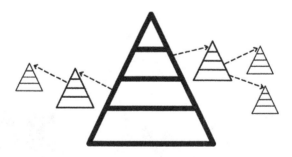

FIGURE 105: Part of why this works – part of why it is possible for the introduction of more options to ameliorate the impetus for conflict by giving people multiple pathways to satisfy their unwavering core desires – is because of the fractal nature of the human psyche. Human desires, as we discussed previously, are causally interlinked and they are infinitely granular. Desires spawn desires ad infinitum. As far as I know, there is no bottom limit to this process. The result is a hyper-complex snow-flake-shaped

never-ending fractal of desire-hierarchies, all emerging from the core desires. If you recall the cosmological analogy of human desire, just like the universe expanded from a single point called a singularity (according to the big bang theory), a single point of singular, self-causing core desires spawns the entire infinitely-expanding universe of human wants.

REVISITING HOW THE UPWARD CYCLE BREAKS DOWN

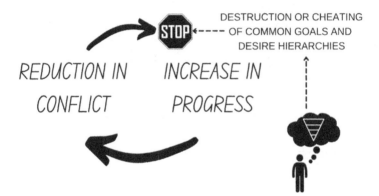

FIGURE 106: How does the upward cycle break down? Because someone, some group, or even some inanimate circumstances flip the common set of ideals, cheat the common set of ideals, or otherwise cheapen the common set of ideals.

IT IS YOU VERSUS THEM: ARGUE FOR THE RIGHT HIERARCHY

FIGURE 107: It's you versus them. There's always a "them" seeking to shift the hierarchy of ideals one way or the other. It may

even be a part of everyone – even of the leader himself – against the "better angels of our nature." The arc of the moral universe bends toward justice insofar as leaders argue for the best values.

BATTLES WITHIN THE SAME MORAL FRAMEWORK

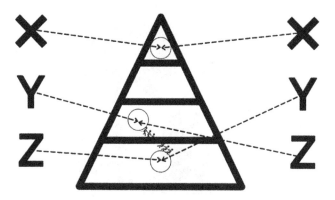

FIGURE 108: Most people tend to agree on the core desires, from which unique universes of desire emerge. Most people tend to agree on the core desires but, based on different upbringings, culturalization, and myriad other factors, they disagree on sub-desires (or "how" to manifest the core desires), as well as on where those sub-desires sit in the hierarchy. Most disagreement is not on which desires should be subordinate to which.

A MORE REALISTIC PORTRAYAL OF DIFFERENT HIERARCHIES

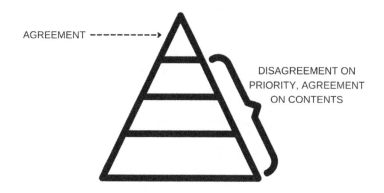

FIGURE 109: Simply put, most people you will encounter tend to agree with most other people on the core desires and values at

the source of their desire hierarchies and on the core desires and values that exist in the hierarchy. Most disagreement will be on which desires and values (and which actions emerging from them) take priority as means to the same ends (the core desires).

IT IS YOU VERSUS THEM: ARGUE FOR THE RIGHT HIERARCHY

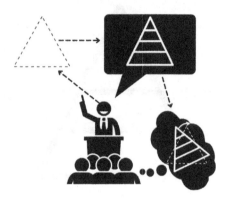

FIGURE 110: Let's bridge everything to one master framework and connect that master framework to the five-step process. Your role as a leader is to identify, to the best of your ability, the best possible hierarchy of values and desires. Then, your goal is to communicate this best possible hierarchy of values and desires to the people under your charge, and to do so in the best possible way.

.................................Chapter Summary.................................

- Human desires and values exist in hierarchies. The core, self-caused, inherent desires sit at the top.
- People can be pulled in two separate directions by two conflicting desire-hierarchies. This is an internal war.
- The same principles apply to groups: groups can be internally pulled toward two conflicting hierarchies of desires.
- Conflict increases the proclivity for future conflict by mitigating progress (or the potential for progress).
- Progress increases the proclivity for future progress by mitigating the impulse to conflict.
- Progress provides people multiple options for satisfying their deeper desires, eliminating the need for conflict.

Claim These Free Resources that Will Help You Unleash the Power of Your Words and Speak with Confidence. Visit www.speakforsuccesshub.com/toolkit for Access.

30 Free Video Lessons

We'll send you one free video lesson every day for 30 days, written and recorded by Peter D. Andrei. Days 1-10 cover authenticity, the prerequisite to confidence and persuasive power. Days 11-20 cover building self-belief and defeating communication anxiety. Days 21-30 cover how to speak with impact and influence, ensuring your words change minds instead of falling flat. Authenticity, self-belief, and impact – this course helps you master three components of confidence, turning even the most high-stakes presentations from obstacles into opportunities.

SPEAK FOR SUCCESS COLLECTION BOOK

VIII

DECODING HUMAN NATURE CHAPTER

III

FRAMEWORK ONE:

The Life-Fore Eight

THE LIFE-FORCE EIGHT

T HE LIFE-FORCE EIGHT DESIRES ARE FUNDAMENTAL to human psychology. They are some of the most fundamental human desires, and they speak unmistakably to us. We cannot ignore them. We are designed to ensure that we satisfy these needs.

WHAT ARE THE LIFE-FORCE EIGHT DESIRES?

Where do they come from? Evolution. It's that simple. Humans who have acquired the genes (through mutation) that create these desires were more likely to survive, and pass them forward. Thus, these "life-force eight" desires are incredibly powerful. They literally keep us alive, and we have genes that *force* these desires into our minds. In other words: if one of these desires is not met, our brains are screaming at us to "fix it now."

When do we see them? Everywhere. Almost every single thing people do relates to these desires in some manner. Again, that's why they are so powerful.

How do you use them? Your communication, whether in public speaking or in writing, can focus on these desires. Explicitly, or implicitly, you can invoke these desires and tap into the powerful forces that drive every single human action.

It's simple: people do things because they hear words that make them do things. Almost always. And those persuasive, powerful, moving words almost always use these life-force eight desires directly or indirectly.

A quick tip: this applies to all of the basic human needs and desires identified in this chapter. Here it is: don't try to force them into your communication. Instead, find the desires that naturally fit the subject of your communication, and use them. Don't unnaturally force in desires that are not related.

SURVIVAL, ENJOYMENT OF LIFE, LIFE EXTENSION

Historical Example: "You ask, What is our policy? I will say; 'It is to wage war, by sea, land and air, with all our might and with all the strength that God can give us: to wage war against a monstrous tyranny, never surpassed in the dark lamentable catalogue of human crime. That is our policy.' You ask, What is our aim? I can answer with one word: Victory-victory at all costs, victory in spite of all terror, victory however long and hard the road may be; for without victory there is no survival." – Winston Churchill

ENJOYMENT OF FOOD AND BEVERAGES

Historical Example: "In the Lord's Prayer, the first petition is for daily bread. No one can worship God or love his neighbor on an empty stomach." – Woodrow Wilson

Freedom from fear, pain, and danger: "We know that America thrives when every person can find independence and pride in their work; when the wages of honest labor liberate families from the brink of hardship. We are true to our creed when a little girl born into the bleakest poverty knows that she has the same chance to succeed as anybody else, because she is an American; she is free, and she is equal, not just in the eyes of God but also in our own. [...] We, the people, still believe that every citizen deserves a basic measure of security and dignity. We must make the hard choices to reduce the cost of health care and the size of our deficit. But we reject the belief that America must choose between caring for the generation that built this country and investing in the generation that will build its future. For we remember the lessons of our past, when twilight years were spent in poverty and parents of a child with a disability had nowhere to turn." – Barack Obama

COMFORTABLE LIVING CONDITIONS

Comfortable living conditions: "Recognizing economic health as an indispensable basis of military strength and the free world's peace, we shall strive to foster everywhere, and to practice ourselves, policies that encourage productivity and profitable trade. For the impoverishment of any single people in the world means danger to the well-being of all other peoples." – Dwight D. Eisenhower

TO BE SUPERIOR, WINNING, KEEPING UP

Historical Example: "America will start winning again, winning like never before." – Donald Trump

SUPERIORITY IS RELATIVE NOT ABSOLUTE

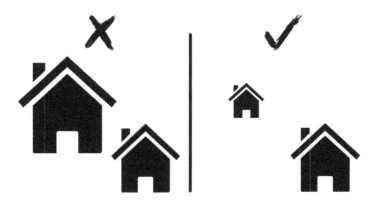

FIGURE 111: The two houses are the same absolute size, but superiority is determined by relative size. Someone may enjoy the size of their house when it is bigger than the neighboring houses but wish it were bigger if the surrounding homes are.

CARE AND PROTECTION OF LOVED ONES

Historical Example: "Our Founders saw themselves in the light of posterity. We can do no less. Anyone who has ever watched a child's eyes wander into sleep knows what posterity is. Posterity is the world to come; the world for whom we hold our ideals, from whom we have borrowed our planet, and to whom we bear sacred responsibility. We must do what America does best: offer more opportunity to all and demand responsibility from all." – Bill Clinton

SOCIAL APPROVAL

Historical Example: "Respecting the United Nations as the living sign of all people's hope for peace, we shall strive to make it not merely an eloquent symbol but an effective force. And in our quest for an honorable peace, we shall neither compromise, nor tire, nor ever cease. By these rules of conduct, we hope to be known to all peoples." – Dwight D. Eisenhower

.................................Chapter Summary.................................

- The life-force eight desires are deeply impactful. We are evolutionary wired to pay attention to these.
- We can rarely, if ever, turn these desires off. They are not only wired into us; they are hardwired.
- Appealing to these desires, as a result, offers your communication a tremendous amount of influence.
- You may not be able to appeal to these directly. They call for finesse and subtly. Appeal in a subtextual manner.
- Most people in developed countries have met these desires. In this case, you can appeal to them by proxy.
- Appeal to empathy for those who may not have met these desires. Appeal to generous impulses.

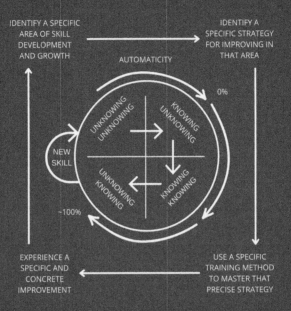

How do anxious speakers turn into articulate masters of the craft? Here's how: With the bulletproof, scientifically-proven, 2,500-year-old (but mostly forgotten) process pictured above.

First, we identify a specific area of improvement. Perhaps your body language weakens your connection with the audience. At this point, you experience "unknowing unknowing." You don't know you don't know the strategy you will soon learn for improving in this area.

Second, we choose a specific strategy for improving in this area. Perhaps we choose "open gestures," a type of gesturing that draws the audience in and holds attention.

At this point, you experience "knowing unknowing." You know you don't know the strategy. Your automaticity, or how automatically you perform the strategy when speaking, is 0%.

Third, we choose a specific drill or training method to help you practice open gestures. Perhaps you give practice speeches and perform the gestures. At this point, you experience "knowing knowing." You know you know the strategy.

And through practice, you formed a weak habit, so your automaticity is somewhere between 0% and 100%.

Fourth, you continue practicing the technique. You shift into "unknowing knowing." You forgot you use this type of gesture, because it became a matter of automatic habit. Your automaticity is 100%.

And just like that, you've experienced a significant and concrete improvement. You've left behind a weakness in communication and gained a strength. Forever. Every time you speak, you use this type of gesture, and you do it without even thinking about it. This alone can make the difference between a successful and unsuccessful speech.

Now repeat. Master a new skill. Create a new habit. Improve in a new area. How else could we improve your body language? What about the structure of your communication? Your persuasive strategy? Your debate skill? Your vocal modulation? With this process, people gain measurable and significant improvements in as little as one hour. Imagine if you stuck with it over time. This is the path to mastery. This is the path to unleashing the power of your words.

Access your 18 free PDF resources, 30 free video lessons, and 2 free workbooks from this link: www.speakforsuccesshub.com/toolkit

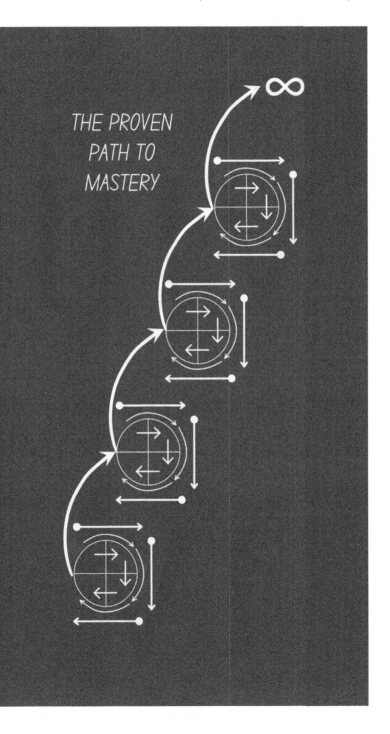

THE PROVEN
PATH TO
MASTERY

SPEAK FOR SUCCESS COLLECTION BOOK

VIII

DECODING HUMAN NATURE CHAPTER

IV

FRAMEWORK TWO:

The Learned Nine

THE LEARNED NINE

MAYBE YOU CAN'T CONNECT YOUR SPEECH to a life-force eight desire. My first response is to try harder. You'll find a way. My second response is that you can also connect it to one of these learned desires. Luckily for you, these are almost as powerful as the life-force eight. And they are much easier to engineer into your communication.

WHAT ARE THE LEARNED DESIRES?

Where do they come from? We've progressed as a society, so for most people, the eight life-force desires are fulfilled. But out of those desires arise the nine learned desires. In other words, we've learned over time that satisfying these desires will end up satisfying our basic human needs: the life-force eight.

When do we see them? These are a lot more common in everyday life. The life-force eight basic human needs and human desires occur behind the scenes. These learned desires are outward manifestations that often satisfy a deeper desire.

How do you use them? Use these when you want to invoke a basic human need or human desire, like one of the life-force eight, without explicitly calling it out.

You'll find it a lot easier to invoke these desires. And they'll still engage the core human needs on some level.

TO BE INFORMED

Historical Example: "A third place to build the Great Society is in the classrooms of America. There your children's lives will be shaped. Our society will not be great until every young mind is set free to scan the farthest reaches of thought and imagination. We are still far from that goal. Today, 8 million adult Americans, more than the entire population of Michigan, have not finished 5 years of school. Nearly 20 million have not finished 8 years of school. Nearly 54 million — more than one quarter of all America — have not even finished high school. Each year more than 100,000 high school graduates, with proved ability, do not enter college because they cannot afford it. And if we cannot educate today's youth, what will we do in 1970 when elementary school enrollment will be 5 million greater than 1960? And high school enrollment will rise by 5 million. College enrollment will increase by more than 3 million. In many places, classrooms are overcrowded and curricula are outdated. Most of our qualified teachers are underpaid, and many of our paid teachers are unqualified. So we must give every child a place to sit and a teacher to learn from. Poverty must not be a bar to learning, and learning must offer an escape from poverty. But more classrooms and more teachers are not enough. We must seek an educational system which grows in excellence as it grows in size. This means better training for our teachers. It means preparing youth to enjoy their hours of leisure as well as their hours of labor. It means exploring new techniques of teaching, to find new ways to stimulate the love of learning and the capacity for creation." – Lyndon B. Johnson

TO SATISFY CURIOSITY

Historical Example: "We meet at a college noted for knowledge, in a city noted for progress, in a State noted for strength, and we stand in need of all three, for we meet in an hour of change and challenge, in a decade of hope and fear, in an age of both knowledge and ignorance. The greater our knowledge increases, the greater our ignorance unfolds. Despite the striking fact that most of the scientists that the world has ever known are alive and working today, despite the fact that this Nation's own scientific manpower is doubling every 12 years in a rate of growth more than three times that of our population as a whole, despite that, the vast stretches of the unknown and the unanswered and the unfinished still far outstrip our collective comprehension." – John F. Kennedy

VISUALIZING THE TWO MODES OF CURIOSITY-BUILDING

SET OF POSSIBLE KNOWLEDGE

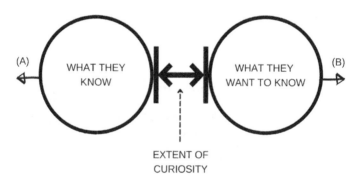

FIGURE 112: You can increase curiosity by moving what they know from what they want to know (A), moving what they want to know from what they know (B), or both.

CLEANLINESS OF BODY AND SURROUNDINGS

Historical Example: "Many of you will live to see the day, perhaps 50 years from now, when there will be 400 million Americans — four-fifths of them in urban areas. In the remainder of this century urban population will double, city land will double, and we will have to build homes, highways, and facilities equal to all those built since this country was first settled. So in the next 40 years we must re-build the entire urban United States. Aristotle said: 'Men come together in cities in order to live, but they remain together in order to live the good life.' It is harder and harder to live the good life in American cities today. The catalog of ills is long: there is the decay of the centers and the despoiling of the suburbs. There is not enough housing for our people or transportation for our traffic. Open land is vanishing and old landmarks are violated. Worst of all expansion is eroding the precious and time honored values of community with neighbors and communion with nature. The loss of these values breeds loneliness and boredom and indifference. Our society will never be great until our cities are great. Today the frontier of imagination and innovation is inside those cities and not beyond their borders. New experiments are already going on. It will be the task of your generation to make the American city a place where future generations will come, not only to live but to live the good life." – Lyndon B. Johnson

EFFICIENCY

Historical Example: "Hand in hand with this we must frankly recognize the overbalance of population in our industrial centers and, by engaging on a national scale in a redistribution, endeavor to provide a better use of the land for those best fitted for the land. The task can be helped by definite efforts to raise the values of agricultural products and with this the power to purchase the output of our cities. It can be helped by preventing realistically the tragedy of the growing loss through foreclosure of our small homes and our farms. It can be helped by insistence that the Federal, State, and local governments act forthwith on the demand that their cost be drastically reduced. It can be helped by the unifying of relief activities which today are often scattered, uneconomical, and unequal." – Franklin Delano Roosevelt

CONVENIENCE

Historical Example: "It can be helped by national planning for and supervision of all forms of transportation and of communications and other utilities which have a definitely public character." – Franklin Delano Roosevelt

DEPENDABILITY AND QUALITY

Historical Example: "It is a place where man can renew contact with nature. It is a place which honors creation for its own sake and for what it adds to the understanding of the race. It is a place where men are more concerned with the quality of their goals than the quantity of their goods." – Lyndon B. Johnson

EXPRESSION OF BEAUTY AND STYLE

Historical Example: "The Great Society is a place where every child can find knowledge to enrich his mind and to enlarge his talents. It is a place where leisure is a welcome chance to build and reflect, not a feared cause of boredom and restlessness. It is a place where the city of man serves not only the needs of the body and the demands of commerce but the desire for beauty and the hunger for community." – Lyndon B. Johnson

ECONOMY AND PROFIT

Historical Example: "Well, this administration's objective will be a healthy, vigorous, growing economy that provides equal opportunity for all Americans, with no barriers born of bigotry or discrimination. Putting America back to work means putting all Americans back to work. Ending inflation means freeing all Americans from the terror of runaway living costs. All must share in the productive work of this 'new beginning' and all must share in the bounty of a revived economy. With the idealism and fair play which are the core of our system and our strength, we can have a strong and prosperous America at peace with itself and the world." – Ronald Reagan

BARGAINS

Historical Example: "In the days ahead I will propose removing the roadblocks that have slowed our economy and reduced productivity. Steps will be taken aimed at restoring the balance between the various levels of government Progress. may be slow – measured in inches and feet, not miles – but we will progress. Is it time to reawaken this industrial giant, to get government back within its means, and to lighten our punitive tax burden. And these will be our first priorities, and on these principles, there will be no compromise." – Ronald Reagan

................................Chapter Summary................................

- The life-force eight desires are, to an extent, primordial. You can consider them "core" desires.
- The learned nine emerge from the life-force eight. The life-force eight cause the learned nine.
- We have learned that satisfying these nine desires is likely to satisfy our core desires.
- It is easier to appeal to the learned nine than it is to appeal to the life-force eight directly.
- As a result, you can draw on the persuasive power of the life-force eight indirectly by touching on the learned nine.
- The learned nine are more versatile, offering you more ways of appealing to them – subtextual, explicit, indirect, etc.

SPEAK FOR SUCCESS COLLECTION BOOK

VIII

DECODING HUMAN NATURE CHAPTER

V

FRAMEWORK THREE:

The Six Core Drives

THE SIX CORE HUMAN DRIVES

T HE SIX CORE HUMAN DRIVES HAVE BEEN identified as pursuits upon which a great deal of human action centers. They are emergent; they are not as fundamental as the life-force eight. Nonetheless, they are immensely powerful persuasive tools.

WHAT ARE THE CORE HUMAN DRIVES?

Where do they come from? These core human drives are what we do to satisfy our basic human needs and human desires. These drives are forces so motivating that they are, in a way, basic human desires on their own. We are so driven to do these things that we *need* them, and thus, you can use them as human desires.

When do we see them? In Josh Kaufman's best-selling business book *The Personal MBA*, he summarizes some previous psychological research and presents these desires. (I've added a sixth one, he presented five, and the research he initially cited presented four. Is someone going to present a seventh?). We see them in business. Every time a drive is unfulfilled, a business pops up to fulfill it. On a personal level, every time a drive is unfulfilled, an action is performed to fulfill it.

How do you use them? Use these when you want a basic framework of human motivators at your fingertips. These are broad, high-level desires. What they lack in specificity, they make up for in versatility. In other words, these are extremely easy to use.

THE DRIVE TO ACQUIRE

Historical Example: "Look at Europe. During the Fifties and Sixties, several European countries provided all their citizens with health care coverage, day care and other services for children, labor laws which facilitate the organization of trade unions, a statutory "social wage" for all workers, union and non-union, providing one month paid vacations, retention of pay while caring for sick family members, pensions and other services. In the year 2000 A.D., most workers in our country do not have these basic rights. In fact, according to the World Health Organization, the United States was ranked 37th among nations in the world regarding the quality of health care a country provides its people. This is not only embarrassing but also unacceptable. Western European countries provided for their people thirty to fifty years ago. Why can't we do it now in a period of economic boom? It's possible. We can make a difference. Together we can chart a new course." – Ralph Nader

THE DRIVE TO BOND

Historical Example: "I am loth to close. We are not enemies, but friends. We must not be enemies. Though passion may have strained, it must not break our bonds of affection. The mystic chords of memory, stretching from every battle-field, and patriot grave, to every living heart and hearthstone, all over this broad land, will yet swell the chorus of the Union, when again touched, as surely they will be, by the better angels of our nature." – Abraham Lincoln

THE DRIVE TO LEARN

Historical Example: "We set sail on this new sea because there is new knowledge to be gained, and new rights to be won, and they must be won and used for the progress of all people. [...] The growth of our science and education will be enriched by new knowledge of our universe and environment, by new techniques of learning and mapping and observation, by new tools and computers for industry, medicine, the home as well as the school. Technical institutions, such as Rice, will reap the harvest of these gains." – John F. Kennedy

THE DRIVE TO DEFEND

Historical Example: "We dare not tempt them with weakness. For only when our arms are sufficient beyond doubt can we be certain beyond doubt that they will never be employed." – John F. Kennedy

THE DRIVE TO FEEL

Historical Example: "The purpose of protecting the life of our Nation and preserving the liberty of our citizens is to pursue the happiness of our people. Our success in that pursuit is the test of our success as a Nation." – Lyndon B. Johnson

THE DRIVE TO IMPROVE

Historical Example: "We believed then and now there are no limits to growth and human progress when men and women are free to follow their dreams." – Ronald Reagan

.................................Chapter Summary.................................

- The six core human drives indirectly overlap with the preceding frameworks. This is common.
- These drives are compelling because you can appeal to them fairly directly without seeming too blunt.
- Maslow's Hierarchy of Needs (which we will discuss shortly) arranges drives in a hierarchy of progression.
- These human drives are not arranged in a hierarchy of progression. One does not require another.

- Different people experience different levels of these drives – some people are fully motivated by one but no others.
- Appeal to the drives that your audience is experiencing. Appeal to who you are actually speaking to.

KEY INSIGHT:

The Drive to Improve, What Abraham Maslow Called the Self-Actualization Need, Is One of the Deepest and Most Powerful.

We Are Tormented by the Potential We Know We Left Unfulfilled. We Know the Human Spirit Is Too Precious to Waste.

Claim These Free Resources that Will Help You Unleash the Power of Your Words and Speak with Confidence. Visit www.speakforsuccesshub.com/toolkit for Access.

2 Free Workbooks

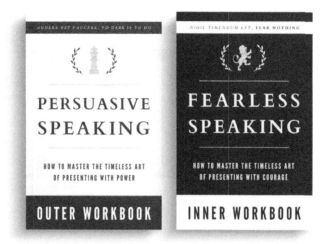

We'll send you two free workbooks, including long-lost excerpts by Dale Carnegie, the mega-bestselling author of *How to Win Friends and Influence People* (5,000,000 copies sold). *Fearless Speaking* guides you in the proven principles of mastering your inner game as a speaker. *Persuasive Speaking* guides you in the time-tested tactics of mastering your outer game by maximizing the power of your words. All of these resources complement the Speak for Success collection.

SPEAK FOR SUCCESS COLLECTION BOOK

VIII

DECODING HUMAN NATURE CHAPTER

VI

FRAMEWORK FOUR:

Maslow's Hierarchy of Needs

MASLOW'S HIERARCHY OF NEEDS

M ASLOW'S HIERARCHY OF NEEDS IS one of the most well-known, foundational, and renowned frameworks of human motivation and desires. Most people's understanding of what those around them want is limited to this hierarchy, however. Its ubiquity crowds out the sheer variety and the true extent of human desires.

WHAT IS MASLOW'S HIERARCHY OF NEEDS?

Where do they come from? These basic human needs, like the life-force eight, come from evolution. And they are arranged in a pyramid; in a hierarchy. I'll explain this later.

When do we see them? We see them *constantly.* When you see someone who doesn't seem to want to strive to achieve their fullest potential, you are seeing this at play. You might wondering, "why aren't they trying to move forward?" This framework of basic human needs presents an answer.

How do you use them? Use these when you want to motivate an audience. Use the hierarchy model to identify what level your audience is on, so you can match your message to it. Here's how this model works: the needs are specifically arranged in a pyramid. And you can't achieve the upper needs unless you fulfill the needs before it. In other words, if someone's physiological needs are not met (no food, warmth, or water), they likely aren't thinking about self-actualizing their fullest potential.

So, what you have to do when using this model to tap into your audience's desires, is this: meet them at the level of the hierarchy they are on. If they are missing belongingness and love, don't try to motivate them to self-actualize. I repeat: gear your communication to the level of the hierarchy your audience is on. You can reference previous rungs on the ladder that have been fulfilled, but not future ones. It won't make sense. People will think "I don't have food. Why are you talking to me about fulfilling my potential?"

PHYSIOLOGICAL NEEDS: FOOD, WATER, HEAT, REST

Historical Example: "A second evil which plagues the modern world is that of poverty. Like a monstrous octopus, it projects its nagging, prehensile tentacles in lands and villages all over the world. Almost two-thirds of the peoples of the world go to bed hungry at night. They are undernourished, ill-housed, and shabbily clad. Many of them have no houses or beds to sleep in. Their only beds are the sidewalks of the cities and the dusty roads of the villages. Most of these poverty-stricken children of God have never seen a physician or a dentist." – Martin Luther King

SAFETY NEEDS: SECURITY, SAFETY

Historical Example: "We, the people, still believe that every citizen deserves a basic measure of security and dignity. We must make the hard choices to reduce the cost of health care and the size of our deficit. But we reject the belief that America must choose between caring for the generation that built this country and investing in the generation that will build its future." – Barack Obama

THE FIRST LEVEL OF MASLOW'S HIERARCHY

BASIC NEEDS

SAFETY NEEDS:
SECURITY, SAFETY

PHYSIOLOGICAL NEEDS:
FOOD, WATER, WARMTH, REST

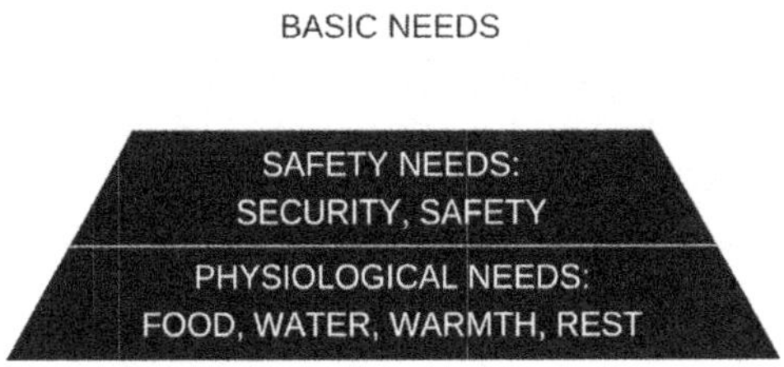

FIGURE 113: This is the first level of Maslow's Hierarchy.

BELONGINGNESS AND LOVE NEEDS

Historical Example: "For we know that our patchwork heritage is a strength, not a weakness. We are a nation of Christians and Muslims, Jews and Hindus, and non-believers. We are shaped by every language and culture, drawn from every end of this Earth; and because we have tasted the bitter swill of civil war and segregation, and emerged from that dark chapter stronger and more united, we cannot help but believe that the old hatreds shall someday pass; that the lines of tribe shall soon dissolve; that as the world grows smaller, our common humanity shall reveal itself; and that America must play its role in ushering in a new era of peace. [...] It is now our generation's task to carry on what those pioneers began. For our journey is not complete until our wives, our mothers and daughters can earn a living equal to their efforts. Our journey is not complete until our gay brothers and sisters are treated like anyone else under the law for if we are truly created equal, then surely the love we commit to one another must be equal as well. Our journey is not complete until no citizen is forced to wait for hours to exercise the right to vote. Our journey is not complete until we find a better way to welcome the striving, hopeful immigrants who still see America as a land of opportunity until bright young students and engineers are enlisted in our workforce rather than expelled from our country. Our journey is not complete until all our children, from the streets of Detroit to the hills of Appalachia, to the quiet lanes of Newtown, know that they are cared for and cherished and always safe from harm." – Barack Obama

ESTEEM NEEDS

Historical Example: "No man can fully grasp how far and how fast we have come, but condense, if you will, the 50,000 years of man's recorded history in a time span of but a half-century. Stated in these terms, we know very little about the first 40 years, except at the end of them advanced man had learned to use the skins of animals to cover them. Then about 10 years ago, under this standard, man emerged from his caves to construct other kinds of shelter. Only five years ago man learned to write and use a cart with wheels. Christianity began less than two years ago. The printing press came this year, and then less than two months ago, during this whole 50-year span of human history, the steam engine provided a new source of power. Newton explored the meaning of gravity. Last month electric lights and telephones and automobiles and airplanes became available. Only last week did we develop penicillin and television and nuclear power, and now if America's new spacecraft succeeds in reaching Venus, we will have literally reached the stars before midnight tonight. This is a breathtaking pace, and such a pace cannot help but create new ills as it dispels old, new ignorance, new problems, new dangers. Surely the opening vistas of space promise high costs and hardships, as well as high reward." – John F. Kennedy

THE SECOND LEVEL OF MASLOW'S HIERARCHY

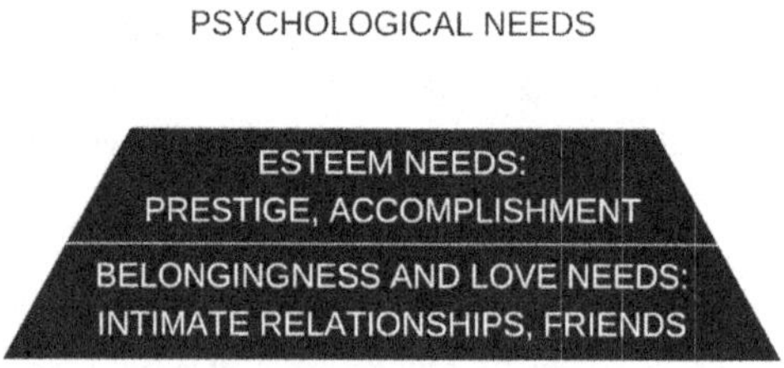

PSYCHOLOGICAL NEEDS

ESTEEM NEEDS:
PRESTIGE, ACCOMPLISHMENT
BELONGINGNESS AND LOVE NEEDS:
INTIMATE RELATIONSHIPS, FRIENDS

FIGURE 114: This is the second level of the hierarchy.

SELF-ACTUALIZATION NEEDS

Historical Example: "We choose to go to the moon. We choose to go to the moon in this decade and do the other things, not because they are easy, but because they are hard, because that goal will serve to organize and measure the best of our energies and skills, because that challenge is one that we are willing to accept, one we are unwilling to postpone, and one which we intend to win, and the others, too." – John F. Kennedy

THE THIRD LEVEL OF MASLOW'S HIERARCHY

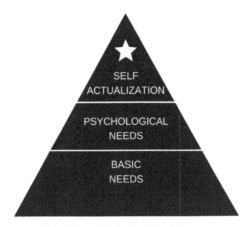

FIGURE 115: This is the entire hierarchy.

TARGET THE RIGHT LEVEL

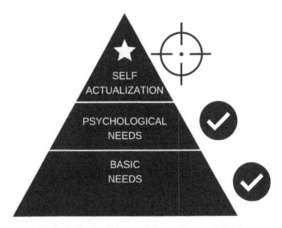

FIGURE 116: Target the level your audience is on – not above or below. In most professional situations in most developed countries, that means targeting the self-actualization need (and in some cases, the esteem needs).

................................Chapter Summary................................

- Maslow's Hierarchy of Needs is perhaps the oldest and most well-known framework of desires.
- People must progress in the hierarchy: upper levels require the preceding levels.

- When someone attains success in one of the lower levels, they move on to the higher level.
- The self-actualization need may be impossible to "fulfill." It may be an ongoing quest.
- As a result, appealing to the self-actualization need can be a deeply impactful and bottomless persuasive well.
- Appeal to the drives that your audience is experiencing. Appeal to who you are actually speaking to.

KEY INSIGHT:

Self-Actualization Is Not a "One-and-Done" Attainment.

Rather, It Is the Progressive Realization of One's Highest Ideal. Can It Ever Be Fully Reached? Or Can It Merely Be Approached?

Moreover, Is It a Fixed and Stagnant Ideal? Or Does It Change Over Time?

Claim These Free Resources that Will Help You Unleash the Power of Your Words and Speak with Confidence. Visit www.speakforsuccesshub.com/toolkit for Access.

18 Free PDF Resources

12 Iron Rules for Captivating Story, 21 Speeches that Changed the World, 341-Point Influence Checklist, 143 Persuasive Cognitive Biases, 17 Ways to Think On Your Feet, 18 Lies About Speaking Well, 137 Deadly Logical Fallacies, 12 Iron Rules For Captivating Slides, 371 Words that Persuade, 63 Truths of Speaking Well, 27 Laws of Empathy, 21 Secrets of Legendary Speeches, 19 Scripts that Persuade, 12 Iron Rules For Captivating Speech, 33 Laws of Charisma, 11 Influence Formulas, 219-Point Speech-Writing Checklist, 21 Eloquence Formulas

SPEAK FOR SUCCESS COLLECTION BOOK

VIII

DECODING HUMAN NATURE CHAPTER

VII

FRAMEWORK FIVE:
16-Need Theory

16-NEED THEORY

MASLOW'S HIERARCHY OF NEEDS AND the six core human drives are broad. 16-need theory is more specific. As you will see, these two frameworks overlap to an extent.

WHAT IS THE 16-NEED THEORY?

Where do they come from? An Explorable article explains it pretty well (the article is licensed under creative commons, so I'll just go ahead and quote from it). Here is the URL: https://explorable.com/16-basic-desires-theory.

"The 16 Basic Desires Theory is a theory of motivation proposed by Steven Reiss, Psychology and Psychiatry professor emeritus at the Ohio State University in Ohio, USA. The concept for this theory originated from the time when Reiss was hospitalized during the 90s. As he was being treated in the hospital, he was able to observe the devotion and hard work of the nurses who took care of him. As he saw how the nurses loved their work, he began to ask himself questions about what gives happiness to a person."

"From the questions 'What makes a person happy?', 'What makes another person happy?' and 'What makes me happy?', Professor Reiss started to search for answer to these questions in the field of motivational research. He found out that there was little emphasis and no analytical models for the structure of human desires. Following his recovery, he commenced his own series of studies about human desires. In his vigorous research, he found out that there are 16 essential needs and values he called 'basic desires,' all of which are drives that motivate all humans. After conducting studies that involved more than 6,000 people, Professor Reiss came up with these 16 basic desires."

When do we see them? "Professor Reiss developed a scientific test procedure called the 'Reiss Profile' that can be used to measure the shape of the basic desires of an individual. The purpose behind measuring the intensity of a basic desire of an individual is to identify a person's 'point of happiness.' As humans are unique, each of us will have a different profile from one another. The profile is represented by a colored bar chart. A strongly active desire is shown in the chart as a 'green' value, whereas a 'red' value means a poorly active desire. The middle value is the 'yellow' value and means that the basic desire depends upon the context of a particular situation. The red value can also be called as 'high striving,' while the green value is also termed as 'low striving.'"

How do you use them? To understand the Reiss Profile, let's put the basic desire "power" in the limelight. A person who has a strong basic desire for power (high striving or green value on the Reiss Profile) is likely to take the leadership role in a group of people. He is a challenge-seeker and a hard-worker for the sake of reaching his goals and ambitions.

On the other hand, an individual who has a weak basic desire for power (low striving or red value on the Reiss Profile) is one that does not like to assume leadership roles, and is nondirective of others, and even of himself. So, here's how to use this: find the profile of your audience members and cater to that. Build an audience persona. Try your best to determine which of these 16 your audience are "high-striving" for. Then, cater your communication specifically to that set of desires.

THE NEED TO BE UNITED WITH THE SOCIAL FABRIC

Historical Example: "I have a dream that one day on the red hills of Georgia, the sons of former slaves and the sons of former slave owners will be able to sit down together at the table of brotherhood. I have a dream that one day even the state of Mississippi, a state sweltering with the heat of injustice, sweltering with the heat of oppression will be transformed into an oasis of freedom and justice. I have a dream that my four little children will one day live in a nation where they will not be judged by the color of their skin but by the content of their character. I have a dream today. I have a dream that one day down in Alabama with its vicious racists, with its governor having his lips dripping with the words of interposition and nullification, one day right down in Alabama little black boys and black girls will be able to join hands with little white boys and white girls as sisters and brothers. I have a dream today." – Martin Luther King

CURIOSITY, THE NEED TO GAIN KNOWLEDGE

Historical Example: "Along the way, Americans produced a great middle class and security in old age; built unrivaled centers of learning and opened public schools to all; split the atom and explored the heavens; invented the computer and the microchip..." – Bill Clinton

SUSTENENCE, THE NEED FOR FOOD

Historical Example: "There are people in the world so hungry, that God cannot appear to them except in the form of bread." – Mahatma Ghandi

THE NEED TO PROTECT ONE'S FAMILY

Historical Example: "This is the heart of our task. With a new vision of government, a new sense of responsibility, a new spirit of community, we will sustain America's journey. The promise we sought in a new land we will find again in a land of new promise. In this new land, education will be every citizen's most prized possession. Our schools will have the highest standards in the world, igniting the spark of possibility in the eyes of every girl and every boy. And the doors of higher education will be open to all. The knowledge and power of the Information Age will be within reach not just of the few, but of every classroom, every library, every child. Parents and children will have time not only to work, but to read and play together. And the plans they make at their kitchen table will be those of a better home, a better job, the certain chance to go to college. Our streets will echo again with the laughter of our children, because no one will try to shoot them or sell them drugs anymore. Everyone who can work, will work, with today's permanent under class part of tomorrow's growing middle class. New miracles of medicine at last will reach not only those who can claim care now, but the children and hardworking families too long denied. We will stand mighty for peace and freedom, and maintain a strong defense against terror and destruction. Our children will sleep free from the threat of nuclear, chemical or biological weapons. Ports and airports, farms and factories will thrive with trade and innovation and ideas. And the world's greatest democracy will lead a whole world of democracies." – Bill Clinton

HONOR, THE NEED TO FOLLOW A CULTURE'S VALUES

Historical Example: "America's vital interests and our deepest beliefs are now one. From the day of our Founding, we have proclaimed that every man and woman on this earth has rights, and dignity, and matchless value, because they bear the image of the Maker of Heaven and earth. Across the generations we have proclaimed the imperative of self-government, because no one is fit to be a master, and no one deserves to be a slave. Advancing these ideals is the mission that created our Nation. It is the honorable achievement of our fathers. Now it is the urgent requirement of our nation's security, and the calling of our time." – George H.W. Bush

IDEALISM, THE NEED FOR SOCIAL JUSTICE

Historical Example: "To those people in the huts and villages of half the globe struggling to break the bonds of mass misery, we pledge our best efforts to help them help themselves, for whatever period is required – not because the communists may be doing it, not because we seek their votes, but because it is right." – John F. Kennedy

INDEPENDENCE, THE NEED TO BE SELF-RELIANT

Historical Example: "From our first days as a nation, we have put our faith in free markets and free enterprise as the engine of America's wealth and prosperity. More than citizens of any other country, we are rugged individualists, a self-reliant people with a healthy skepticism of too much government." – Barack Obama

ORDER, THE NEED FOR CONTROLLED ENVIRONMENTS

Historical Example: "By 1980, we knew it was time to renew our faith, to strive with all our strength toward the ultimate in individual freedom consistent with an orderly society." – Ronald Reagan

PHYSICAL ACTIVITY, THE NEED FOR EXERCISE

Historical Example: "Schools are growing gardens. They're moving beyond just pizza and tater tots to lunches filled with fresh produce and whole grains. Companies are actually rewarding employees for eating right and going to the gym. And it seems like everyone's running out to buy those fitness bracelets. [...] I mean, just think about what our work together means for a child born today. Maybe that child will be one of the 1.6 million kids attending healthier daycare centers where fruits and vegetables have replaced cookies and juice. And when that child starts school, maybe she'll be one of the over 30 million kids eating the healthier school lunches that we fought for. Maybe she'll be – yes! Maybe she'll be one of the 2 million kids with a Let's Move! salad bar in her school, or one of the nearly 9 million kids in Let's Move! Active Schools who are getting 60 minutes of physical activity a day, or one of the 5 million kids soon attending healthier after-school programs. Maybe that child will be one of the 70 million people living in Let's Move! City, Towns or Counties so she can walk to school on new sidewalks, participate in a summer meal program, join a local athletic league. Maybe that child will be one of the 3.6 million folks in underserved areas who finally have somewhere to buy groceries – groceries that are a whole lot healthier since food and beverage companies cut 6.4 trillion calories from their products." – Michelle Obama

POWER, THE NEED FOR CONTROL OVER OTHERS

Historical Example: "We will lead not merely by the example of our power but by the power of our example." – Joe Biden

SAVING, THE NEED TO ACCUMULATE

Historical Example: "As a result of these bipartisan efforts, America's finances were in great shape by the year 2000. We went from deficit to surplus. America was actually on track to becoming completely debt-free, and we were prepared for the retirement of the Baby Boomers." – Barack Obama

SOCIAL CONTACT, THE NEED FOR RELATIONSHIPS

Historical Example: "But there has always been another thread running throughout our history – a belief that we are all connected; and that there are some things we can only do together, as a nation." – Barack Obama

SOCIAL STATUS, THE NEED FOR SOCIAL SIGNIFICANCE

Historical Example: "We hear much of special interest groups. Our concern must be for a special interest group that has been too long neglected. It knows no sectional boundaries or ethnic and racial divisions, and it crosses political party lines. It is made up of men and women who raise our food, patrol our streets, man our mines and our factories, teach our children, keep our homes, and heal us when we are sick – professionals, industrialists, shopkeepers, clerks, cabbies, and truckdrivers. They are, in short, 'We the people,' this breed called Americans. [...] We have every right to dream heroic dreams. Those who say that we are in a time when there are no heroes just don't know where to look. You can see heroes every day going in and out of factory gates. Others, a handful in number, produce enough food to feed all of us and then the world beyond. You meet heroes across a counter – and they are on both sides of that counter. There are entrepreneurs with faith in themselves and faith in an idea who create new jobs, new wealth and opportunity. They are individuals and families whose taxes support the Government and whose voluntary gifts support church, charity, culture, art, and education. Their patriotism is quiet but deep. Their values sustain our national life. I have used the words 'they' and 'their' in speaking of these heroes. I could say 'you' and 'your' because I am addressing the heroes of whom I speak – you, the citizens of this blessed land. Your dreams, your hopes, your goals are going to be the dreams, the hopes, and the goals of this administration, so help me God." – Ronald Reagan

TRANQUILITY, THE NEED TO BE PROTECTED

Historical Example: "We the people of the United States, in order to form a more perfect union, establish justice, insure domestic tranquility, provide for the common defense, promote the general welfare, and secure the blessings of liberty to ourselves and our posterity, do ordain and establish this Constitution for the United States of America." – Preamble of the Constitution

VENGEANCE, THE NEED TO PUNISH AN AGGRESSOR

Historical Example: "In company with our brave Allies and brothers-in-arms on other Fronts you will bring about the destruction of the German war machine, the elimination of Nazi tyranny over oppressed peoples of Europe, and security for ourselves in a free world. Your task will not be an easy one. Your enemy is well trained, well equipped, and battle-hardened. He will fight savagely. But this is the year 1944. Much has happened since the Nazi triumphs of 1940-41. The United Nations have inflicted upon the Germans great defeats, in open battle, man-to-man. Our air offensive has seriously reduced their strength in the air and their capacity to wage war on the ground. Our Home Fronts have given us an overwhelming superiority in weapons and munitions of war, and placed at our disposal great reserves of trained fighting men. The tide has turned. The free men of the world are marching together to victory." – Dwight D. Eisenhower

..................................Chapter Summary..................................

- Every audience is different. Every individual is different. Humans and human motivations are infinitely diverse.
- Create an audience persona: Develop a comprehensive and non-superficial picture of who your audience members are.
- Cultivate an understanding of their motivations; cultivate an understanding of which of the 16-needs drives them.

- Ensure this describes the wide swath of your audience, not only some individual members. Appeal to what they share.
- When you discover the desires for which your audience members are "high striving," you know what to target.
- Of course, it is entirely possible that more than a single desire dominates your audience's motivational pallet.

KEY INSIGHT:

If People Seek Status But You Want to Motivate Compassion, Trying to Arm-Wrestle Their Motives Won't Always Work.

Sometimes, You Must Connect Compassion to Status, And Channel Preexisting Motives In a New and Better Direction.

SPEAK FOR SUCCESS COLLECTION BOOK

VIII

DECODING HUMAN NATURE CHAPTER

VIII

FRAMEWORK SIX:
ERG Theory

ERG THEORY

E RG THEORY IS ANOTHER BROAD MODEL of the human needs and desires. It is well-documented, well-supported, and well-suited for persuasive communication. It helps to have multiple models to view the human needs and desires, and it helps that some of them are specific while some of them are broad. All of these models are just tools in your persuasive toolbox. The more, the merrier.

WHAT IS ERG THEORY?

Where do they come from? These needs come from Maslow's Hierarchy of Needs. They build upon Maslow's Hierarchy of needs, by organizing Maslow's basic human needs into "existence," "relatedness," and "growth" buckets. However, each of these three can be treated as a basic human need on their own.

When do we see them? Any time we see Maslow's Hierarchy of Needs, particularly the necessary order in which they are achieved. People progress from wanting existence, to wanting relatedness, to wanting growth. Many of the other basic human needs and human desires fall under these three categories.

How do you use them? The same way you would use Maslow's Hierarchy of Needs. If your audience is struggling with existence needs (food, water, warmth), then they don't care as much about relatedness (social connections, bonds, family), or growth (self-improvement, progress, and achievement). If your audience is struggling with growth needs, they still care about food, water, and warmth. Those needs just aren't their predominant human desires based on their positions in life. So, if you recall from our discussion of Maslow's Hierarchy of Needs, you use the ERG model in your public speaking, communicating, or writing by following this rule: match your communication to the level your audience is on.

EXISTENCE, I WANT TO EXIST

Historical Example: "In such a spirit on my part and on yours we face our common difficulties. They concern, thank God, only material things. Values have shrunken to fantastic levels; taxes have risen; our ability to pay has fallen; government of all kinds is faced by serious curtailment of income; the means of exchange are frozen in the currents of trade; the withered leaves of industrial enterprise lie on every side; farmers find no markets for their produce; the savings of many years in thousands of families are gone. More important, a host of unemployed citizens face the grim problem of existence, and an equally great number toil with little return. Only a foolish optimist can deny the dark realities of the moment." – Franklin Delano Roosevelt

RELATEDNESS, AFTER I CAN EXIST, I WANT TO RELATE

Historical Example: "An idea born in revolution and renewed through two centuries of challenge. An idea tempered by the knowledge that, but for fate we, the fortunate and the unfortunate, might have been each other. An idea ennobled by the faith that our nation can summon from its myriad diversity the deepest measure of unity." – Bill Clinton

GROWTH, AFTER I RELATE, I WANT TO GROW

Historical Example: "We must simplify our tax system, make it more fair, and bring the rates down for all who work and earn. We must think anew and move with a new boldness, so every American who seeks work can find work; so the least among us shall have an equal chance to achieve the greatest things – to be heroes who heal our sick, feed the hungry, protect peace among nations, and leave this world a better place. [...] The time has come for a new American emancipation – a great national drive to tear down economic barriers and liberate the spirit of enterprise in the most distressed areas of our country. My friends, together we can do this, and do it we must, so help me God. From new freedom will spring new opportunities for growth, a more productive, fulfilled and united people, and a stronger America – an America that will lead the technological revolution, and also open its mind and heart and soul to the treasures of literature, music, and poetry, and the values of faith, courage, and love." – Ronald Reagan

ERG THEORY GRAFTS ONTO MASLOW'S HIERARCHY

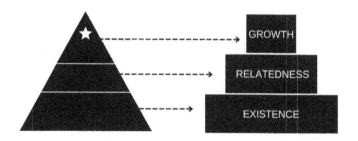

FIGURE 117: ERG theory grafts onto Maslow's Hierarchy.

...............................Chapter Summary...............................

- Maslow's Hierarchy of Needs is as follows: physiological, safety, love, esteem, and self-actualization.
- The ERG model stands for the "existence, relatedness, growth" model.

- The ERG model directly grafts onto Maslow's Hierarchy. It is a sort of meta-framework.
- Existence envelops physiological and safety needs. First, before anything else, people want to extend existence.
- Relatedness envelops love and belonging and esteem needs. After ensuring existence, people want to belong.
- Growth envelops self-actualization. After ensuring existence and belonging, people want to grow.

KEY INSIGHT:

The ERG Model Exemplifies How Frameworks Can Be Abstracted. It Is a Generalization of Maslow's Hierarchy of Needs.

But It Is No Less Useful, Significant, and Illuminating.

Claim These Free Resources that Will Help You Unleash the Power of Your Words and Speak with Confidence. Visit www.speakforsuccesshub.com/toolkit for Access.

30 Free Video Lessons

We'll send you one free video lesson every day for 30 days, written and recorded by Peter D. Andrei. Days 1-10 cover authenticity, the prerequisite to confidence and persuasive power. Days 11-20 cover building self-belief and defeating communication anxiety. Days 21-30 cover how to speak with impact and influence, ensuring your words change minds instead of falling flat. Authenticity, self-belief, and impact – this course helps you master three components of confidence, turning even the most high-stakes presentations from obstacles into opportunities.

SPEAK FOR SUCCESS COLLECTION BOOK

VIII

DECODING HUMAN NATURE CHAPTER

FRAMEWORK SEVEN:
Spiritual Needs

SPIRITUAL NEEDS

T HESE NEEDS ARE NOT ORGANIZED by any particular framework for human desires, but by their fundamentally spiritual characteristics. By my estimation, "spiritual" is the best word to describe them. You may consider them by another label if you so choose. You may call them "meta-psychological needs" (not things your psychology needs, but how your psychology wants your psychology to be).

WHAT ARE THE SPIRITUAL NEEDS?

Where do they come from? I couldn't tell you. It's a grand mystery where the spirituality needs come from. And I'm not going to come up with some explanation that teeters precariously on the line between fact and fiction.

When do we see them? In the actions of people who have the basic human needs, like food, water, shelter, financial security, etc. In the actions of the world's notables. But most importantly, in ourselves.

How do you use these? In your communication or public speaking (like the examples show you), use them to truly move audiences on a fundamental, emotional, human level. Use them to get incredible action out of people. Use them to speak to the bedrock spiritual principles that motivate people.

ULTIMATE SELF-REALIZATION OR SELF-ACCEPTANCE

Historical Example: "I believe in American belonging because of an experience you are part of right here tonight. Looking out at you and remembering how it felt to be an Indiana teenager, wondering if he would ever belong in this world. Wondering if something deep inside him meant that he would forever be an outsider. That he might never wear the uniform, never be accepted, never even know love. Now that same person is standing in front of you, a mayor, a veteran, happily married, and one step closer to becoming the next president of the United States. That is the America we are building. That is the America so many Iowans chose tonight. If you are ready to build an American life defined by belonging, this is our chance. If you're ready to build an American politics defined by boldness, this is our chance. If you are ready to build an American future defined by unity in the face of our greatest challenges, this is our chance." – Pete Buttigieg

KEY INSIGHT:

We Want to Become The Person
We Want to Be.

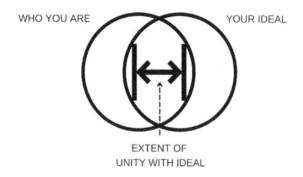

UNITIVE ATTAINMENT OF YOUR IDEAL

SET OF POSSIBLE CHARACTER TRAITS

WHO YOU ARE   YOUR IDEAL

EXTENT OF
UNITY WITH IDEAL

FIGURE 118: Uniting with your ideal means "acting how the best version of yourself would act."

THE NEED TO REACH OUR POTENTIAL

Historical Example: "We will be judged, you and I, for how we resolve the cascading crises of our era. Will we rise to the occasion? Will we master this rare and difficult hour? Will we meet our obligations and pass along a new and better world for our children? I believe we must and I believe we will. And when we do, we will write the next chapter in the American story. It's a story that might sound something like a song that means a lot to me. It's called 'American Anthem' and there is one verse stands out for me: 'The work and prayers of centuries have brought us to this day. What shall be our legacy? What will our children say? Let me know in my heart, when my days are through; America, America, I gave my best to you.' Let us add our own work and prayers to the unfolding story of our nation. If we do this then when our days are through our children and our children's children will say of us they gave their best. They did their duty. They healed a broken land." – Joe Biden

KEY INSIGHT:

The Sense of Our Precious Potential
Slipping Away with Time Is a Deep
Motivator with Great Urgency.

UNITIVE ATTAINMENT OF YOUR POTENTIAL

SET OF CONCIEVABLE ACCOMPLISHMENTS

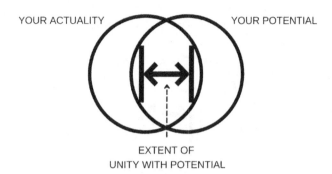

YOUR ACTUALITY   YOUR POTENTIAL

EXTENT OF
UNITY WITH POTENTIAL

FIGURE 119: Uniting with your potential means "actualizing the highest possible extent of your potential."

INSPIRATION, SPONTANEOUS INSIGHT OR EMOTION

Historical Example: "To match the magnitude of our tasks, we need the energies of our people – enlisted not only in grand enterprises, but more importantly in those small, splendid efforts that make headlines in the neighborhood newspaper instead of the national journal. With these, we can build a great cathedral of the spirit –each of us raising it one stone at a time, as he reaches out to his neighbor, helping, caring, doing. I do not offer a life of uninspiring ease. I do not call for a life of grim sacrifice. I ask you to join in a high adventure – one as rich as humanity itself, and as exciting as the times we live in. The essence of freedom is that each of us shares in the shaping of his own destiny. Until he has been part of a cause larger than himself, no man is truly whole. The way to fulfillment is in the use of our talents; we achieve nobility in the spirit that inspires that use. As we measure what can be done, we shall promise only what we know we can produce, but as we chart our goals we shall be lifted by our dreams." – Richard Nixon

BEING ACCEPTED BY OTHERS

Historical Example: "What our citizens must know is this: America faces a disease that is fatal and spreading. And this calls for urgency, not panic. It calls for compassion, not blame. And it calls for understanding, not ignorance. It's also important that America not reject those who have the disease, but care for them with dignity and kindness." – Ronald Reagan

A CONNECTION TO A TRANSCENDENT ENTITY

Historical Example: "I am the son of a black man from Kenya and a white woman from Kansas. I was raised with the help of a white grandfather who survived a Depression to serve in Patton's Army during World War II and a white grandmother who worked on a bomber assembly line at Fort Leavenworth while he was overseas. I've gone to some of the best schools in America and lived in one of the world's poorest nations. I am married to a black American who carries within her the blood of slaves and slaveowners – an inheritance we pass on to our two precious daughters. I have brothers, sisters, nieces, nephews, uncles and cousins, of every race and every hue, scattered across three continents, and for as long as I live, I will never forget that in no other country on Earth is my story even possible. It's a story that hasn't made me the most conventional candidate. But it is a story that has seared into my genetic makeup the idea that this nation is more than the sum of its parts – that out of many, we are truly one." – Barack Obama

TRANSFORMATION, MOVING TOWARD YOUR TOP IDEAL

Historical Example: "To that work I now turn, with all the authority of my office. I ask the Congress to join with me. But no president, no Congress, no government, can undertake this mission alone. My fellow Americans, you, too, must play your part in our renewal. I challenge a new generation of young Americans to a season of service; to act on your idealism by helping troubled children, keeping company with those in need, reconnecting our torn communities. There is so much to be done; enough indeed for millions of others who are still young in spirit to give of themselves in service, too." – Bill Clinton

THE COMPLETION OF PERSONAL OR GLOBAL AFFAIRS

Historical Example: "And so, my fellow Americans, at the edge of the 21st century, let us begin with energy and hope, with faith and discipline, and let us work until our work is done." – Bill Clinton

DEFINITION, KNOWING WHO YOU ARE

Historical Example: "The crisis we are facing today does not require of us the kind of sacrifice that Martin Treptow and so many thousands of others were called upon to make. It does require, however, our best effort, and our willingness to believe in ourselves and to believe in our capacity to perform great deeds; to believe that together, with God's help, we can and will resolve the problems which now confront us. And, after all, why shouldn't we believe that? We are Americans. God bless you, and thank you." – Ronald Reagan

A MORAL COMPASS AND ASSOCIATED BELIEF SYSTEM

Historical Example: "The purpose of protecting the life of our Nation and preserving the liberty of our citizens is to pursue the happiness of our people. Our success in that pursuit is the test of our success as a Nation." – Lyndon B. Johnson

A SET OF VALUES PRIZED ABOVE MERE ATTAINMENTS

Historical Example: "Many centuries ago, Saint Augustine, a saint of my church, wrote that a people was a multitude defined by the common objects of their love. What are the common objects we love that define us as Americans? I think I know. Opportunity. Security. Liberty. Dignity. Respect. Honor. And, yes, the truth." – Joe Biden

A SET OF BELIEFS ABOUT HOW THE WORLD WORKS

Historical Example: "So, as we begin, let us take inventory. We are a nation that has a government – not the other way around. And this makes us special among the nations of the Earth. Our Government has no power except that granted it by the people. It is time to check and reverse the growth of government which shows signs of having grown beyond the consent of the governed. It is my intention to curb the size and influence of the Federal establishment and to demand recognition of the distinction between the powers granted to the Federal Government and those reserved to the States or to the people. All of us need to be reminded that the Federal Government did not create the States; the States created the Federal Government. Now, so there will be no misunderstanding, it is not my intention to do away with government. It is, rather, to make it work-work with us, not over us; to stand by our side, not ride on our back. Government can and must provide opportunity, not smother it; foster productivity, not stifle it. If we look to the answer as to why, for so many years, we achieved so much, prospered as no other people on Earth, it was because here, in this land, we unleashed the energy and individual genius of man to a greater extent than has ever been done before. Freedom and the dignity of the individual have been more available and assured here than in any other place on Earth. The price for this freedom at times has been high, but we have never been unwilling to pay that price. It is no coincidence that our present troubles parallel and are proportionate to the intervention and intrusion in our lives that result from unnecessary and excessive growth of government." – Ronald Reagan

SELF-IDENTITY THROUGH CONTRAST

Historical Example: "Above all, we must realize that no arsenal, or no weapon in the arsenals of the world, is so formidable as the will and moral courage of free men and women. It is a weapon our adversaries in today's world do not have. It is a weapon that we as Americans do have. Let that be understood by those who practice terrorism and prey upon their neighbors." – Ronald Reagan

UNITIVE ATTAINMENT OF A CONTRASTING ENTITY

SET OF POSSIBLE QUALITIES, BELIEFS, ETC.

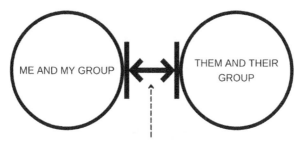

EXTENT OF ANTITHESIS,
EXTENT OF DEFINITION THROUGH CONTRAST

FIGURE 120: We crave self-definition through contrast; self-definition not only by who we are but who we are not.

DEVELOPING PERSONAL COMPETENCE

Historical Example: "We in our turn have an assured confidence that we shall be able to leave this heritage unwasted and enlarged to our children and our children's children. To do so we must show, not merely in great crises, but in the everyday affairs of life, the qualities of practical intelligence, of courage, of hardihood, and endurance, and above all the power of devotion to a lofty ideal, which made great the men who founded this Republic in the days of Washington, which made great the men who preserved this Republic in the days of Abraham Lincoln." – Theodore Roosevelt

FREEDOM OF THOUGHT, SPEECH, ASSOCIATON…

Historical Example: "Great nations of the world are moving toward democracy through the door to freedom. Men and women of the world move toward free markets through the door to prosperity. The people of the world agitate for free expression and free thought through the door to the moral and intellectual satisfactions that only liberty allows. We know what works: Freedom works. We know what's right: Freedom is right. We know how to secure a more just and prosperous life for man on Earth: through free markets, free speech, free elections, and the exercise of free will unhampered by the state." – George H. W. Bush

UNITIVE ATTAINMENT OF FREEDOM

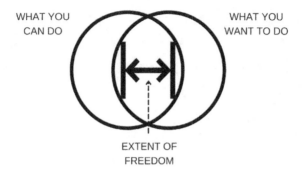

FIGURE 121: Freedom is being able to do what you want.

HOPE, BELIEVING IN A BETTER FUTURE

Historical Example: "Hope is the bedrock of this nation. The belief that our destiny will not be written for us, but by us, by all those men and women who are not content to settle for the world as it is, who have the courage to remake the world as it should be." – Barack Obama

A GROUP RALLIED AROUND A COMMON IDENTITY

Historical Example: "Above all, Democrats still believe in the American idea – its principles, its purpose, and its promise. We know that four more years of the crass, craven, corrupt leadership we have seen from Donald Trump and the Republican Party will damage our character and our country beyond repair. We pray, as Langston Hughes did, 'O, let America be America again – the land that never has been yet – and yet must be – the land where every man is free.' Democrats call on all Americans to come together and seize this last, best chance to restore the soul of our nation—and vote this November to ensure our greatest days are still to come." – Democratic Party Platform

BEING COMPLETED BY SOMETHING EXTERNAL

Historical Example: "Injustice anywhere is a threat to justice everywhere. We are caught in an inescapable network of mutuality, tied in a single garment of destiny. Whatever affects one directly, affects all indirectly." – Martin Luther King

THE DESIRE TO BE UNDERSTOOD BY OTHER PEOPLE

Historical Example: "I understand that many Americans view the future with some fear and trepidation. I understand they worry about their jobs, about taking care of their families, about what comes next. I get it." – Joe Biden

LIVING IN TRANQUILITY, STABILITY, AND CALM

Historical Example: "My fellow Americans, as we look back at this remarkable century, we may ask, can we hope not just to follow, but even to surpass the achievements of the 20th century in America and to avoid the awful bloodshed that stained its legacy? To that question, every American here and every American in our land today must answer a resounding 'Yes.'" – Bill Clinton

BEING ACCEPTED BY ONESELF

Historical Example: "Taking a word like gay and applying it to myself, I was still years away from being able to do that, even in my own mind. I wasn't coming back to a family. More than that, I had no idea what it was like to be in love, and the idea that here I am, I'm a grown-ass man, I own a home, I'm the mayor of my city, I'm a military officer and if I get killed over there I will go to my grave not knowing what it's like to be in love." – Pete Buttigieg

LEGACY, LEAVING SOMETHING BEHIND

Historical Example: "On the eve of our struggle for independence a man who might have been one of the greatest among the Founding Fathers, Dr. Joseph Warren, President of the Massachusetts Congress, said to his fellow Americans, 'Our country is in danger, but not to be despaired of... On you depend the fortunes of America. You are to decide the important questions upon which rests the happiness and the liberty of millions yet unborn. Act worthy of yourselves.' Well, I believe we, the Americans of today, are ready to act worthy of ourselves, ready to do what must be done to ensure happiness and liberty for ourselves, our children and our children's children." – Ronald Reagan

KNOWING, THE DESIRE TO DISCOVER NEW TRUTHS

Historical Example: "The growth of our science and education will be enriched by new knowledge of our universe and environment, by new techniques of learning and mapping and observation, by new tools and computers for industry, medicine, the home as well as the school. Technical institutions, such as Rice, will reap the harvest of these gains." – John F. Kennedy

TRUTH, THE DESIRE TO FIND AND KNOW WHAT IS TRUE

Historical Example: "And, yes, the truth. Recent weeks and months have taught us a painful lesson. There is truth and there are lies. Lies told for power and for profit. And each of us has a duty and responsibility, as citizens, as Americans, and especially as leaders – leaders who have pledged to honor our Constitution and protect our nation – to defend the truth and to defeat the lies." – Joe Biden

THE DESIRE TO EXPERIENCE INNER TRANQUILITY

Historical Example: "Nobody can hurt me without my permission. [...] Each one has to find his peace from within. And peace to be real must be unaffected by outside circumstances." – Mahatma Ghandi

A WAY TO EXPLAIN THE HUMAN EXPERIENCE

Historical Example: "Science investigates; religion interprets. Science gives man knowledge, which is power; religion gives man wisdom, which is control. Science deals mainly with facts; religion deals mainly with values. The two are not rivals." – Martin Luther King

GOD, THE DESIRE TO EXPERIENCE A HIGHER BEING

Historical Example: "My friends, before I begin the expression of those thoughts that I deem appropriate to this moment, would you permit me the privilege of uttering a little private prayer of my own. And I ask that you bow your heads: Almighty God, as we stand here at this moment my future associates in the Executive branch of Government join me in beseeching that Thou will make full and complete our dedication to the service of the people in this throng, and their fellow citizens everywhere. Give us, we pray, the power to discern clearly right from wrong, and allow all our words and actions to be governed thereby, and by the laws of this land. Especially we pray that our concern shall be for all the people regardless of station, race or calling. May cooperation be permitted and be the mutual aim of those who, under the concepts of our Constitution, hold to differing political faiths; so that all may work for the good of our beloved country and Thy glory. Amen." – Dwight D. Eisenhower

MEANING, THE DESIRE TO DISCOVER A PURPOSE

Historical Example: "Efforts and courage are not enough without purpose and direction." – John F. Kennedy

UNITIVE ATTAINMENT OF A TRANSCENDENT MEANING

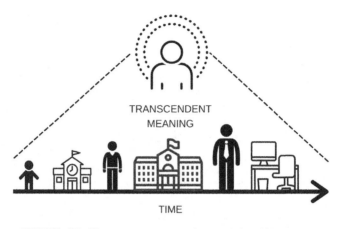

TRANSCENDENT
MEANING

TIME

FIGURE 122: We crave a transcendent meaning. We crave a purpose that supersedes all lesser purposes. We crave an ultimate goal, an ultimate reason, and a cosmic significance that transcends the day-to-day of our lives. And I believe we have this, if we know where to look.

VISION, SOMETHING TO AIM AT AND WORK TOWARD

Historical Example: "But if I were to say, my fellow citizens, that we shall send to the moon, 240,000 miles away from the control station in Houston, a giant rocket more than 300 feet tall, the length of this football field, made of new metal alloys, some of which have not yet been invented, capable of standing heat and stresses several times more than have ever been experienced, fitted together with a precision better than the finest watch, carrying all the equipment needed for propulsion, guidance, control, communications, food and survival, on an untried mission, to an unknown celestial body, and then return it safely to earth, re-entering the atmosphere at speeds of over 25,000 miles per hour, causing heat about half that of the temperature of the sun – almost as hot as it is here today – and do all this, and do it right, and do it first before this decade is out – then we must be bold." – John F. Kennedy

KEY INSIGHT:

We Are Aiming Creatures. Committing to An Aim Organizes, Inspires, Integrates, and Motivates Us.

UNITIVE ATTAINMENT OF A HOPEFUL VISION

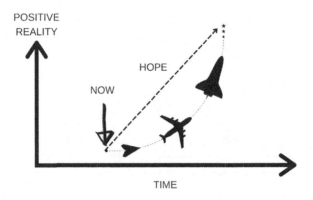

FIGURE 123: No matter how bright our present moment is, we will always turn our gaze toward a brighter future. Humans are striving, questing, and hopeful and creatures. Some say the tragedy of success is gaining what you hoped for but losing your hope.

GENEROSITY, GIVING TO OUR FELLOW HUMANS

Historical Example: "Together, we resolved that a great nation must care for the vulnerable, and protect its people from life's worst hazards and misfortune." – Barack Obama

DISTINCTION, BEING DIFFERENT AND "MORE THAN"

Historical Example: "We become not a melting pot but a beautiful mosaic. Different people, different beliefs, different yearnings, different hopes, different dreams." – Jimmy Carter

THE DESIRE TO BE HEARD AND ATTENDED TO

Historical Example: "The great challenge of this conference is to give voice to women everywhere whose experiences go unnoticed, whose words go unheard. [...] The voices of this conference and of the women at Huairou must be heard loud and clear. [...] If there is one message that echoes forth from this conference, it is that human rights are women's rights... And women's rights are human rights. Let us not forget that among those rights are the right to speak freely. And the right to be heard." – Hillary Clinton

NOSTALGIA, THE DESIRE TO RESURRECT THE PAST

Historical Example: "So to all Americans, in every city near and far, small and large, from mountain to mountain, and from ocean to ocean, hear these words: You will never be ignored again. Your voice, your hopes, and your dreams will define our American destiny. And your courage and goodness and love will forever guide us along the way. Together, We will make America strong again. We will make wealthy again. We will make America proud again. We will make America safe again. And yes, together, we will make America great again. Thank you. God bless you. And God bless America." – Donald Trump

THE COLOR PALLETTE OF EMOTIONS AND DESIRES

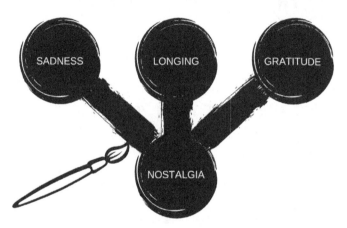

FIGURE 124: Emotions combine into ever-more-complex permutations. Desires do as well. I do not know what the limit to this combinatorial process is. But I have not found it. I don't know if there is one. Some psychologists believe the psyche is bottomless and infinitely complex. If this is true, this combinatorial process has no limit.

FEELING CONNECTED TO PEOPLE, PLACES, THINGS...

Historical Example: "You have given me a great responsibility – to stay close to you, to be worthy of you, and to exemplify what you are. Let us create together a new national spirit of unity and trust. Your strength can compensate for my weakness, and your wisdom can help to minimize my mistakes. Let us learn together and laugh together and work together and together, confident that in the end we will triumph together in the right." – Jimmy Carter

UNITIVE ATTAINMENT OF A CONNECTED BEING

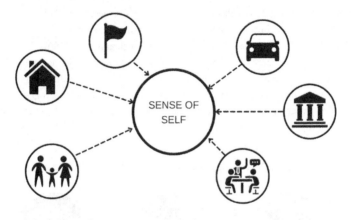

FIGURE 125: We want to conceive of our being as a connected piece of a puzzle of meaningful pieces.

VIRTUE, THE DESIRE TO FIT YOUR IDEA OF GOOD

Historical Example: "The American dream endures. We must once again have full faith in our country – and in one another. I believe America can be better. We can be even stronger than before. [...] We have already found a high degree of personal liberty, and we are now struggling to enhance equality of opportunity. Our commitment to human rights must be absolute, our laws fair, our natural beauty preserved; the powerful must not persecute the weak, and human dignity must be enhanced. We have learned that 'more' is not necessarily 'better,' that even our great Nation has its recognized limits, and that we can neither answer all questions nor solve all problems. We cannot afford to do everything, nor can we afford to lack boldness as we meet the future. So, together, in a spirit of individual sacrifice for the common good, we must simply do our best." – Jimmy Carter

CLARITY, FREEDOM FROM CONFUSION

Historical Example: "So I want to talk to you today about three places where we begin to build the Great Society – in our cities, in our countryside, and in our classrooms." – Lyndon B. Johnson

UNITIVE ATTAINMENT OF UNDERSTANDING

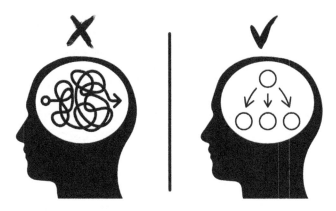

FIGURE 126: We want to understand and organize reality into manageable narratives and frameworks.

ALIGNMENT, FREEDOM FROM COGNITIVE DISSONANCE,

Historical Example: "Profound and powerful forces are shaking and remaking our world, and the urgent question of our time is whether we can make change our friend and not our enemy. This new world has already enriched the lives of millions of Americans who are able to compete and win in it. But when most people are working harder for less; when others cannot work at all; when the cost of health care devastates families and threatens to bankrupt many of our enterprises, great and small; when fear of crime robs law-abiding citizens of their freedom; and when millions of poor children cannot even imagine the lives we are calling them to lead, we have not made change our friend. We know we have to face hard truths and take strong steps. But we have not done so. Instead, we have drifted, and that drifting has eroded our resources, fractured our economy, and shaken our confidence." – Bill Clinton

A SIMPLE WAY TO DEFINE ONE'S PERSON OR GROUP

Historical Example: "Ours was the first society openly to define itself in terms of both spirituality and of human liberty. It is that unique self-definition which has given us an exceptional appeal, but it also imposes on us a special obligation, to take on those moral duties which, when assumed, seem invariably to be in our own best interests." – Jimmy Carter

.................................Chapter Summary.................................

- It is a grand mystery where the spiritual needs come from. It is possibly even debatable if the "spiritual" label fits.

- Regardless, these desires are deeply powerful, and the evidence for their existence is strong.
- You can conceive of these desires as further elucidating the "self-actualization" level of Maslow's Hierarchy.
- You can also conceive of these desires as further elucidating the "growth" layer of the ERG model.
- Appealing to these desires often achieves a level of extraordinary inspiration and motivation.
- Use these tactfully. Use them gently. Observe the examples of historical speakers.

KEY INSIGHT:

There Is Such a Thing as Complexity-Induced Anxiety, And It Can Manifest Physical Symptoms While Also Paralyzing Our Efforts.

Offering Clarity and Simplicity that Does Not Distort the Essential Truths of the Matter At Hand Is a Great and Empowering Gift.

Claim These Free Resources that Will Help You Unleash the Power of Your Words and Speak with Confidence. Visit www.speakforsuccesshub.com/toolkit for Access.

2 Free Workbooks

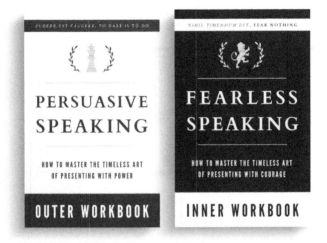

We'll send you two free workbooks, including long-lost excerpts by Dale Carnegie, the mega-bestselling author of *How to Win Friends and Influence People* (5,000,000 copies sold). *Fearless Speaking* guides you in the proven principles of mastering your inner game as a speaker. *Persuasive Speaking* guides you in the time-tested tactics of mastering your outer game by maximizing the power of your words. All of these resources complement the Speak for Success collection.

SPEAK FOR SUCCESS COLLECTION BOOK

VIII

DECODING HUMAN NATURE CHAPTER

FRAMEWORK EIGHT:
Economic Desires

ECONOMIC DESIRES

H ERE WE DEVIATE FROM THE PATTERN OF THE previous examples. While political figures do speak to the economic desires, these are extremely specific; the best examples are drawn from the commercial world. I draw most of the examples from the copywriting of the main sales page for serial entrepreneur Russel Brunson's software company ClickFunnels and the other examples from other software companies. Why? There's no real reason: it's just arbitrary. I suppose it exemplifies how broadly applicable the desires are.

WHAT ARE THE BASIC ECONOMIC HUMAN DESIRES?

Where do they come from? These are how people separate the good products from the bad ones. And know this: when I say product, that doesn't only mean a physical product. Ideas are products. Plans are products. Suggestions to your boss at work are products. Many of these economic desires apply not only to physical products, but to that expanded definition of product. If these economic human desires are not met, a person probably won't buy a product. Luckily for you, you'll know exactly what they are, and how to express them for easy persuasive communication.

When do we see them? We see them in effective marketing. If someone was convinced to purchase a product by any marketing message, it probably had most or all of these values in it. Why? Because this is how people determine if something is worth buying. And remember what I said about our definition of product: these often dictate whether someone will subscribe to a school of thought, too.

How do you use them? When you are selling a product or service. They act as a checklist. If you simply ask yourself "have I covered efficacy?" or "speed?" or how about "reliability?" and run through the entire list, you're guaranteed to touch on each of the economic values in your pitch. This means your audience will at the very least *logically* think it is a good product. You'll notice that for many of the economic values, there is a "comparative" value. All that means is "does this product satisfy this economic desire more than the other options?"

EFFICACY, HOW WELL DOES IT WORK?

Historical Example: "We deliver observability that's more than metrics, logs, and traces. Plus, support for the technologies you use most, and precise answers through a full-stack topological model and unparalleled AI engine. So, you can automate operations and collaborate better." – Dynatrace

RELATIVE EFFICACY, DOES IT BEAT ALTERNATIVES?

Historical Example: "Dynatrace: The Leader in Cloud Monitoring." – Dynatrace

SPEED, HOW QUICKLY DOES IT WORK?

Historical Example: "Quickly Create Beautiful Sales Funnels That Convert Your Visitors into Leads And Then Customers..." – ClickFunnels Landing Page

RELIABILITY, CAN I DEPEND ON IT TO DELIVER?

Historical Example: "Join 111,770 entrepreneurs who are actively using ClickFunnels to easily get their products and message out to the world!" – ClickFunnels Landing Page

RELATIVE RELIABILITY, IS IT THE MOST DEPENDABLE?

Historical Example: "111.7K users, 1.64B contacts, 8.45M funnels, $10.8B processed." – ClickFunnels Landing Page

PRODUCT-PROBLEM FIT, DOES IT FIX MY PROBLEM?

Historical Example: "What's A Funnel...? What Exactly Is the Difference Between A Website and A Sales Funnel? ClickFunnels Is A Website and Sales Funnel Builder For Entrepreneurs. Yes, ClickFunnels was created so that entrepreneurs like you, who aren't programmers and who don't know how to code, can easily build beautiful pages inside of a sales funnel, to gow your company online!" – ClickFunnels Landing Page

EASE OF USE, HOW MUCH EFFORT DOES IT REQUIRE?

Historical Example: "'I've been building out my new funnel inside of ClickFunnels, and after doing it, the idea of using anything else is daunting to me. I would have had to have membership software, landing pages, order forms and then still figure out how to tie them all together. I'll never have to go through that again because of ClickFunnels!'" – ClickFunnels Landing Page

RELATIVE EASE OF USE, IS THERE AN EASIER OPTION?

Historical Example: "In Less Than 10 Minutes, You Can Create What Would Have Taken Your Tech Team Weeks To Do..." – ClickFunnels Landing Page

FLEXIBILITY, HOW MANY THINGS DOES IT DO?

Historical Example: "Quickly Build Smart Sales Funnels That Convert! Create High Converting Pages Using Our 'Drag N Drop' Editor. Run Smart Affiliate Programs Inside Your Funnels. Create Smart Email, Text and Messenger Follow-Up Funnels!" – ClickFunnels Landing Page

RELATIVE FLEXIBILITY, DO OTHER OPTIONS DO MORE?

Historical Example: "ClickFunnels Gives You the Tools and Strategies You Need in One Convenient Spot! Yes, ClickFunnels Gives You the Tools and Strategies You Need to Market, Sell, AND Deliver Your Products Online. Simply Drag and Drop Webpage Editor! Quickly Build Sales Funnels That Convert! Smart Shopping Cart With 1 Click Upsells! Email and Facebook Marketing Automation! Everything Organized in One Simple Dashboard!" – ClickFunnels Landing Page

STATUS, DOES IT IMPROVE HOW OTHERS SEE ME?

Historical Example: "Timeless Style: Rolex's Datejust is the archetype of the classic watch thanks to functions and aesthetics that never go out of fashion." – Rolex

AESTHETIC APPEAL, HOW GOOD DOES IT LOOK?

Historical Example: "Quickly Create Beautiful Sales Funnels..." – ClickFunnels Landing Page

EMOTION, HOW DOES IT MAKE ME FEEL?

Historical Example: "Get ready to be amazed in five minutes or less." – Dynatrace

COST, HOW MUCH DO I HAVE TO GIVE UP TO GET THIS?

Historical Example: "Start Free 14 Day Trial Now, Build Your First Funnel For FREE Right Now!" – ClickFunnels Landing Page

...............................Chapter Summary...............................

- These desires are perhaps more practical than the spiritual desires, for example. They are more tangible.
- These desires often act as a checklist and as a result, they determine our buying behavior.
- If a product or service exceeds a sufficient number of these qualities, we buy. If not, we don't.

- Everyone has a different requisite number of economic values a product must meet.
- Everyone often has a "keystone economic value" – if you check this box, it outweighs all the others.
- Use these when formulating ideas for products or services. They will increase demand.

KEY INSIGHT:

The Commercial Applications of the Human Desires Are Widespread and Significant.

SPEAK FOR SUCCESS COLLECTION BOOK

VIII

DECODING HUMAN NATURE CHAPTER

XI

FRAMEWORK NINE:

Robbin's Six Needs

ROBBIN'S SIX NEEDS

T HESE SIX BASIC HUMAN NEEDS WILL TEACH you exactly how to motivate people. It will teach you how to make yourself a leader who others will gladly rally around. These six human needs are simple, powerful, and easy to use, like the "certainty" need.

WHAT ARE ROBBIN'S SIX NEEDS?

Where do these come from? Tony Robbins, success coach and motivational speaker (amongst many other impressive pursuits) has identified these as the core motivating desires of the people he has met. The first four needs are defined as needs of the personality and the last two are identified as needs of the spirit.

When do we see them? He argues that almost all actions people take are manifestations of one or more of these basic human needs. I agree with him. I disagree that there are only six human desires, though, as you can see by now.

How do you use them? When you want to lead people. When you want to convince people. When you want to persuade audiences as a public speaker.

CERTAINTY YOU CAN AVOID PAIN AND GAIN PLEASURE

Historical Example: "That we are in the midst of crisis is now well understood. Our nation is at war against a far-reaching network of violence and hatred. Our economy is badly weakened, a consequence of greed and irresponsibility on the part of some, but also our collective failure to make hard choices and prepare the nation for a new age. Homes have been lost, jobs shed, businesses shuttered. Our health care is too costly, our schools fail too many – and each day brings further evidence that the ways we use energy strengthen our adversaries and threaten our planet. These are the indicators of crisis, subject to data and statistics. Less measurable, but no less profound, is a sapping of confidence across our land; a nagging fear that America's decline is inevitable, that the next generation must lower its sights. Today I say to you that the challenges we face are real. They are serious and they are many. They will not be met easily or in a short span of time. But know this America: They will be met." – Barack Obama

UNCERTAINTY AND VARIETY, THE NEED FOR NOVELTY

Historical Example: "Many years ago the great British explorer George Mallory, who was to die on Mount Everest, was asked why did he want to climb it. He said, 'Because it is there.' Well, space is there, and we're going to climb it, and the moon and the planets are there, and new hopes for knowledge and peace are there. And, therefore, as we set sail we ask God's blessing on the most hazardous and dangerous and greatest adventure on which man has ever embarked. Thank You." – John F. Kennedy

VISUALIZING CERTAINTY

FIGURE 127: Too much certainty bores us. Humans were made to quest into the dangerous unknown.

VISUALIZING UNCERTAINTY

FIGURE 128: Too much certainty scares us. Humans were made to preserve themselves.

BRIDGING UNCERTAINTY AND CERTAINTY

FIGURE 129: We must place one foot firmly in order and certainty and the other firmly in chaos and uncertainty. We must straddle the thin line between chaos and order. This reconciles this dialectic of our being.

SIGNIFICANCE, FEELING UNIQUE, IMPORTANT, NEEDED

Historical Example: "President Pitzer, Mr. Vice President, Governor, Congressman Thomas, Senator Wiley, and Congressman Miller, Mr. Webb, Mr. Bell, scientists, distinguished guests, and ladies and gentlemen: I appreciate your president having made me an honorary visiting professor, and I will assure you that my first lecture will be very brief. I am delighted to be here, and I'm particularly delighted to be here on this occasion. We meet at a college noted for knowledge, in a city noted for progress, in a State noted for strength, and we stand in need of all three..." – John F. Kennedy

CONNECTION AND LOVE, A FEELING OF UNION

Historical Example: "My purpose is to be, in my action, just and constitutional; and yet practical, in performing the important duty, with which I am charged, of maintaining the unity, and the free principles of our common country." – Abraham Lincoln

GROWTH, EXPANDING CAPACITY AND CAPABILITY

Historical Example: "To be sure, we are behind, and will be behind for some time in manned flight. But we do not intend to stay behind, and in this decade, we shall make up and move ahead. The growth of our science and education will be enriched by new knowledge of our universe and environment, by new techniques of learning and mapping and observation, by new tools and computers for industry, medicine, the home as well as the school. Technical institutions, such as Rice, will reap the harvest of these gains. And finally, the space effort itself, while still in its infancy, has already created a great number of new companies, and tens of thousands of new jobs. Space and related industries are generating new demands in investment and skilled personnel, and this city and this State, and this region, will share greatly in this growth. What was once the furthest outpost on the old frontier of the West will be the furthest outpost on the new frontier of science and space. Houston, your City of Houston, with its Manned Spacecraft Center, will become the heart of a large scientific and engineering community. During the next 5 years the National Aeronautics and Space Administration expects to double the number of scientists and engineers in this area, to increase its outlays for salaries and expenses to $60 million a year; to invest some $200 million in plant and laboratory facilities; and to direct or contract for new space efforts over $1 billion from this Center in this City. To be sure, all this costs us all a good deal of money. This year's space budget is three times what it was in January 1961, and it is greater than the space budget of the previous eight years combined. That budget now stands at $5,400 million a year – a staggering sum, though somewhat less than we pay for cigarettes and cigars every year. Space expenditures will soon rise some more, from 40 cents per person per week to more than 50 cents a week for every man, woman and child in the United Stated, for we have given this program a high national priority – even though I realize that this is in some measure an act of faith and vision, for we do not now know what benefits await us. But if I were to say, my fellow citizens, that we shall send to the moon, 240,000 miles away from the control station in Houston, a giant rocket more than 300 feet tall, the length of this football field, made of new metal alloys, some of which have not yet been invented, capable of standing heat and stresses several times more than have ever been experienced, fitted together with a precision better than the finest watch, carrying all the equipment needed for propulsion, guidance, control, communications, food and survival, on an untried mission, to an unknown celestial body, and then return it safely to earth, re-entering the atmosphere at speeds of over 25,000 miles per hour, causing heat about half that of the temperature of the sun – almost as hot as it is here today – and do all this, and do it right, and do it first before this decade is out – then we must be bold." – John F. Kennedy

KEY INSIGHT:

We Want to Feel Our Characters and Capabilities Growing In Strength; the Ground Under Our Feet Consequently Solidifying.

VISUALIZING GROWTH

FIGURE 130: Balancing order and chaos is keeping one foot in each. Growth is expanding the overall scope of the order we create as well as the chaos we confront.

CONTRIBUTION, SERVICE, AND SUPPORT OF OTHERS

Historical Example: "We must think anew and move with a new boldness, so every American who seeks work can find work; so the least among us shall have an equal chance to achieve the greatest things – to be heroes who heal our sick, feed the hungry, protect peace among nations, and leave this world a better place." – Ronald Reagan

...............................Chapter Summary..................................

- Tony Robbins has identified these six core needs based on a lifetime of experience dealing with people.
- The first four needs are considered "needs of the personality," describing more outward-facing desires.
- The last two needs are considered "needs of the spirit," describing more inward-facing desires.
- Appeal to people on both levels: appeal to the needs of the personality and the needs of the spirit.
- As with all desires, note any particularly powerful desires in your audience and cater specifically to those.
- As with all desires, people may be motivated by any number of these desires. We all have a different motivational profile.

Claim These Free Resources that Will Help You Unleash the Power of Your Words and Speak with Confidence. Visit www.speakforsuccesshub.com/toolkit for Access.

18 Free PDF Resources

12 Iron Rules for Captivating Story, 21 Speeches that Changed the World, 341-Point Influence Checklist, 143 Persuasive Cognitive Biases, 17 Ways to Think On Your Feet, 18 Lies About Speaking Well, 137 Deadly Logical Fallacies, 12 Iron Rules For Captivating Slides, 371 Words that Persuade, 63 Truths of Speaking Well, 27 Laws of Empathy, 21 Secrets of Legendary Speeches, 19 Scripts that Persuade, 12 Iron Rules For Captivating Speech, 33 Laws of Charisma, 11 Influence Formulas, 219-Point Speech-Writing Checklist, 21 Eloquence Formulas

SPEAK FOR SUCCESS COLLECTION BOOK

VIII

DECODING HUMAN NATURE CHAPTER

XII

FRAMEWORK TEN:

Russel's Core Four

RUSSEL'S CORE FOUR DESIRES

T HESE ARE CYNICAL, like "vanity." Cynicism is often realism, however, and this cynicism is by no means the blind cynicism of the world-weary.

WHAT ARE BERTRAND RUSSEL'S CORE FOUR HUMAN DESIRES?

Where do they come from? These come from Bertrand Russel's Nobel Prize acceptance speech. Let me quote him: "All human activity is prompted by desire. There is a wholly fallacious theory advanced by some earnest moralists to the effect that it is possible to resist desire in the interests of duty and moral principle. I say this is fallacious, not because no man ever acts from a sense of duty, but because duty has no hold on him unless he desires to be dutiful. If you wish to know what men will do, you must know not only, or principally, their material circumstances, but rather the whole system of their desires with their relative strengths."

When do we see them? In the restless pursuit of some infinite and insatiable desire. I'll let Mr. Russel explain: "Man differs from other animals in one very important respect, and that is that he has some desires which are, so to speak, infinite, which can never be fully gratified, and which would keep him restless even in Paradise. The boa constrictor, when he has had an adequate meal, goes to sleep, and does not wake until he needs another meal. Human beings, for the most part, are not like this."

How do you use them? When you see these desires in someone, they are probably extremely deep-rooted. Some people try to avoid pursuing these. They are seen as negative ambition. But if you see someone manifesting these, chances are there's a lot more to it. Chances are they seek it on a level much deeper than they let on. That means they are easy but powerful persuasive buttons you can push. That said, chances are everyone expresses these to a small degree, so they are universally applicable.

ACQUISITIVENESS FOR MATERIAL POSSESSIONS

Historical Example: "The wish to possess as much as possible of goods, or the title to goods." – Bertrand Russel

RIVALRY, THE WISH TO DEFEAT AN OPPONENT

Historical Example: "A great many men will cheerfully face impoverishment if they can thereby secure complete ruin for their rivals, hence the present level of taxation." – Bertrand Russel

VANITY, THE DESIRE FOR PRAISE AND ATTENTION

Historical Example: "[It] is one of the most fundamental desires of the human heart. It can take innumerable forms, from buffoonery to the pursuit of posthumous fame." – Bertrand Russel

POWER, THE DESIRE TO IMPOSE OUR WILL ON OTHERS

Historical Example: "Many people prefer glory to power, but on the whole these people have less effect upon the course of events than those who prefer power to glory: power, like vanity, is insatiable." – Bertrand Russel

...............................Chapter Summary...............................

- Bertrand Russel's core four desires are more cynical, elucidating the cunning aspects of our personality.
- These four desires represent our more malevolent impulses. They reveal a drive to control and dominate.
- While these desires are generally frowned upon, you can channel them into productive pursuits.
- Rivalry can motivate excellence instead of mutual destruction. Competition can produce progress.
- Vanity can be transformed into the desire to stand as a positive example of one's ideals.
- Acquisitiveness can drive us to create products and services that other people want to patronize, thereby creating value.

Email Peter D. Andrei, the author of the Speak for Success collection and the President of Speak Truth Well LLC directly.

pandreibusiness@gmail.com

SPEAK FOR SUCCESS COLLECTION BOOK

VIII

DECODING HUMAN NATURE CHAPTER

XIII

FRAMEWORK ELEVEN:

Fear-Based Needs

FEAR NEEDS

F EAR IS A POWERFUL FORCE. It can sell millions of products, elect presidents, and move minds and hearts. And these following desires are all based in fear.

WHAT ARE THE FEAR NEEDS AND DESIRES?

Where do they come from? These are all desires based in the freedom from some fear. The fears that keep us up at night, and that torment us daily, all touch upon the basic human desires. In other words, these are all desires that are the *absence* of something we fear.

When do we see them? When someone is behaving in a defensive way. This doesn't mean that they respond "defensively" to criticism, but that they seem to be protecting themselves against some perceived fear. The reason they are acting that way is to achieve their basic human need of freedom from that fear.

How do you use them? These are insanely powerful. So, use them carefully. If you can be subtle, that's even better. Use these in a classic "fear appeal" model: "You are in danger. You are especially vulnerable to this danger. You can protect yourself. You can protect yourself with this action."

FREEDOM FROM LOSS

Historical Example: "Our land of new promise will be a nation that meets its obligations, a nation that balances its budget, but never loses the balance of its values. A nation where our grandparents have secure retirement and health care, and their grandchildren know we have made the reforms necessary to sustain those benefits for their time. A nation that fortifies the world's most productive economy even as it protects the great natural bounty of our water, air, and majestic land." – Bill Clinton

FREEDOM FROM DANGER

Historical Example: "We will stand mighty for peace and freedom, and maintain a strong defense against terror and destruction. Our children will sleep free from the threat of nuclear, chemical or biological weapons." – Bill Clinton

FREEDOM FROM BEING LEFT OUT

Historical Example: "By gathering in Beijing, we are focusing world attention on issues that matter most in the lives of women and their families: access to education, health care, jobs, and credit, the chance to enjoy basic legal and human rights and participate fully in the political life of their countries." – Hillary Clinton

FREEDOM FROM CRITICISM

Historical Example: "Criticism may not be agreeable, but it is necessary. It fulfills the same function as pain in the human body. It calls attention to an unhealthy state of things." – Winston Churchill

FREEDOM FROM BAD DECISIONS

Historical Example: "You and I are told increasingly we have to choose between a left or right. Well I'd like to suggest there is no such thing as a left or right. There's only an up or down – up toward man's old-aged dream, the ultimate in individual freedom consistent with law and order, or down to the ant heap of totalitarianism. And regardless of their sincerity, their humanitarian motives, those who would trade our freedom for security have embarked on this downward course." – Ronald Reagan

FREEDOM FROM DISAPPOINTING OTHERS

Historical Example: "There can be no real peace while one American is dying some place in the world for the rest of us. We're at war with the most dangerous enemy that has ever faced mankind in his long climb from the swamp to the stars, and it's been said if we lose that war, and in so doing lose this way of freedom of ours, history will record with the greatest astonishment that those who had the most to lose did the least to prevent its happening. [...] Freedom is never more than one generation away from extinction. We didn't pass it to our children in the bloodstream. It must be fought for, protected, and handed on for them to do the same, or one day we will spend our sunset years telling our children and our children's children what it was once like in the United States where men were free." – Ronald Reagan

FREEDOM FROM LOSS OF AUTONOMY

Historical Example: "Not too long ago, two friends of mine were talking to a Cuban refugee, a businessman who had escaped from Castro, and in the midst of his story one of my friends turned to the other and said, 'We don't know how lucky we are.' And the Cuban stopped and said, 'How lucky you are? I had someplace to escape to.' And in that sentence he told us the entire story. If we lose freedom here, there's no place to escape to. This is the last stand on earth." – Ronald Reagan

FREEDOM FROM SEPARATION

Historical Example: "What Latinos should look at is comparing this president to the president we have is outrageous. Number one, we didn't lock people up in cages. We didn't separate families. We didn't do all of those things, number one. Number two, this is the president who came along with the DACA program, no one had ever done that before, the president sent legislation to desk saying he wants to find a pathway for the

11 million undocumented in the United States of America. This is the president has done a great deal, so I'm proud to have served with him. What I would do as president is several more things because things have changed." – Joe Biden

FREEDOM FROM GUILT

Historical Example: "Now, I want to be clear about this because sometimes in our debates with our friends on the other side of the political spectrum, this may not be clear, so let me just repeat it once again, as Americans, we understand that some folks are going to earn more than others. We don't resent success..." – Barack Obama

FREEDOM FROM [INSERT HARM]

Historical Example: "Five score years ago, a great American, in whose symbolic shadow we stand today, signed the Emancipation Proclamation. This momentous decree came as a great beacon light of hope to millions of Negro slaves who had been seared in the flames of withering injustice. It came as a joyous daybreak to end the long night of their captivity. But 100 years later, the Negro still is not free. One hundred years later, the life of the Negro is still sadly crippled by the manacles of segregation and the chains of discrimination. One hundred years later, the Negro lives on a lonely island of poverty in the midst of a vast ocean of material prosperity. One hundred years later the Negro is still languished in the corners of American society and finds himself in exile in his own land. And so we've come here today to dramatize a shameful condition. This will be the day when all of God's children will be able to sing with new meaning: My country, 'tis of thee, sweet land of liberty, of thee I sing. Land where my fathers died, land of the pilgrims' pride, from every mountainside, let freedom ring. And if America is to be a great nation, this must become true. And so let freedom ring from the prodigious hilltops of New Hampshire. Let freedom ring from the mighty mountains of New York. Let freedom ring from the heightening Alleghenies of Pennsylvania. Let freedom ring from the snowcapped Rockies of Colorado. Let freedom ring from the curvaceous slopes of California. But not only that, let freedom ring from Stone Mountain of Georgia. Let freedom ring from Lookout Mountain of Tennessee. Let freedom ring from every hill and molehill of Mississippi. From every mountainside, let freedom ring. And when this happens, and when we allow freedom ring, when we let it ring from every village and every hamlet, from every state and every city, we will be able to speed up that day when all of God's children, black men and white men, Jews and Gentiles, Protestants and Catholics, will be able to join hands and sing in the words of the old Negro spiritual: Free at last. Free at last. Thank God almighty, we are free at last." – Martin Luther King

RELIEF

Historical Example: "This generation of Americans has been tested by crises that steeled our resolve and proved our resilience. A decade of war is now ending. An economic recovery has begun." – Barack Obama

ESCAPE

Historical Example: "We, therefore, the Representatives of the united States of America, in General Congress, Assembled, appealing to the Supreme Judge of the world for the rectitude of our intentions, do, in the Name, and by Authority of the good People of these Colonies, solemnly publish and declare, That these United Colonies are, and of Right ought to be Free and Independent States; that they are Absolved from all Allegiance to the British Crown, and that all political connection between them and the State of Great Britain, is and ought to be totally dissolved; and that as Free and Independent States, they have full Power to levy War, conclude Peace, contract Alliances, establish Commerce, and to do all other Acts and Things which Independent States may of right do. And for the support of this Declaration, with a firm reliance on the protection of divine Providence, we mutually pledge to each other our Lives, our Fortunes and our sacred Honor." – Declaration of Independence

.................................Chapter Summary.................................

- Fear is one of the most powerful and impactful desires. It can hold more sway over our actions than any of the others.
- Do not instigate fear. Do not fabricate fear. Fear-mongering is an unethical persuasive strategy.
- To use fear ethically, offer a solution to a preexisting fear. Do not create the fear yourself, however.
- Broadly speaking, fear needs emerge from our loss aversion: Loss hurts us more than an equivalent gain.
- Present benefits of your position not only in the form of gains, but in the form of "freedoms from."
- Present what they will gain, but also what they will protect themselves from losing.

KEY INSIGHT:

One of the Greatest Factors Motivating Ethical Behavior Is Rightfully Fearing the Consequences of Unethical Behavior.

SPEAK FOR SUCCESS COLLECTION BOOK

VIII

DECODING HUMAN NATURE CHAPTER

XIV

FRAMEWORK TWELVE:

Emergent Human Desires of the Modern Era

HUMAN DESIRES OF THE MODERN ERA

W E HAVE A WHOLE NEW SET OF DESIRES that have emerged out of our modern way of life; desires which may have been (and probably were) present in the days of old, but which have risen in prominence since the advent of modernity.

WHAT ARE THE HUMAN NEEDS OF THE MODERN ERA?

Where do they come from? These desires are relatively new. Did we always want "more time?" Not as much as we wanted to hunt for our next meal so we didn't die. But since we're now far removed from our natural state of chasing our base desires (the life-force eight), we have new desires. Now we would all love more time to do things we love.

When do we see them? In the new habits people have developed. In the common complaints you've heard before. "I wish I had more time." "I wish I got promoted." "I wish I started saving earlier."

How do you use them? They are natural to fit into your communication. And the best part is that they will resonate with pretty much everyone.

ACHIEVING OUR PERSONAL DEFINITION OF HAPPINESS

Historical Example: "The purpose of protecting the life of our Nation and preserving the liberty of our citizens is to pursue the happiness of our people. Our success in that pursuit is the test of our success as a Nation." – Lyndon B. Johnson

CONSERVING FINANCIAL RESOURCES

Historical Example: "But I have an uncomfortable feeling that this prosperity isn't something on which we can base our hopes for the future. No nation in history has ever survived a tax burden that reached a third of its national income. Today, 37 cents out of every dollar earned in this country is the tax collector's share, and yet our government continues to spend 17 million dollars a day more than the government takes in. We haven't balanced our budget 28 out of the last 34 years. We've raised our debt limit three times in the last twelve months, and now our national debt is one and a half times bigger than all the combined debts of all the nations of the world. We have 15 billion dollars in gold in our treasury; we don't own an ounce. Foreign dollar claims are 27.3 billion dollars. And we've just had announced that the dollar of 1939 will now purchase 45 cents in its total value." – Ronald Reagan

CONSERVING OUR LIMITED TIME AND ENERGY

Historical Example: "We must act today in order to preserve tomorrow. And let there be no misunderstanding – we are going to begin to act, beginning today." – Ronald Reagan

BUILDING LARGER AND LARGER SOCIAL NETWORKS

Historical Example: "Across the world, we see them embraced, and we rejoice. Our hopes, our hearts, our hands, are with those on every continent who are building democracy and freedom. Their cause is America's cause." – Bill Clinton

PEOPLE WANT TO RISE TO POSITIONS OF STATUS,

Historical Example: "This beautiful capital, like every capital since the dawn of civilization, is often a place of intrigue and calculation. Powerful people maneuver for position and worry endlessly about who is in and who is out, who is up and who is down, forgetting those people whose toil and sweat sends us here and pays our way. Americans deserve better, and in this city today, there are people who want to do better. And so I say to all of us here, let us resolve to reform our politics, so that power and privilege no longer shout down the voice of the people. Let us put aside personal advantage so that we can feel the pain and see the promise of America. Let us resolve to make our government a place for what Franklin Roosevelt called 'bold, persistent experimentation,' a government for our tomorrows, not our yesterdays. Let us give this capital back to the people to whom it belongs." – Bill Clinton

THE DESIRE FOR TRANSCENDENT MEANING

Historical Example: "My friends, we are not the sum of our possessions. They are not the measure of our lives. In our hearts we know what matters. We cannot hope only to leave our children a bigger car, a bigger bank account. We must hope to give them a sense of what it means to be a loyal friend, a loving parent, a citizen who leaves his home, his neighborhood and town better than he found it. What do we want the men and women who work with us to say when we are no longer there? That we were more driven to succeed than anyone around us? Or that we stopped to ask if a sick child had gotten better, and stayed a moment there to trade a word of friendship?" – George Bush

WINNING POWER AND POSITION, AND TO LEAD

Historical Example: "We have become a great nation, forced by the fact of its greatness into relations with the other nations of the earth, and we must behave as beseems a people with such responsibilities. Toward all other nations, large and small, our attitude must be one of cordial and sincere friendship. We must show not only in our words, but in our deeds, that we are earnestly desirous of securing their good will by acting toward them in a spirit of just and generous recognition of all their rights. But justice and generosity in a nation, as in an individual, count most when shown not by the weak but by the strong. While ever careful to refrain from wrongdoing others, we must be no less insistent that we are not wronged ourselves. We wish peace, but we wish the peace of justice, the peace of righteousness. We wish it because we think it is right and not because we are afraid. No weak nation that acts manfully and justly should ever have cause to fear us, and no strong power should ever be able to single us out as a subject for insolent aggression." – Theodore Roosevelt

TO AVOID LOSS (MORE THAN TO ATTAIN GAIN)

Historical Example: "But the evil has come with the good, and much fine gold has been corroded. With riches has come inexcusable waste. We have squandered a great part of what we might have used, and have not stopped to conserve the exceeding bounty of nature, without which our genius for enterprise would have been worthless and impotent, scorning to be careful, shamefully prodigal as well as admirably efficient. We have been proud of our industrial achievements, but we have not hitherto stopped thoughtfully enough to count the human cost, the cost of lives snuffed out, of energies overtaxed and broken, the fearful physical and spiritual cost to the men and women and children upon whom the dead weight and burden of it all has fallen pitilessly the years through. The groans and agony of it all had not yet reached our ears, the solemn, moving undertone of our life, coming up out of the mines and factories, and out of every home where the struggle had its intimate and familiar seat. With the great Government went many deep secret things which we too long delayed to look into and scrutinize with candid, fearless eyes. The great Government we loved has too often been made use of for private and selfish purposes, and those who used it had forgotten the people." – Woodrow Wilson

WHY LOSS HURTS MORE THAN GAIN FEELS GOOD

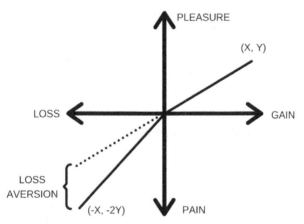

FIGURE 131: Loss hurts us more than an equivalent gain pleases us. This is known as loss aversion.

TO BE AND TO HAVE A STEP ABOVE WHAT IS AVERAGE

Historical Example: "Let me start with the economy, and a basic fact: the United States of America, right now, has the strongest, most durable economy in the world. We're in the middle of the longest streak of private-sector job creation in history. More than 14 million new jobs; the strongest two years of job growth since the '90s; an unemployment rate cut in half. Our auto industry just had its best year ever. Manufacturing has created nearly 900,000 new jobs in the past six years. And we've done all this while cutting our deficits by almost three-quarters. [...] The United States of America is the most powerful nation on Earth. Period. It's not even close. We spend more on our military than the next eight nations combined. Our troops are the finest fighting force in the history of the world. No nation dares to attack us or our allies because they know that's the path to ruin. Surveys show our standing around the world is higher than when I was elected to this office, and when it comes to every important international issue, people of the world do not look to Beijing or Moscow to lead – they call us." – Barack Obama

ATTAINING SYMBOLS OF SUCCESS AND STATUS

Historical Example: "This is the first time in history that this ceremony has been held, as you have been told, on this West Front of the Capitol. Standing here, one faces a magnificent vista, opening up on this city's special beauty and history. At the end of this open mall are those shrines to the giants on whose shoulders we stand. Directly in front of me, the monument to a monumental man: George Washington, Father of our country. A man of humility who came to greatness reluctantly. He led America out of revolutionary victory into infant nationhood. Off to one side, the stately memorial to Thomas Jefferson. The Declaration of Independence flames with his eloquence. And then beyond the Reflecting Pool the dignified columns of the Lincoln Memorial. Whoever would understand in his heart the meaning of America will find it in the life of Abraham Lincoln. Beyond those monuments to heroism is the Potomac River, and on the far shore the sloping hills of Arlington National Cemetery with its row on row of simple white markers bearing crosses or Stars of David. They add up to only a tiny fraction of the price that has been paid for our freedom." – Ronald Reagan

KEY INSIGHT:

Symbols of Success Are Not Always Obvious. They Often Speak Subconsciously.

WE WANT TO WIN IN THE SYMBOL-STATUS INTERFACE

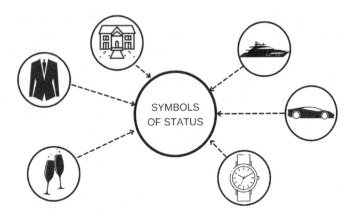

FIGURE 132: We seek to immerse ourselves in a web of symbols revealing our status to the world.

PEOPLE WANT TO ESCAPE ANXIETY AND UNEASE

Historical Example: "I am certain that my fellow Americans expect that on my induction into the Presidency I will address them with a candor and a decision which the present situation of our Nation impels. This is preeminently the time to speak the truth, the whole truth, frankly and boldly. Nor need we shrink from honestly facing conditions in our country today. This great Nation will endure as it has endured, will revive and will prosper. So, first of all, let me assert my firm belief that the only thing we have to fear is fear itself – nameless, unreasoning, unjustified terror which paralyzes needed efforts to convert retreat into advance." – Franklin Delano Roosevelt

PEOPLE WANT TO WORK LESS AND REST MORE

Historical Example: "We will no longer accept 46 percent of all new income going to the top 1 percent, while millions of Americans are forced to work 2 or 3 jobs just to survive and over half of our people live paycheck to paycheck, frightened to death about what happens to them financially if their car breaks down or their child becomes sick. Today, we fight for a political revolution." – Bernie Sanders

TO FILL LESS TIME WITH INVOLUNTARY ACTIVITY

Historical Example: "Over the next four and one half months, this campaign must challenge the campaigns of the Bush and Gore duopoly in every locality by running with the people. When Americans go to work, wondering who will take care of their elderly parents or their children, irritated by the endless traffic jams, stifled by their lack of rights in the corporate workplace, ripped off by unscrupulous sellers and large companies, put on telephone hold for the longest times before you get an answer to a simple question- so much for this modern telecommunications age, beset by having to pay for health care you cannot afford or drug prices you shouldn't have to suffer, aghast at how little time your frenzied life leaves you for children, family, friends and community, overcome by the sheer ugliness of commercial strips and sprawls and incessantly saturating advertisements, repelled by the voyeurism of the mass media and the commercialization of childhood, upset at the rejection of the wisdoms of our elders and forebears, anxious over the ways your tax dollars are being misused, feeling that there needs to be more to life than the desperate rat race to make ends meet, then think about becoming a part of a progressive movement of Greens, of this citizens' campaign, to change the political economy so that healthy environments, healthy communities, and healthy people become its overwhelming reason for being." – Ralph Nader

ADEQUACY, PEOPLE WANT TO BE ENOUGH

Historical Example: "We have every right to dream heroic dreams. Those who say that we are in a time when there are no heroes just don't know where to look. You can see heroes every day going in and out of factory gates. Others, a handful in number, produce enough food to feed all of us and then the world beyond. You meet heroes across a counter – and they are on both sides of that counter. There are entrepreneurs with faith in themselves and faith in an idea who create new jobs, new wealth and opportunity. They are individuals and families whose taxes support the Government and whose voluntary gifts support church, charity, culture, art, and education. Their patriotism is quiet but deep. Their values sustain our national life. I have used the words 'they' and 'their' in speaking of these heroes. I could say 'you' and 'your' because I am addressing the heroes of whom I speak – you, the citizens of this blessed land. Your dreams, your hopes, your goals are going to be the dreams, the hopes, and the goals of this administration, so help me God." – Ronald Reagan

KEY INSIGHT:

Part of Us Wants to Grow and Rise to the Challenges Facing Us. Another Part Begs Us to Pretend We're Good Enough Already.

WHAT DOES IT MEAN TO BE ENOUGH?

SET OF POSSIBLE QUALITIES

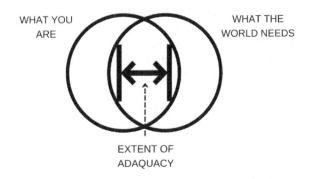

WHAT YOU ARE

WHAT THE WORLD NEEDS

EXTENT OF ADAQUACY

FIGURE 133: People want to be what they need to be.

ESTEEM, PEOPLE WANT TO FEEL LOVED

Historical Example: "As we bind up the internal wounds of Watergate, more painful and more poisonous than those of foreign wars, let us restore the golden rule to our political process, and let brotherly love purge our hearts of suspicion and of hate." – Gerald Ford

LIBERATION FROM LASTING PAST TRAUMAS

Historical Example: "We have a place, all of us, in a long story – a story we continue, but whose end we will not see. It is the story of a new world that became a friend and liberator of the old, a story of a slave-holding society that became a servant of freedom, the story of a power that went into the world to protect but not possess, to defend but not to conquer. It is the American story – a story of flawed and fallible people, united across the generations by grand and enduring ideals." – George W. Bush

RESPECT, SELF-RESPECT, RESPECT FROM OTHERS

Historical Example: "History, faith, and reason show the way, the way of unity. We can see each other not as adversaries but as neighbors. We can treat each other with dignity and respect. We can join forces, stop the shouting, and lower the temperature. [...] Let us listen to one another. Hear one another. See one another. Show respect to one another. Politics need not be a raging fire destroying everything in its path. [...] What are the common objects we love that define us as Americans? I think I know. Opportunity. Security. Liberty. Dignity. Respect. Honor. And, yes, the truth." – Joe Biden

CONFIDENCE, SELF-LOVE, AND SELF-BELIEF

Historical Example: "We can stop sending our children to schools with corridors of shame and start putting them on a pathway to success. We can stop talking about how great teachers are and start rewarding them for their greatness by giving them more pay and more support. We can do this with our new majority. We can harness the ingenuity of farmers and scientists, citizens and entrepreneurs to free this nation from the tyranny of oil and save our planet from a point of no return. [...] For when we have faced down impossible odds, when we've been told we're not ready or that we shouldn't try or that we can't, generations of Americans have responded with a simple creed that sums up the spirit of a people: Yes, we can. Yes, we can. Yes, we can. It was a creed written into the founding documents that declared the destiny of a nation: Yes, we can. It was whispered by slaves and abolitionists as they blazed a trail towards freedom through the darkest of nights: Yes, we can. It was sung by immigrants as they struck out from distant shores and pioneers who pushed westward against an unforgiving wilderness: Yes, we can. It was the call of workers who organized, women who reached for the ballot, a president who chose the moon as our new frontier, and a king who took us to the mountaintop and pointed the way to the promised land: Yes, we can, to justice and equality. Yes, we can, to opportunity and prosperity. Yes, we can heal this nation. Yes, we can repair this world. Yes, we can." – Barack Obama

INCLUSION, PEOPLE WANT TO BE INCLUDED

Historical Example: "We are running for them. This campaign is giving voice to them. It has room for everyone because no matter who you voted for in elections past. For that matter, no matter who you caucused for tonight, we welcome you in our campaign and you belong in the future that we are building for America. Whether you're a young woman with autism in Muscatine or a veteran battling addiction in Clermont, you belong. Whether you clean hotel rooms in Las Vegas or are getting a new business up and running in Charleston, you belong." – Pete Buttigieg

INTELLECTUALLY STIMULATING WORK AND LIFE

Historical Example: "Today, we say to our young people that we want you to get the best education that you can, regardless of the income of your family. Good jobs require a good education. That is why we are going to make public colleges and universities tuition free, and substantially lower the outrageous level of student debt that currently exists. America once had the best educated workforce in the world, and we are going to make that happen again." – Bernie Sanders

..................................Chapter Summary..................................

- Desire never ends by satisfying desires. With the satisfaction of one desire, two more often emerge.

- Trying to meet human desires is like trying to slay a hydra: We always find something else to want.
- We may even conceive of a "desire for desire." We may want to want. We will always turn our eye toward the next peak.
- We have constructed a world in which most people in developed countries have met their primordial desires.
- As a result, new desires have emerged. These are the emergent needs of the modern era.
- They link back to the core desires but stand discretely on their own. They are often more complex to satisfy.

KEY INSIGHT:

Physical Courage Is a Deeply Admirable Character Trait. In the Modern World, Intellectual Courage Should Be Just as Admirable.

It Takes Courage to Kill Beloved But Outdated Systems of Thought and Belief. It's Easy to Blind Ourselves to the Shortcomings of What We Know And Love. But It Is Also Dangerous.

Claim These Free Resources that Will Help You Unleash the Power of Your Words and Speak with Confidence. Visit www.speakforsuccesshub.com/toolkit for Access.

30 Free Video Lessons

We'll send you one free video lesson every day for 30 days, written and recorded by Peter D. Andrei. Days 1-10 cover authenticity, the prerequisite to confidence and persuasive power. Days 11-20 cover building self-belief and defeating communication anxiety. Days 21-30 cover how to speak with impact and influence, ensuring your words change minds instead of falling flat. Authenticity, self-belief, and impact – this course helps you master three components of confidence, turning even the most high-stakes presentations from obstacles into opportunities.

SPEAK FOR SUCCESS COLLECTION BOOK

VIII

DECODING HUMAN NATURE CHAPTER

XV

FRAMEWORK THIRTEEN:
Weakness Needs

WEAKNESS NEEDS

H UMANS ARE AT ONCE INCOMPREHENSIBLY strong and undeniably weak. We all have a set of basic human needs and human desires that arise from our weakness.

WHAT ARE THE WEAKNESS NEEDS?

Where do they come from? These come from our weakest impulses. Undeniably, almost every single human being has at least one of these impulses. Probably more.

When do we see them? We see them in people acting from a place of fear. We see them in people not playing to win, just playing not to lose. We see them in people who live their lives molded around the desire to defend themselves from a set of fears. To a degree, that describes all of us.

How do you use them? Use these when you see them. Know that even when they aren't manifested in an obvious way, they are probably still there. The hyper-successful CEO? He or she probably suffers from more of these than they admit. In fact, much of what they do is to satisfy these "weak" basic human needs. Meeting expectations, getting approval, and preventing rejection, for example.

PREVENTING THE REOCCURENCE OF PAST FAILURES

Historical Example: "The American dream endures. We must once again have full faith in our country – and in one another. I believe America can be better. We can be even stronger than before. Let our recent mistakes bring a resurgent commitment to the basic principles of our Nation, for we know that if we despise our own government we have no future. We recall in special times when we have stood briefly, but magnificently, united. In those times no prize was beyond our grasp." – Jimmy Carter

ASSOCIATIVE RELATIONSHIPS TO PEOPLE AND IDEAS

Historical Example: "The physical configuration of the earth has separated us from all of the Old World, but the common brotherhood of man, the highest law of all our being, has united us by inseparable bonds with all humanity." – Calvin Coolidge

SIMPLICITY, THE DESIRE TO ESCAPE COMPLEXITY

Historical Example: "Such a moment calls for hopeful and audacious voices from communities like ours. And yes, it calls for a new generation of leadership. The principles that will guide my campaign are simple enough to fit on a bumper sticker: freedom, security, and democracy." – Pete Buttigieg

GUIDANCE FROM AN EXPERT OR AUTHORITY FIGURE

Historical Example: "It is to be hoped that the normal balance of executive and legislative authority may be wholly adequate to meet the unprecedented task before us. But it may be that an unprecedented demand and need for undelayed action may call for temporary departure from that normal balance of public procedure. I am prepared under my constitutional duty to recommend the measures that a stricken nation in the midst of a stricken world may require. These measures, or such other measures as the Congress may build out of its experience and wisdom, I shall seek, within my constitutional authority, to bring to speedy adoption. But in the event that the Congress shall fail to take one of these two courses, and in the event that the national emergency is still critical, I shall not evade the clear course of duty that will then confront me. I shall ask the Congress for the one remaining instrument to meet the crisis – broad Executive power to wage a war against the emergency, as great as the power that would be given to me if we were in fact invaded by a foreign foe. For the trust reposed in me I will return the courage and the devotion that befit the time. I can do no less." – Franklin Delano Roosevelt

REVEALING THE AGE-OLD STORYTELLING FORMULA

FIGURE 134: This is an archetypal, age-old storytelling framework. A hero has a problem and meets a guide who gives him a plan he can use to solve it. He acts on the plan and this results either in success or failure. The role of the guide is essential. We seek a guiding hand. We seek assistance and experience.

VICTIMIZATION, THE ABILITY TO BLAME OTHERS

Historical Example: "Well, I don't think they really do like the economy. Go back and talk to the old neighbors in the middle-class neighborhoods you grew up in. The middle class is getting killed. The middle class is getting crushed and the working class has no way up as a consequence of that. You have, for example, farmers in the Midwest, 40 percent of them could pay, couldn't pay their bills last year. You have most Americans, if they've received the bill for 400 dollars or more, they'd have to sell something or borrow the money. The middle class is not, is behind the eight ball. We have to make sure that they have an even shot. We have to eliminate significant number of these god-awful tax cuts that were given to the very wealthy. We have to invest in education. We have to invest in healthcare. We have to invest in those things that make a difference in the lives of middle-class people so they can maintain their standard of living. That's not being done, and the idea that we're growing, we're not growing. The wealthy, very wealthy are growing. Ordinary people are not growing. They are not happy with where they are, and that's why we must change this presidency now." – Joe Biden

THE VICTIM, PERPETRATOR, BENEVOLENCE MODEL

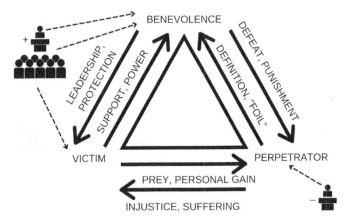

FIGURE 135: The victim, perpetrator, and benevolence model is a persuasive structure that presents the audience as victims of a perpetrator (like the speaker's opponents) while presenting the speaker (or his solution or team) as the benevolent force for good that will defeat the perpetrator, heal the victim, and restore justice. The audience can be both the victims – appealing to the victimization need – or people the speaker is inviting into the benevolent force for good.

THE DESIRE TO MEET THE EXPECTATIONS OF OTHERS

Historical Example: "On the eve of our struggle for independence a man who might have been one of the greatest among the Founding Fathers, Dr. Joseph Warren, President of the Massachusetts Congress, said to his fellow Americans, 'Our country is in danger, but not to be despaired of.... On you depend the fortunes of America. You are to decide the important questions upon which rests the happiness and the liberty of millions yet unborn. Act worthy of yourselves.'" – Ronald Reagan

THE DESIRE TO RECEIVE APPROVAL FROM OTHERS

Historical Example: "And as we renew ourselves here in our own land, we will be seen as having greater strength throughout the world. We will again be the exemplar of freedom and a beacon of hope for those who do not now have freedom." – Ronald Reagan

TO HAVE OUR WANTS AND BELIEFS VALIDATED

Historical Example: "At the center of this movement is a crucial conviction, that a nation exists to serve its citizens. Americans want great schools for their children, safe neighborhoods for their families, and good jobs for themselves. These are just and reasonable demands of righteous people and a righteous public, but for too many of our citizens a different reality exists." – Donald Trump

TO FIT IN AS A MEMBER OF A SUPPORTIVE GROUP

Historical Example: "The grandest of these ideals is an unfolding American promise that everyone belongs, that everyone deserves a chance, that no insignificant person was ever born." – George W Bush

THE DESIRE TO RECEIVE ATTENTION FROM OTHERS

Historical Example: "What truly matters is not which party controls our government, but whether our government is controlled by the people. January 20th, 2017 will be remembered as the day the people became the rulers of this nation again. The forgotten men and women of our country, will be forgotten no longer. Everyone is listening to you now. You came by the tens of millions to become part of a historic movement, the likes of which the world has never seen before." – Donald Trump

RECIPROCATION AND COOPERATION FROM OTHERS

Historical Example: "To our sister republics south of our border, we offer a special pledge – to convert our good words into good deeds – in a new alliance for progress – to assist free men and free governments in casting off the chains of poverty. But this peaceful revolution of hope cannot become the prey of hostile powers. Let all our neighbors know that we shall join with them to oppose aggression or subversion anywhere in the Americas. And let every other power know that this Hemisphere intends to remain the master of its own house. [...] Finally, to those nations who would make themselves our adversary, we offer not a pledge but a request: that both sides begin

244 | Decoding Human Nature

anew the quest for peace, before the dark powers of destruction unleashed by science engulf all humanity in planned or accidental self-destruction. [...] So let us begin anew – remembering on both sides that civility is not a sign of weakness, and sincerity is always subject to proof. Let us never negotiate out of fear. But let us never fear to negotiate. Let both sides explore what problems unite us instead of belaboring those problems which divide us. Let both sides, for the first time, formulate serious and precise proposals for the inspection and control of arms – and bring the absolute power to destroy other nations under the absolute control of all nations. Let both sides seek to invoke the wonders of science instead of its terrors. Together let us explore the stars, conquer the deserts, eradicate disease, tap the ocean depths and encourage the arts and commerce. Let both sides unite to heed in all corners of the earth the command of Isaiah – to 'undo the heavy burdens... [and] let the oppressed go free.'" – John F. Kennedy

...............................Chapter Summary...............................

- The weakness needs emerge from our fragility and our less desirable and less virtuous qualities.
- The impulses themselves are often (but not always) qualities people seek to transcend and overcome.
- However, you can channel them toward positive ends. You can use them to motivate virtues.
- Much like the fear needs, you can twist the weakness needs to serve the ends of progress.
- You can use the desire for reciprocation to empower positive, fair, and moral relations and arrangements.
- You can use the desire for meeting external expectations as a bad quality to motivate a good thing: enthusiastic action.

KEY INSIGHT:

Human Desires Must Not Be Given Into Entirely Nor Entirely Eradicated. They Should Be Channeled, Integrated, and Negotiated with.

Claim These Free Resources that Will Help You Unleash the Power of Your Words and Speak with Confidence. Visit www.speakforsuccesshub.com/toolkit for Access.

2 Free Workbooks

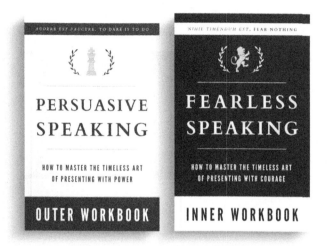

We'll send you two free workbooks, including long-lost excerpts by Dale Carnegie, the mega-bestselling author of *How to Win Friends and Influence People* (5,000,000 copies sold). *Fearless Speaking* guides you in the proven principles of mastering your inner game as a speaker. *Persuasive Speaking* guides you in the time-tested tactics of mastering your outer game by maximizing the power of your words. All of these resources complement the Speak for Success collection.

SPEAK FOR SUCCESS COLLECTION BOOK

VIII

DECODING HUMAN NATURE CHAPTER

XVI

FRAMEWORK FOURTEEN:
Malevolent Desires

MALEVOLENT DESIRES

H UMANS HAVE A SET OF IMMORAL BASIC needs and desires, which you can channel into productive and moral directions with the correct approach.

WHAT ARE THE MALEVOLENT DESIRES?

Where do they come from? These desires are tribal. They are primitive. They are primal. They are engineered into us by evolution. They stem from the influence of the negative-ego. Freud would have called it the "id." Much of what goes wrong in the world is the product of these desires.

When do we see them? In people who are vindictive. In people who are selfish. In people who are constantly striving, but never arriving, and almost always striving at the expense of others. But also, in almost everybody, to some lesser degree.

How do you use them? As you will see, these are double edged swords, and you can strike with the positive edge if you are cognizant of the desires.

REVENGE, THROWING STONES AT OUR ENEMIES

Historical Example: "Our problems – Our problems are both acute and chronic, yet all we hear from those in positions of leadership are the same tired proposals for more Government tinkering, more meddling, and more control – all of which led us to this sorry state in the first place. Can anyone look at the record of this Administration and say, 'Well done?' Can anyone compare the state of our economy when the Carter Administration took office with where we are today and say, 'Keep up the good work?' Can anyone look at our reduced standing in the world today and say, 'Let's have four more years of this?' I believe the American people are going to answer these questions, as you've answered them, in the first week in November and their answer will be, 'No – we've had enough.'" – Ronald Reagan

THE DESIRE TO BE PART OF A SUPERIOR GROUP

Historical Example: "This right now is the greatest country on Earth." – Michelle Obama

COMPETING AND WINNING TO SATISFY EGO DEMANDS

Historical Example: "Within these last 19 months at least 45 satellites have circled the earth. Some 40 of them were "made in the United States of America" and they were far more sophisticated and supplied far more knowledge to the people of the world than those of the Soviet Union. [...] To be sure, we are behind, and will be behind for some time in manned flight. But we do not intend to stay behind, and in this decade, we shall make up and move ahead." – John F. Kennedy

THE DESIRE TO PASS JUDGEMENT ONTO OTHERS

Historical Example: "Plenty is at our doorstep, but a generous use of it languishes in the very sight of the supply. Primarily this is because the rulers of the exchange of mankind's goods have failed, through their own stubbornness and their own incompetence, have admitted their failure, and abdicated. Practices of the unscrupulous money changers stand indicted in the court of public opinion, rejected by the hearts and minds of men. True they have tried, but their efforts have been cast in the pattern of an outworn tradition. Faced by failure of credit they have proposed only the lending of more money. Stripped of the lure of profit by which to induce our people to follow their false leadership, they have resorted to exhortations, pleading tearfully for restored confidence. They know only the rules of a generation of self-seekers. They have no vision, and when there is no vision the people perish. The money changers have fled from their high seats in the temple of our civilization. We may now restore that temple to the ancient truths. The measure of the restoration lies in the extent to which we apply social values more noble than mere monetary profit." – Franklin Delano Roosevelt

STATUS, PRESTIGE, ELITISM, BEING A SPECIAL GROUP

Historical Example: "I say that the United States of America is a unique experiment in history. I believe in American exceptionalism. I wasn't for sending ground forces into Libya. It would have been counterproductive, but we are an inspiration to these people. I know because I've looked them in the eyes, and they looked at me. They look to America for inspiration and leadership." – John McCain

AGGRESSION, NOT ONLY AGAINST AGGRESSORS

Historical Example: "Even though large tracts of Europe and many old and famous States have fallen or may fall into the grip of the Gestapo and all the odious apparatus of Nazi rule, we shall not flag or fail. We shall go on to the end, we shall fight in France, we shall fight on the seas and oceans, we shall fight with growing confidence and growing strength in the air, we shall defend our Island, whatever the cost may be, we shall fight on the beaches, we shall fight on the landing grounds, we shall fight in the fields and in the streets, we shall fight in the hills; we shall never surrender, and even if, which I do not for a moment believe, this Island or a large part of it were subjugated and starving, then our Empire beyond the seas, armed and guarded by the British Fleet, would carry on the struggle, until, in God's good time, the New World, with all its power and might, steps forth to the rescue and the liberation of the old." – Winston Churchill

GREED, TO AMASS MORE THAN WE COULD EVER NEED

Historical Example: "That we are in the midst of crisis is now well understood. Our nation is at war against a far-reaching network of violence and hatred. Our economy is badly weakened, a consequence of greed and irresponsibility on the part of some, but also our collective failure to make hard choices and prepare the nation for a new age." – Barack Obama

IMPORTANCE, THE DESIRE TO BE IMPORTANT

Historical Example: "We hear much of special interest groups. Our concern must be for a special interest group that has been too long neglected. It knows no sectional boundaries or ethnic and racial divisions, and it crosses political party lines. It is made up of men and women who raise our food, patrol our streets, man our mines and our factories, teach our children, keep our homes, and heal us when we are sick – professionals, industrialists, shopkeepers, clerks, cabbies, and truckdrivers. They are, in short, 'We the people,' this breed called Americans." – Ronald Reagan

......................Chapter Summary...............................

- We may see these desires as further elucidating the framework outlined by Bertrand Russel.
- Much like weakness and fear needs, these are undesirable desires that most people seek to transcend.
- Nonetheless, you can use them to fuel a persuasive fire that produces drastically positive results in the real world.
- You can twist the desire for aggression into a motivation to protect others by beating back aggressors.
- You can twist the desire for superiority into a productive desire for excellence.
- You can twist the desire for revenge into an inward-oriented motivation to improve and grow.

KEY INSIGHT:

The Desire For Importance Is the Desire to "Be Someone." It Can Motivate Great Altruism, But Also Poisonous Vanity.

Claim These Free Resources that Will Help You Unleash the Power of Your Words and Speak with Confidence. Visit www.speakforsuccesshub.com/toolkit for Access.

18 Free PDF Resources

12 Iron Rules for Captivating Story, 21 Speeches that Changed the World, 341-Point Influence Checklist, 143 Persuasive Cognitive Biases, 17 Ways to Think On Your Feet, 18 Lies About Speaking Well, 137 Deadly Logical Fallacies, 12 Iron Rules For Captivating Slides, 371 Words that Persuade, 63 Truths of Speaking Well, 27 Laws of Empathy, 21 Secrets of Legendary Speeches, 19 Scripts that Persuade, 12 Iron Rules For Captivating Speech, 33 Laws of Charisma, 11 Influence Formulas, 219-Point Speech-Writing Checklist, 21 Eloquence Formulas

SPEAK FOR SUCCESS COLLECTION BOOK

VIII

DECODING HUMAN NATURE CHAPTER

XVII

FRAMEWORK FIFTEEN:

Esteem Needs

ESTEEM NEEDS

B ROKEN DOWN, THE ESTEEM NEEDS ARE some of the most powerful persuasive buttons. And this chapter will teach you exactly how to use them.

WHAT ARE THE ESTEEM NEEDS?

Where do they come from? They were first identified in Maslow's Hierarchy of Needs. But they can be broken down much further.

When do we see them? We see them in people who seem to be "living for others." They do what others want them to, seeking to gain esteem.

How do you use them? At the risk of sounding like a broken record, you use these by including them in your communication. But a bonus tip for these specifically: don't press them too hard. People don't want to desire esteem. So, if you are obvious in your use of these desires, you'll receive resistance.

ADMIRATION, BEING PRAISED BY OTHERS

Historical Example: "Senator Hatfield, Mr. Chief Justice, Mr. President, Vice President Bush, Vice President Mondale, Senator Baker, Speaker O'Neill, Reverend Moomaw, and my fellow citizens: To a few of us here today, this is a solemn and most momentous occasion; and yet, in the history of our Nation, it is a commonplace occurrence. The orderly transfer of authority as called for in the Constitution routinely takes place as it has for almost two centuries and few of us stop to think how unique we really are. In the eyes of many in the world, this every-four-year ceremony we accept as normal is nothing less than a miracle." – Ronald Reagan

POPULARITY, BEING LIKED BY MANY OTHERS

Historical Example: "The American people have summoned the change we celebrate today. You have raised your voices in an unmistakable chorus. You have cast your votes in historic numbers. And you have changed the face of Congress, the presidency and the political process itself. Yes, you, my fellow Americans have forced the spring." – Bill Clinton

SATISFYING OUR POSSESSIVE IMPULSES

Historical Example: "This country belongs to the people and whenever they shall grow weary of their government they can exercise their constitutional right to amend it, or revolutionary right to dismember it or overthrow it." – Abraham Lincoln

WANTING TO BE THE OBJECT OF OTHERS' ENVY

Historical Example: "Thomas Jefferson believed that to preserve the very foundations of our nation, we would need dramatic change from time to time. Well, my fellow citizens, this is our time. Let us embrace it. Our democracy must be not only the envy of the world but the engine of our own renewal. There is nothing wrong with America that cannot be cured by what is right with America." – Bill Clinton

...............................Chapter Summary..................................

- These needs are discrete and they stand alone, but you can conceive them as elucidating Maslow's "esteem" level.
- These needs often motivate those who "live for others," seeking to earn admiration and praise.
- These needs are not inherently destructive if they are properly balanced in a broader hierarchy of desire.
- These needs can become destructive if they begin to dominate an individual's desire hierarchy.
- You can appeal to these needs in such a way that you motivate positive action.
- These needs call for subtle, gentle appeals, not direct or explicit ones.

KEY INSIGHT:

Envy Is More Complicated Than It Appears. Someone Envies What They Envy, But Also That Someone Else Is the Object of Envy. Envy Envies Envy.

SPEAK FOR SUCCESS COLLECTION BOOK

VIII

DECODING HUMAN NATURE CHAPTER

XVIII

FRAMEWORK SIXTEEN:
Primordial Needs

PRIMAL HUMAN NEEDS

T HESE ARE AS FOUNDATIONAL AS THE LIFE-FORCE eight. They further elucidate the fundamental, evolutionarily-engineered desires motivating us.

WHAT ARE THE PRIMAL HUMAN NEEDS?

Where do they come from? These are wired so deep into our minds. Why? Because thousands of years ago, they helped us survive. People who had the gene that created these desires were more likely to survive and pass those genes onto their offspring.

When do we see them? We see them in the common actions we all take. Why do we work? Why do we try to earn money? Why do we exercise? The answers seem obvious. But we do it to satisfy our primal basic human needs and human desires.

How do you use them? Use these implicitly, not explicitly. That will make it more subtle, and these in particular demand subtlety.

SURVIVAL, THE DESIRE TO EXTEND LIFE

Historical Example: "The world is still engaged in a massive armaments race designed to ensure continuing equivalent strength among potential adversaries. We pledge perseverance and wisdom in our efforts to limit the world's armaments to those necessary for each nation's own domestic safety. And we will move this year a step toward ultimate goal – the elimination of all nuclear weapons from this Earth. We urge all other people to join us, for success can mean life instead of death." – Jimmy Carter

THE DESIRE TO LIVE AWAY FROM ALL THREATS

Historical Example: "Our streets will echo again with the laughter of our children, because no one will try to shoot them or sell them drugs anymore. Everyone who can work, will work, with today's permanent under class part of tomorrow's growing middle class. New miracles of medicine at last will reach not only those who can claim care now, but the children and hardworking families too long denied. We will stand mighty for peace and freedom, and maintain a strong defense against terror and destruction. Our children will sleep free from the threat of nuclear, chemical or biological weapons." – Bill Clinton

THE DESIRE TO DEFEND WHAT IS OURS FROM FOES

Historical Example: "Our forbearance should never be misunderstood. Our reluctance for conflict should not be misjudged as a failure of will. When action is required to preserve our national security, we will act. We will maintain sufficient strength to prevail if need be, knowing that if we do so we have the best chance of never having to use that strength." – Ronald Reagan

THE DESIRE TO PROVIDE FOR OUR OFFSPRING

Historical Example: "Well, I believe we, the Americans of today, are ready to act worthy of ourselves, ready to do what must be done to ensure happiness and liberty for ourselves, our children and our children's children." – Ronald Reagan

..................................Chapter Summary..................................

- These needs are similar to the life-force eight in that they are primordial, fundamental, and basic.
- These needs are closer to the label of "core" than a framework like the emergent modern needs, for example.
- These needs, as a result, are nearly inalienable. People can hardly resist answering the call of these desires.
- These needs, to put it in other words, often sit subconsciously at or near the top of people's hierarchies.
- The desire to provide for children is one of the most noble and powerful motivations to apply persuasively.
- You can link appeals to these needs very closely to appeals to other needs, and they often overlap.

KEY INSIGHT:

The Best Solutions to Problems Do Not Merely Treat the Problem's Symptoms Now, But Work Across Time, Across Place, and Across Different Groups of People.

SPEAK FOR SUCCESS COLLECTION BOOK

VIII

DECODING HUMAN NATURE CHAPTER

XIX

FRAMEWORK SEVENTEEN:
My 7P Model

MY 7P MODEL

A FTER RESEARCHING THIS SUBJECT for a long, long time, and diving deep into the dark depths of human desires, I've come up with this model. It is, in part, a particular categorization of the other identified needs.

People: we desire meaningful relationships with people. Purpose: we desire a defined purpose. Progress: we desire progress towards our defined purpose. Plan: we desire a plan for achieving our purpose. Protection: we desire to protect ourselves and our property and our purpose. Property: we desire to gain more property (but don't think of this strictly as material property – think of it as "things we take ownership of.") Passion: we desire to center our lives around a main activity we are passionate about.

In other words: people want to progress towards a purpose they are passionate about with the right people and a plan, and they want to protect their property and get new property.

...............................Chapter Summary...............................

- This a simple model I have developed by observation of the other frameworks.
- It can be conceived as a checklist: if an endeavor appeals to all seven of the items, people will be motivated.
- This framework – like all of the frameworks – can also be used to structure goals and tasks.
- Appealing to these desires in a persuasive message is only one of their applications.
- You can use them to structure motivational jobs for employees, for example.
- It is an easy exercise to graft other frameworks onto this one, and to see how they interrelate.

Claim These Free Resources that Will Help You Unleash the Power of Your Words and Speak with Confidence. Visit www.speakforsuccesshub.com/toolkit for Access.

30 Free Video Lessons

We'll send you one free video lesson every day for 30 days, written and recorded by Peter D. Andrei. Days 1-10 cover authenticity, the prerequisite to confidence and persuasive power. Days 11-20 cover building self-belief and defeating communication anxiety. Days 21-30 cover how to speak with impact and influence, ensuring your words change minds instead of falling flat. Authenticity, self-belief, and impact – this course helps you master three components of confidence, turning even the most high-stakes presentations from obstacles into opportunities.

SPEAK FOR SUCCESS COLLECTION BOOK

VIII

DECODING HUMAN NATURE CHAPTER

XX

ADVANCED STRATEGIES:

Little-Known Strategies to Empower Your Message

ADVANCED STRATEGIES FOR INSTANTLY BOOSTING THE PERSUASIVE POWER OF THE HUMAN NEEDS AND HUMAN DESIRES

I F INVOKING THE BASIC HUMAN NEEDS and innate human desires that motivate basically everyone isn't persuasive enough for you, then this chapter will be great. Why? Because you'll learn the proven strategies that can make a "need invocation statement" much more persuasive. In other words, these are all tools you can use to modify your invocation statements, and techniques you can stack up in a persuasive pyramid. Are you ready? Let's dive in.

AGITATORS

Agitators are wonderful. Why? Because they instantly add force and persuasive power to your statements that invoke the basic human needs and desires. An agitator is a statement right after the invocation of a basic human desire that is designed specifically to intensify that desire. Want to jump to an example? Let's grab one of our old ones, for the human need of victimization (predicated on the psychological fact that personal responsibility is often a heavy burden, and blaming externalities is easy). If you recall, the definition is this: victimization, the excuse to blame other people, events, or institutions for one's problems to avoid taking personal responsibility. And our example was this (remember, this does not necessarily reflect – or not reflect – my political views: I am acting as an investigator and a guide, not a judge):

"Well, I don't think they really do like the economy. Go back and talk to the old neighbors in the middle-class neighborhoods you grew up in. The middle class is getting killed. The middle class is getting crushed and the working class has no way up as a consequence of that. You have, for example, farmers in the Midwest, 40 percent of them could pay, couldn't pay their bills last year. You have most Americans, if they've received the bill for 400 dollars or more, they'd have to sell something or borrow the money. The middle class is not, is behind the eight ball. We have to make sure that they have an even shot. We have to eliminate significant number of these god-awful tax cuts that were given to the very wealthy. We have to invest in education. We have to invest in healthcare. We have to invest in those things that make a difference in the lives of middle-class people so they can maintain their standard of living. That's not being done, and the idea that we're growing, we're not growing. The wealthy, very wealthy are growing. Ordinary people are not growing. They are not happy with where they are, and that's why we must change this presidency now." – Joe Biden

There are already agitators in there. Can you find them? I've italicized them. Here they are: "Well, I don't think they really do like the economy. Go back and talk to the old neighbors in the middle-class neighborhoods you grew up in. The middle class is getting *killed.* The middle class is getting *crushed* and the working class has no way up as a consequence of that. You have, for example, farmers in the Midwest, 40 percent of them could pay, couldn't pay their bills last year. You have most Americans, if they've received the bill for 400 dollars or more, they'd have to sell something or borrow the money. The middle class is not, is behind the eight ball. We have to make sure that they have an even shot. We have to eliminate significant number of these *god-awful* tax cuts that were given to the very wealthy. We have to invest in education. We have to invest in healthcare. We have to invest in those things that make a difference in the lives of middle-class people so they can maintain their standard of living. That's not being done, and the idea that we're growing, we're not growing. The wealthy, very wealthy are growing. Ordinary people are not growing. They are not happy with where they are, and that's why we must change this presidency now."

Words like "killed," "crushed," and "god-awful" are evocative words that connote victimization and have a definitively emotional character. They are not particularly necessary. They are only there to agitate and intensify the human desire of victimization. To elaborate: victimization is a two-fold need. People want victimization to avoid taking responsibility for problems, but this then comes with a second fold: the desire to beat back the injustice, and defeat the unfair externalities. Although, often, the burden of personal responsibility can be heavier than the burden of externalities. Thus, we see "pretend" solutions that don't solve the problem, but serve as fake actions designed to fool people into thinking they're doing something about it. This is not just my musing: this is supported by extensive psychological testimony. Now let's go ahead and add some new agitators to this invocation of victimization:

"Well, I don't think they really do like the economy, *when two degree-holding adults have to work six jobs between themselves to make sure their kids don't go hungry.* Go back and talk to the old neighbors in the *dying* middle-class neighborhoods you grew up in. The middle class is getting *killed*. The middle class is getting *crushed* and the working class has no way up as a consequence of that, *guaranteeing a crushing cycle of intergenerational poverty and suffering and generating a modern-day caste system.* You have, for example, *struggling* farmers in the Midwest, 40 percent of them could pay, couldn't pay their bills last year. You have most *hard-working and honest* Americans, if they've received the bill for 400 dollars or more – *the amount of money some so-called elite Americans make in one minute* – they'd have to sell something *near and dear to their hearts* or borrow the money. The middle class is not, is behind the eight ball – *not getting what they deserve, what they've earned, what America promised them, or what humans need to flourish. The middle class is suffering. The middle class is suffocating. The middle class is drowning. And it's not just the people you know, it's most Americans.* We have to make sure that they have an even shot. We have to eliminate significant number of these *god-awful* tax cuts that were given to the very wealthy. We have to invest in education. We have to invest in healthcare. We have to invest in those things that make a difference in the lives of middle-class people so they can maintain their standard of living. That's not being done, and the idea that we're growing, we're not growing. The wealthy, very wealthy are growing. Ordinary people are not growing. They are not happy with where they are, and that's why we must change this presidency now."

Let's talk about this. First, we'll discuss the impact of agitators. Then, how these particular agitators function. Here's the impact: when someone invokes a need that is salient to you, you will inevitably feel a gut feeling, a sort of pull towards that person and what they are saying. You will feel some dissonance, and perhaps a want-got gap. Or maybe you'll feel sad, or happy, or whatever; the point is that you'll be feeling *something*, and feeling, or emotion, is the key to persuasion. *All agitators do is intensify that feeling.*

If the invocation of a need happened to make you feel a stark want-got gap, a distinct difference between what you want and what you have, then agitators will intensify that feeling of psychological discomfort. In other words: there is a hole poked your feeling that you have enough. Agitators widen that hole, and calls to action provide a means to fill that gap (note how Biden ended the segment).

Now, why do these particular agitators work? What kinds of agitators do we have in our toolbox? Plenty. I'll just go over the ones I used.

First, we have connotative, evocative word injections. You might think this is immoral, but the point of this need-invocation is, quite frankly, to inspire (whether it reflects reality is a different story – and obviously it should) a sense of unfairness and injustice, to satisfy people's aversion to blaming themselves for their problems, and to create psychological discomfort that can be alleviated by a specific action. So, let's check out some connotative, evocative words we injected to fabricate those emotions. These are simple but powerful words we simply shoved into the original words: "dying, struggling, hard-working and honest, near and dear to their hearts."

Some of these are obvious. For example, it's obvious that words like the following serve to agitate the negative emotions: "dying" and "struggling."

So, let me explain: "hard-working and honest" in reference to the victims connotes and evokes a contrast between their hard-working, responsible ways and the people who are hurting them. Contrasts are persuasive. This subtle intensifier is so subtle that it is more likely than most agitators to bypass the logical filter and drive home its influence directly to the subconscious mind.

"Near and dear to their hearts" is quite subtle too: it evokes a sense of loss, and makes the problems produced for the victims by the victimizers more defined. People will imagine an item near and dear to their hearts when they hear this phrase; it will be an image so specific to each individual that it could not be directly conjured by the speaker, and as a result, it will intensify the sentiment because personally specific emotion is the most intense.

Our second type of agitator: repetition. The more ways you can find to say the same sentiment, the more reinforced that sentiment will be. If it's a key phrase, you can actually repeat it in its entirety, once and perhaps twice. But in other cases, direct repetition makes you sound crazy, if it is not a key phrase, if it is longer than a handful of words, and if it is in sequence. For example: let's say you want to emphasize how your solution is the one key to solving a problem. You can't exactly say "this is the one solution to our problem. This is the one solution to our problem. This is the one solution to our problem." But you can say this: "this *one, single* method is the *individual* strategy that *alone* will solve the problem: it is the *unique key* that fits your *unique* lock." Get it? In doing so, you invoked the same sentiment seven times in about 25 words, with single words, and repeated it so many times that it was agitated, and bypassed the logical filter and hit straight at the subconscious. Repetitive agitators for human desire invocations work the same way. This strategy is exemplified by this sequence: *"The middle class is suffering. The middle class is suffocating. The middle class is drowning."*

Our third agitator is intensifying sentence sequels. These are great. Quite simply, this agitator is just tagging another description on the end of a sentence. Let me highlight the intensifying sentence sequels from our previous example: "Well, I don't think they really do like the economy, *when two degree-holding adults have to work six jobs between themselves to make sure their kids don't go hungry.* Go back and talk to the old neighbors in the *dying* middle-class neighborhoods you grew up in. The middle class is getting killed. The middle class is getting crushed and the working class has no way up as a consequence of that, *guaranteeing a crushing cycle of intergenerational poverty and suffering and generating a modern-day caste system.*

How are these constructed? Well, it's easy: identify where you want to place one of these agitators (must be at the end of a sentence), identify something at the end of that sentence that you can say more about, and ask yourself "what more can I say about this that will agitate the emotions and desire I'm trying to create?" For example: "Well, I don't think they really do like the **economy**, *when two degree-holding adults have to work six jobs between themselves to make sure their kids don't go hungry.* Go back and talk to the old neighbors in the *dying* middle-class neighborhoods you grew up in. The middle class is getting killed. The middle class is getting crushed and the working class has no way up as a consequence of **that**, *guaranteeing a crushing cycle of intergenerational poverty and suffering and generating a modern-day caste system.*

See how the sentence sequels are elaborating upon the words "economy," and "that," and doing so in an agitating, intensifying way?

Our fourth agitator is enumeration and interjection. Enumeration and interjection are much like intensifying sentence sequels, except they occur basically anywhere. Here's what this agitator is: breaking down something into descriptive parts, and interjecting that intensifying description in your words. Here's an example: "You have most hard-working and honest Americans, if they've received the bill for 400 dollars or more – *the amount of money some so-called elite Americans make in one minute* – they'd have to sell something near and dear to their hearts or borrow the money. The middle class is not, is behind the eight ball – *not getting what they deserve, what they've earned, what America promised them, or what humans need to flourish. The middle class is suffering.*

Our fifth agitator is group identify and magnification. This agitator accomplishes the following kind of intensification: it makes the problem seem bigger than the individual and it clumps the individual into a group of people who are suffering because of the problem. For example: "And it's not just the people you know, it's most Americans."

This works because group identity is validating, comforting, and because joining a "team" makes one's emotional mind overpower their rational one; the tribal psychology of teams is very powerful and irrational. Think of sports fans who fight each other over miniscule provocations related to their respective teams. And this implicitly invokes the desires to be a part of a group, team, or tribe; and in this case, it invokes those desires with respect to unity by shared victimization, yet another desire.

Our sixth type of agitator is a need specific sentiment. This is a broader kind of agitator: this is adding need-specific sentiments onto your original content. It's just adding *more*. And every need calls for a specific type of sentiment. For victimization, it is these: anger, blame, injustice, and the like. See how all of the other justifiers are geared towards adding more of those sentiments? Those were some specific ways to do it, but anything that adds more need-specific sentiments to your human need and desire invocations is an agitator.

And now, a brief note on morality: there's a difference between tricking people into thinking they are victims of something and intensifying the victimization of people who really are victims of something in order to build the necessary support to end the victimization. I will make no comment as to whether this example fits this framework – it is beside the point. What matters in the context of this book are the techniques themselves: it is up to you to use them morally.

JUSTIFIERS

This one rule of persuasion is much more broadly applicable than just to the human desires. In short: people are more likely to follow a request or suggestion, or believe a stance, if there is a justification for it. And the truth of the justification is less important than its existence. In other words: no justification is the least persuasive, an illogical but existing justification is very persuasive, and a logically sound justification is typically the most persuasive. An illogical but existing justification, and also a justification made without regard to its validity (only to check the audience's mental box of "yes, there is a reason for this") is called a "fake justifier."

We're going to be talking about how to use a fake justifier or a legitimate justifier to make your human desire invocations more persuasive. A justifier is usually connected to a request, suggestion, or claim by words like "because, since, for, to, in order to," and the like. Let us use an example from Biden: "They are not happy with where they are, and that's why we must change this presidency now, because the current president is doing nothing to alleviate this injustice and everything to exacerbate it."

See how simple it is? It's saying "X, because Y," instead of just "X." But want to be even more persuasive? Try a tricolon justifier. A tricolon is three items separated by commas. It's a tool of rhetoric, eloquence, and powerful language, and I cover more of these tools in my other books. A tricolon justifier would be this: "X, because reason one, reason two, and reason three."

But how are justifiers they more broadly applicable? Here's how: any time you want your audience to take an action, you must justify that action. But above that: many of the actions *you* take in persuasive communication must be justified. "I'm calling because…" "I'm speaking to you all about this because…" "I would like to talk about X, because Y…"

PERSONAL STORIES

It's simple: people love stories, and personal stories can invoke a need, build audience trust, and captivate attention all at the same time. So, let me teach you how to use them. In short: you can talk about you fulfilling a desire before invoking it, or you having an unfulfilled desire, or you having an unfilled desire and then how you filled it, or you bearing personal witness to any of the former occurring on behalf of another person or group.

"Well, I don't think they really do like the economy, when two degree-holding adults have to work six jobs between themselves to make sure their kids don't go hungry. Go back and talk to the old neighbors in the dying middle-class neighborhoods you grew up in. The middle class is getting killed. The middle class is getting crushed and the working class has no way up as a consequence of that, guaranteeing a crushing cycle of intergenerational poverty and suffering and generating a modern-day caste system. *I was in my hometown in the industrial Midwest. What did I see? I met a father who used to provide for his family with his factory job – he worked with the utmost diligence and excellence, doing everything with passion and attention to detail, because he cared about what he produced. Then, one day, close to Christmas, he was informed that his job was being taken and given to a robot – and that he could only get severance if he helped the engineers install the robot in the factory. Now, he has to work three backbreaking jobs, making less money than before, and he gets home after his kids have gone to sleep. Is this the America you want?"*

The reason this works is because the audience of a story end up taking on the emotions of the hero in the story, especially if the story is real, and especially if it is about a person who they can see in that moment, who is telling the story about themselves.

NONEXISTENT CALL TO ACTION

Now, I want you to know this: touching on the basic human needs and desires is powerful even if you don't use them to immediately suggest an action (a call to action). Why? Because you captivate attention, increase the perceived value of your communication, and abide by most of the theories we covered by the beginning. Just a brief note before we move on to our final advanced technique for invoking the human desires.

INTENSITY LEVERS

These are like agitators. Let me lay it out as simply as possible: we have needs and desires, but for many of those needs and desire, we feel them with greater intensity towards a specific subject. In other words: we want X on its own, but we want X even more in regards to Y. Everyone has a hierarchy of desires. And for an individual desire, everyone has a hierarchy of things to which that desire can be applied.

Get it? If not, this example will explain: we have the desire to not disappoint others. For each different person, that desire is placed on a value scale against all other desires.

We might want that desire more or less than other desires, all arranged in a hierarchy of how much we want them relative to each other. But within that desire, some people might have a very intense desire to not disappoint certain others, but a less urgent desire to not disappoint different others. Confused? I'll explain.

For example: let's say the desire to not disappoint is someone's 15th most important desire. Within that desire, not disappointing their family in particular could be the most intense, not disappointing their boss could be moderately intense, and not disappointing their friends could be the least intense. These different "grades" of a desire's intensity as it relates to different groups are called intensity levers. They produce the same impact as agitators.

That said: how do you determine which intensity levers to invoke? You can't, exactly. Instead determine the *likely* intensity levers that are at play, but not their relative importance, and enjoy the power of the tricolon, which always comes to the rescue. This produces this sort of structure: "[desire invocation] [connector statement if needed] [intensity lever one] [intensity lever two] [intensity lever three]." This prevents having to guess which intensity lever is most important to someone; a very difficult task, especially if your audience is large and diverse.

As a specific (and extremely non-subtle and rudimentary) example: "[insert action] prevents you from disappointing people who are counting on you," becomes "[insert action] prevents you from disappointing your boss, your friends, and your family, who are all counting on you." Get it? This way, you don't have to pick just one of the intensity levers and risk getting it wrong.

...............................Chapter Summary...............................

- Agitators are rhetorical tools you can use to intensify the strength of your appeals to human desires.
- Justifiers appeal to the logical mind, logically validating the link between your message and what people want.
- You can embed implicit desire-invocations in an agitating story of someone you know or of yourself.
- You do not need an explicit call to action to benefit from appealing to the human desires in your communication.
- Simply touching on them implicitly increases engagement, grabs attention, and portrays value.
- Intensity levers are the subjects that intensify our desires. We want praise, but particularly from a particular source.

SOMETHING WAS MISSING. THIS IS IT.

D ECEMBER OF 2021, I COMPLETED the new editions of the 15 books in the Speak for Success collection, after months of work, and many 16-hour-long writing marathons. The collection is over 1,000,000 words long and includes over 1,700 handcrafted diagrams. It is *the* complete communication encyclopedia. But instead of feeling relieved and excited, I felt uneasy and anxious. Why? Well, I know now. After writing over 1,000,000 words on communication across 15 books, it slowly dawned on me that I had missed the most important set of ideas about good communication. What does it *really* mean to be a good speaker? This is my answer.

THERE ARE THREE DIMENSIONS OF SUCCESS

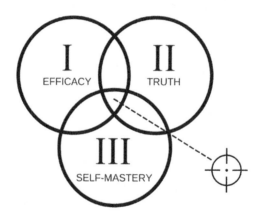

FIGURE I: A good speaker is not only rhetorically effective. They speak the truth, and they are students of self-mastery who experience peace, calm, and deep equanimity as they speak. These three domains are mutually reinforcing.

THE THREE AXES, IN DIFFERENT WORDS

Domain One	Domain Two	Domain Three
Efficacy	Truth	Self-Mastery
Rhetoric	Research	Inner-Peace
Master of Words	Seeker of Truth	Captain of Your Soul
Aristotle's "Pathos"	Aristotle's "Logos"	Aristotle's "Ethos"
Impact	Insight	Integrity
Presence of Power	Proper Perspective	Power of Presence
Inter-Subjective	Objective	Subjective
Competency	Credibility	Character
External-Internal	External	Internal
Verbal Mastery	Subject Mastery	Mental Mastery
Behavioral	Cognitive	Emotional

I realized I left out much about truth and self-mastery, focusing instead on the first domain. On page 27, the practical guide is devoted to domain I. On page 34, the ethical guide is devoted to domain II. We will shortly turn to domain III with an internal guide.

WHAT A GOOD SPEAKER LOOKS LIKE

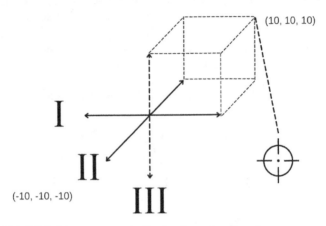

FIGURE II: We can conceptualize the three domains of success as an (X, Y, Z) coordinate plane, with each axis extending between -10 and 10. Your job is to become a (10, 10, 10). A (-10, 10, 10) speaks the truth and has attained self-mastery, but is deeply ineffective. A (10, -10, 10), speaks brilliantly and is at peace, but is somehow severely misleading others. A (10, 10, -10), speaks the truth well, but lives in an extremely negative inner state.

THE THREE AXES VIEWED DIFFERENTLY

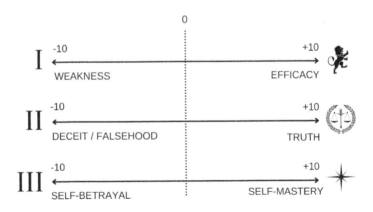

FIGURE III: We can also untangle the dimensions of improvement from representation as a coordinate plane, and instead lay them out flat, as spectrums of progress. A (+10, -10, -10) is a true monster, eloquent but evil. A (10, 10, 10) is a Martin Luther King. A more realistic example is (4, -3, 0): This person is moderately persuasive, bends truth a little too much for comfort (but not horribly), and is mildly anxious about speaking but far from falling apart. Every speaker exists at some point along these axes.

THE EXTERNAL MASTERY PROCESS IS INTERNAL TOO

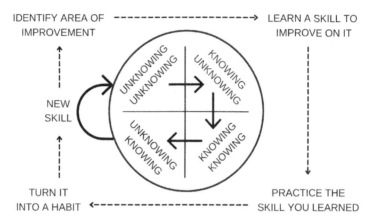

FIGURE IV: The same process presented earlier as a way to achieve rhetorical mastery will also help you achieve self-mastery. Just replace the word "skill" with "thought" or "thought-pattern," and the same cyclical method works.

THE POWER OF LANGUAGE

Language has generative power. This is why many creation stories include language as a primordial agent playing a crucial role in crafting reality. "In the beginning was the Word, and the Word was with God (John 1:1)."

Every problem we face has a story written about its future, whether explicit or implicit, conscious or subconscious. Generative language can rewrite a story that leads downward, turning it into one that aims us toward heaven, and then it can inspire us to realize this story. It can remove the cloud of ignorance from noble possibilities.

And this is good. You can orient your own future upward. That's certainly good for you. You can orient the future upward for yourself and for your family. That's better. And for your friends. That's better. And for your organization, your community, your city, and your country. That's better still. And for your enemies, and for people yet unborn; for all people, at all times, from now until the end of time.

And it doesn't get better than that.

Sound daunting? It is. It is the burden of human life. It is also the mechanism of moral progress. But start wherever you can, wherever you are. Start by acing your upcoming presentation.

But above all, remember this: all progress begins with truth.

Convey truth beautifully. And know thyself, so you can guard against your own proclivity for malevolence, and so you can strive toward self-mastery. Without self-mastery, it's hard, if not nearly impossible, to do the first part; to convey truth beautifully.

Truth, so you do good, not bad; impact, so people believe you; and self-mastery, as an essential precondition for truth and impact. Imagine what the world would be like if everyone were a triple-ten on our three axes. Imagine what good, what beauty, what bliss would define our existence. Imagine what good, what beauty, what bliss *could* define our existence, here and now.

It's up to you.

THE INNER GAME OF SPEAKING

REFER BACK TO THIS INTERNAL GUIDE as needed. These humble suggestions have helped me deliver high-stakes speeches with inner peace, calm, and equanimity. They are foundational, and the most important words I ever put to paper. I hope these ideas help you as much as they helped me.

MASTER BOTH GAMES. Seek to master the outer game, but also the inner game. The self-mastery game comes before the word-mastery game, and even the world-mastery game. In fact, if you treat *any* game as a way to further your self-mastery, setting this as your "game above all games," you can never lose.

ADOPT THREE FOUNDATIONS. Humility: "The other people here probably know something I don't. They could probably teach me something. I could be overlooking something. I could be wrong. They have something to contribute." Passion: "Conveying truth accurately and convincingly is one of the most important things I'll ever do." Objectivity: "If I'm wrong, I change course. I am open to reason. I want to *be* right; I don't just want to seem right or convince others I am."

STRIVE FOR THESE SUPERLATIVES. Be the kindest, most compassionate, most honest, most attentive, most well-researched, and most confident in the room. Be the one who cares most, who most seeks to uplift others, who is most prepared, and who is most thoughtful about the reason and logic and evidence behind the claims.

START BY CULTIVATING THE HIGHEST VIRTUES IN YOURSELF: love for your audience, love for truth, humility, a deep and abiding desire to make the world a better place, the desire to both be heard and to hear, and the desire to both teach and learn. You will find peace, purpose, clarity, confidence, and persuasive power.

START BY AVOIDING THESE TEMPTING MOTIVES. Avoid the desire to "outsmart" people, to overwhelm and dominate with your rhetorical strength, to embarrass your detractors, to win on the basis of cleverness alone, and to use words to attain power for its own sake. Don't set personal victory as your goal. Strive to achieve a victory for truth. And if you discover you are wrong, change course.

LISTEN TO YOURSELF TALK. (Peterson, 2018). See if what you are saying makes you feel stronger, physically, or weaker. If it makes you feel weaker, stop saying it. Reformulate your speech until you feel the ground under you solidifying.

SPEAK FROM A PLACE OF LOVE. It beats speaking from a desire to dominate. Our motivation and purpose in persuasion must be love. It's ethical *and* effective.

LOVE YOUR ENEMIES (OR HAVE NONE). If people stand against you, do not inflame the situation with resentment or anger. It does no good, least of all for you.

AVOID THESE CORRUPTING EMOTIONS: resistance, resentment, and anger. Against them, set acceptance, forgiveness, and love for all, even your enemies.

PLACE YOUR ATTENTION HERE, NOW. Be where you are. Attend to the moment. Forget the past. Forget the future. Nothing is more important than this.

FOCUS ON YOURSELF, BUT NOW. Speaking gurus will tell you to focus solely on your audience. Yes, that works. But so does focusing on yourself, as long as you focus on yourself *now*. Let this focus root you in the present. Don't pursue a mental commentary on what you see. Instead, just watch. Here. Now. No judgment.

ACCEPT YOUR FEAR. Everyone fears something. If you fear speaking, don't fear your fear of speaking too. Don't reprimand yourself for it. Accept it. Embrace it, even. Courage isn't action without fear. Courage is action despite fear.

STARE DOWN YOUR FEAR. To diminish your fear, stare at the object of your fear (and the fear itself), the way a boxer faces off with his opponent before the fight. Hold it in your mind, signaling to your own psyche that you can face your fear.

CHIP AWAY AT YOUR FEAR. The path out of fear is to take small, voluntary steps toward what you fear. Gradual exposure dissolves fear as rain carves stone.

LET THE OUTER SHAPE THE INNER. Your thoughts impact your actions. But your actions also impact your thoughts. To control fear, seek to manage its outward manifestations, and your calm exterior will shape your interior accordingly.

KNOW THAT EGO IS THE ENEMY. Ego is a black storm cloud blocking the warm sunlight of your true self. Ego is the creation of a false self that masquerades as your true self and demands gratification (which often manifests as the destruction of something good). The allure of arrogance is the siren-song of every good speaker. With it comes pride and the pursuit of power; a placing of the outer game before the inner. Don't fall for the empty promises of ego-gratification. Humility is power.

DON'T IDENTIFY WITH YOUR POSITIONS. Don't turn your positions into your psychological possessions. Don't imbue them with a sense of self.

NOTICE TOXIC AVATARS. When person A speaks to person B, they often craft a false idea, a false avatar, of both themselves and their interlocuter: A1 and B1. So does person B: B2 and A2. The resulting communication is a dance of false avatars; A1, B1, B2, and A2 communicate, but not person A and B. A false idea of one's self speaks to a false idea of someone else, who then does the same. This may be why George Bernard Shaw said "the greatest problem in communication is the illusion that it has been accomplished." How do you avoid this dance of false avatars? This conversation between concepts but not people?

Be present. Don't prematurely judge. Let go of your *sense* of self, for just a moment, so your real self can shine forth.

MINE THE RICHES OF YOUR MIND. Look for what you need within yourself; your strengths and virtues. But also acknowledge and make peace with your own capacity for malevolence. Don't zealously assume the purity of your own motives.

RISE ABOVE YOUR MIND. The ability to think critically, reason, self-analyze, and self-criticize is far more important than being able to communicate, write, and speak. Introspect before you extrospect. Do not identify as your mind, but as the awareness eternally watching your mind. Do not be in your mind, but above it.

CLEAR THE FOG FROM YOUR PSYCHE. Know what you believe. Know your failures. Know your successes. Know your weaknesses. Know your strengths. Know what you fear. Know what you seek. Know your mind. Know yourself. Know your capacity for malevolence and evil. Know your capacity for goodness and greatness. Don't hide any part of yourself from yourself. Don't even try.

KNOW YOUR LOGOS. In 500 B.C. Heraclitus defined Logos as "that universal principle which animates and rules the world." What is your Logos? Meditate on it. Sit with it. Hold it up to the light, as a jeweler does with a gem, examining all angles.

KNOW YOUR LIMITS. The more you delineate and define the actions you consider unethical, the more likely you are to resist when they seem expedient.

REMEMBER THAT EVERYTHING MATTERS. There is no insignificant job, duty, role, mission, or speech. Everything matters. Everything seeks to beat back chaos in some way and create order. A laundromat doesn't deal in clean clothes, nor a trash disposal contractor in clean streets. They deal in order. In civilization. In human dignity. Don't ignore the reservoir of meaning and mattering upon which you stand. And remember that it is there, no matter where you stand.

GIVE THE GIFT OF MEANING. The greatest gift you can give to an audience is the gift of meaning; the knowledge that they matter, that they are irreplaceable.

HONOR YOUR INHERITANCE. You are the heir to thousands of years of human moralizing. Our world is shaped by the words of long-dead philosophers, and the gifts they gave us: gems of wisdom, which strengthen us against the dread and chaos of the world. We stand atop the pillars of 4,000 years of myth and meaning. Our arguments and moral compasses are not like planks of driftwood in a raging sea, but branches nourished by an inestimably old tree. Don't forget it.

BE THE PERSON YOU WANT TO BE SEEN AS. How do you want to be seen by your audience? How can you actually be that way, rather than just seeming to be?

HAVE TRUE ETHOS. Ethos is the audience's perception that the speaker has their best interests at heart. It's your job to make sure this perception is accurate.

CHANGE PLACES WITH YOUR AUDIENCE. Put yourself in their shoes, and then be the speaker you would want to listen to, the speaker worthy of your trust.

ACT AS THOUGH THE WHOLE WORLD IS WATCHING. Or as though a newspaper will publish a record of your actions. Or as though you're writing your autobiography with every action, every word, and even every thought. (You are).

ACT WITH AUDACIOUS HONOR. As did John McCain when he called Obama, his political opponent, "a decent family man, [and] citizen, that I just happen to have disagreements with." As did Socrates and Galileo when they refused to betray truth.

ADOPT A MECHANIC'S MENTALITY. Face your challenges the way a mechanic faces a broken engine; not drowning in emotion, but with objectivity and clarity. Identify the problem. Analyze the problem. Determine the solution. Execute the solution. If it works, celebrate. If not, repeat the cycle. This is true for both your inner and outer worlds: your fear of speaking, for example, is a specific problem with a specific fix, as are your destructive external rhetorical habits.

APPLY THE MASTERY PROCESS INTERNALLY. The four-step mastery process is not only for mastering your rhetoric, but also for striving toward internal mastery.

MARSHAL YOURSELF ALONG THE THREE AXES. To marshal means to place in proper rank or position – as in marshaling the troops – and to bring together and order in the most effective way. It is a sort of preparation. It begins with taking complete stock of what is available. Then, you order it. So, marshal yourself along three axes: the rhetorical axis (your points, arguments, rhetorical techniques, key phrases, etc.), the internal axis (your peace of mind, your internal principles, your mental climate, etc.), and the truth axis (your research, your facts, your logic, etc.).

PRACTICE ONE PUNCH 10,000 TIMES. As the martial arts adage says, "I fear not the man who practiced 10,000 punches once, but the man who practiced one punch 10,000 times." So it is with speaking skills and rhetorical techniques.

MULTIPLY YOUR PREPARATION BY TEN. Do you need to read a manuscript ten times to memorize it? Aim to read it 100 times. Do you need to research for one hour to grasp the subject of your speech? Aim to research for ten.

REMEMBER THE HIGHEST PRINCIPLE OF COMMUNICATION: the connection between speaker and audience – here, now – in this moment, in this place.

KNOW THERE'S NO SUCH THING AS A "SPEECH." All good communication is just conversation, with varying degrees of formality heaped on top. It's all just connection between consciousnesses. Every "difference" is merely superficial.

SEE YOURSELF IN OTHERS. What are you, truly? Rene Descartes came close to an answer in 1637, when he said "cogito, ego sum," I think therefore I am. The answer this seems to suggest is that your thoughts are most truly you. But your thoughts (and your character) change all the time. Something that never changes, arguably even during deep sleep, is awareness. Awareness is also the precondition for thought. A computer performs operations on information, but we don't say the computer "thinks." Why? Because it lacks awareness. So, I believe what makes you "you," most fundamentally, is your awareness, your consciousness. And if you accept this claim – which is by no means a mystical or religious one – then you must also see yourself in others. Because while the contents of everyone's consciousness is different, the consciousness itself is identical. How could it be otherwise?

FORGIVE. Yourself. Your mistakes. Your detractors. The past. The future. All.

FREE YOUR MIND. Many of the most challenging obstacles we face are thoughts living in our own minds. Identify these thoughts, and treat them like weeds in a garden. Restore the pristine poise of your mind, and return to equanimity.

LET. Let what has been be and what will be be. Most importantly, let what is be what is. Work to do what good you can do, and accept the outcome.

FLOW. Wikipedia defines a flow state as such: "a flow state, also known colloquially as being in the zone, is the mental state in which a person performing some activity is fully immersed in a feeling of energized focus, full involvement, and enjoyment in the process of the activity. In essence, flow is characterized by the complete absorption in what one does, and a resulting transformation in one's sense of time." Speaking in a flow state transports you and your audience outside of space and time. When I entered deep flow states during my speeches and debates, audience members would tell me that "it felt like time stopped." It felt that way for me too. Speaking in a flow state is a form of meditation. And it both leads to and results from these guidelines. Adhering to them leads to flow, and flow helps you adhere to them.

MEDITATE. Meditation brings your attention to the "here and now." It creates flow. Practice silence meditation, sitting in still silence and focusing on the motions of your mind, but knowing yourself as the entity watching the mind, not the mind itself. Practice aiming meditation, centering your noble aim in your mind, and focusing on the resulting feelings. (Also, speaking in flow is its own meditation).

EMBARK ON THE GRAND ADVENTURE. Take a place wherever you are. Develop influence and impact. Improve your status. Take on responsibility. Develop capacity and ability. Do scary things. Dare to leap into a high-stakes speech with no preparation if you must. Dare to trust your instincts. Dare to strive. Dare to lead. Dare to speak the truth freely, no matter how brutal it is. Be bold. Risk failure. Throw out your notes. The greatest human actions – those that capture our hearts and minds – occur on the border between chaos and order, where someone is daring to act and taking a chance when they know they could fall off the tightrope with no net below. Training wheels kill the sense of adventure. Use them if you need to, but only to lose them as soon as you can. Speak from the heart and trust yourself. Put yourself out there. Let people see the gears turning in your mind, let them see you grappling with your message in real time, taking an exploration in the moment. This is not an automaton doing a routine. It's not robotic or mechanical. That's too much order. It's also not unstructured nonsense. That's too much chaos. There is a risk of failure, mitigated not by training wheels, but by preparation. It is not a perfectly practiced routine, but someone pushing themselves just beyond their comfort zone, right at the cutting-edge of what they are capable of. It's not prescriptive. It's not safe either. The possibility that you could falter and fall in real-time calls out the best from you, and is gripping for the audience. It is also a thrilling adventure. Have faith in yourself, faith that you will say the right words when you need to. Don't think ahead, or backward. Simply experience the moment.

BREAK THE SEVEN LAWS OF WEAKNESS. If your goal is weakness, follow these rules. Seek to control what you can't control. Seek praise and admiration from others. Bend the truth to achieve your goals. Treat people as instruments in your game. Only commit to outer goals, not inner goals. Seek power for its own sake. Let anger and dissatisfaction fuel you in your pursuits, and pursue them frantically.

FAIL. Losses lead to lessons. Lessons lead to wins. If there's no chance of failure in your present task, you aren't challenging yourself. And if you aren't challenging yourself, you aren't growing. And that's the deepest and most enduring failure.

DON'T BETRAY YOURSELF. To know the truth and not say the truth is to betray the truth and to betray yourself. To know the truth, seek the truth, love the truth, and to speak the truth and speak it well, with poise and precision and power… this is to honor the truth, and to honor yourself. The choice is yours.

FOLLOW YOUR INNER LIGHT. As the Roman emperor and stoic philosopher Marcus Aurelius wrote in his private journal, "If thou findest in human life anything better than justice, truth, temperance, fortitude, and, in a word, anything better than thy own mind's self-satisfaction in the things which it enables thee to do according to right reason, and in the condition that is assigned to thee without thy own choice; if, I say, thou seest anything better than this, turn to it with all thy soul, and enjoy that which thou hast found to be the best. But if nothing appears to be better than [this], give place to nothing else." And as Kant said, treat humans as ends, not means.

JUDGE THEIR JUDGMENT. People *are* thinking of you. They *are* judging you. But what is their judgment to you? Nothing. (Compared to your self-judgment).

BREAK LESSER RULES IN THE NAME OF HIGHER RULES. Our values and moral priorities nest in a hierarchy, where they exist in relation to one another. Some are more important than others. If life compels a tradeoff between two moral principles, as it often does, this means there is a right choice. Let go the lesser of the two.

DON'T AVOID CONFLICT. Necessary conflict avoided is an impending conflict exacerbated. Slay the hydra when it has two heads, not twenty.

SEE THE WHOLE BOARD. Become wise in the ways of the world, and learned in the games of power and privilege people have been playing for tens of thousands of years. See the status-struggles and dominance-shuffling around you. See the chess board. But then opt to play a different game; a more noble game. The game of self-mastery. The game that transcends all other games. The worthiest game.

SERVE SOMETHING. Everyone has a master. Everyone serves something. Freedom is not the absence of service. Freedom is the ability to choose your service. What, to you, is worth serving? With your work and with your words?

TAKE RESPONSIBILITY FOR YOUR RIPPLE EFFECT. If you interact with 1,000 people, and they each interact with 1,000 more who also do the same, you are three degrees away from one billion people. Remember that compassion is contagious.

ONLY SPEAK WHEN YOUR WORDS ARE BETTER THAN SILENCE. And only write when your words are better than a blank page.

KNOW THERE IS THAT WHICH YOU DON'T KNOW YOU DON'T KNOW. Of course, there's that you know you don't know too. Recognize the existence of both of these domains of knowledge, which are inaccessible to you in your present state.

REMEMBER THAT AS WITHIN, SO (IT APPEARS) WITHOUT. If you orient your aim toward goals fueled by emotions like insecurity, jealousy, or vengeance, the world manifests itself as a difficult warzone. If you orient your aim toward goals fueled by emotions like universal compassion and positive ambition, the beneficence of the world manifests itself to you. Your aim and your values alter your perception.

ORIENT YOUR AIM PROPERLY. Actions flow from thought. Actions flow from *motives*. If you orient your aim properly – if you aim at the greatest good for the greatest number, at acting forthrightly and honorably – then this motive will fuel right actions, subconsciously, automatically, and without any forethought.

STOP TRYING TO USE SPEECH TO GET WHAT YOU WANT. Try to articulate what you believe to be true as carefully as possible, and then accept the outcome.

USE THE MOST POWERFUL "RHETORICAL" TACTIC. There is no rhetorical tool more powerful than the overwhelming moral force of the unvarnished truth.

INJECT YOUR EXPERIENCE INTO YOUR SPEECH. Speak of what you know and testify of what you have seen. Attach your philosophizing and persuading and arguing to something real, some story you lived through, something you've seen.

DETACH FROM OUTCOME. As Stoic philosopher Epictetus said: "There is only one way to happiness and that is to cease worrying about things which are beyond the power of our will. Make the best use of what is in your power, and take the rest as it happens. The essence of philosophy is that a man should so live that his happiness shall depend as little as possible on external things. Remember to conduct yourself in life as if at a banquet. As something being passed around comes to you, reach out your hand and take a moderate helping. Does it pass you? Don't stop it. It hasn't yet come? Don't burn in desire for it, but wait until it arrives in front of you."

FOCUS ON WHAT YOU CONTROL. As Epictetus said, "It's not what happens to you, but how you react to it that matters. You may be always victorious if you will never enter into any contest where the issue does not wholly depend upon yourself. Some things are in our control and others not. Things in our control are opinion, pursuit, desire, aversion, and, in a word, whatever are our own actions. Things not in our control are body, property, reputation, command, and, in one word, whatever are not our own actions. Men are disturbed not by things, but by the view which they take of them. God has entrusted me with myself. Do not with that all things will go well with you, but that you will go well with all things." Before a high-stakes speech or event, I always tell myself this: "All I want from this, all I aim at, is to conduct what I control, my thoughts and actions, to the best of my ability. Any external benefit I earn is merely a bonus."

VIEW YOURSELF AS A VESSEL. Conduct yourself as something through which truth, brilliantly articulated, flows into the world; not as a self-serving entity, but a conduit for something higher. Speak not for your glory, but for the glory of good.

Made in the USA
Las Vegas, NV
15 December 2023